Super Power, Spoony Bards, and Silverware

Platform Studies
Nick Montfort and Ian Bogost, editors

Racing the Beam: The Atari Video Computer System, Nick Montfort and Ian Bogost, 2009

Codename Revolution: The Nintendo Wii Platform, Steven E. Jones and George K. Thiruvathukal, 2012

The Future Was Here: The Commodore Amiga, Jimmy Maher, 2012

Flash: Building the Interactive Web, Anastasia Salter and John Murray, 2014

I AM ERROR: The Nintendo Family Computer / Entertainment System Platform, Nathan Altice, 2015

Peripheral Vision: Bell Labs, the S-C 4020, and the Origins of Computer Art, Zabet Patterson, 2015

Now the Chips Are Down: The BBC Micro, Alison Gazzard, 2016

Minitel: Welcome to the Internet, Julien Mailland and Kevin Driscoll, 2017

Super Power, Spoony Bards, and Silverware: The Super Nintendo Entertainment System, Dominic Arsenault, 2017

Super Power, Spoony Bards, and Silverware

The Super Nintendo Entertainment System

Dominic Arsenault

The MIT Press   Cambridge, Massachusetts   London, England

This book was set in Filosofia OT by Toppan Best-set Premedia Limited. Printed and bound in the United States of America.

Library of Congress Cataloging-in-Publication Data

Names: Arsenault, Dominic, author.
Title: Super Power, Spoony Bards, and Silverware : the Super Nintendo Entertainment System / Dominic Arsenault.
Description: Cambridge, MA : The MIT Press, 2017. | Series: Platform studies | Includes bibliographical references and index.
Identifiers: LCCN 2016055172 | ISBN 9780262036566 (hardcover : alk. paper)
Subjects: LCSH: Nintendo video games--History. | Nintendō Kabushiki Kaisha. | Nintendo of America Inc. | Video games industry--History.
Classification: LCC GV1469.32 .A76 2017 | DDC 794.809--dc23 LC record available at https://lccn.loc.gov/2016055172

10 9 8 7 6 5 4 3 2 1

Contents

Series Foreword

How can someone create a breakthrough game for a mobile phone or compelling work of art for an immersive 3D environment without understanding that the mobile phone and the 3D environment are different sorts of computing platforms? The best artists, writers, programmers, and designers are well aware of how certain platforms facilitate certain types of computational expression and innovation. Likewise, computer science and engineering have long considered how underlying computing systems can be analyzed and improved. As important as scientific and engineering approaches are, and as significant as work by creative artists has been, there is also much to be learned from the sustained, intensive, humanistic study of digital media. We believe it is time for humanists to seriously consider the lowest level of computing systems and their relationship to culture and creativity.

The Platform Studies series has been established to promote the investigation of underlying computing systems and of how they enable, constrain, shape, and support the creative work that is done on them. The series investigates the foundations of digital media—the computing systems, both hardware and software, that developers and users depend upon for artistic, literary, and gaming development. Books in the series will certainly vary in their approaches, but they will all share certain features:

- a focus on a single platform or a closely related family of platforms
- technical rigor and in-depth investigation of how computing technologies work

- an awareness of and a discussion of how computing platforms exist in a context of culture and society, being developed on the basis of cultural concepts and then contributing to culture in a variety of ways—for instance, by affecting how people perceive computing.

Acknowledgments

Writing this book has taken a number of years, and although I've been alone in penning the words, the long journey of ideas, from vague intuitions to rough shaping to constant chiseling and their final stonecast presence, could never have happened without the excellent people who have surrounded me through these years. I want to thank everyone who has engaged with my hypotheses, listened to my ramblings, and offered support in every way possible. In particular, and although mortally afraid to forget someone, I'd like to thank first Andréanne and Nathan, for being there for me and putting up with me while I rattled away at my keyboard for impossible hours; my close friends and colleagues in the Montreal game studies community, whom I always look forward to seeing, even if that doesn't happen enough: Bernard Perron, for his friendship, support, encouragements and wise advice; Maude Bonenfant, for the inspiring discussions and rich exchanges we keep having; Carl Therrien, Guillaume Roux-Girard, and Simon Dor, for their sustained, positive presence through the years; Martin Picard, for sending me charts and news and sharing ideas during writing (and beyond); Gabrielle Trépanier-Jobin, Louis-Martin Guay, and Danny Godin, for the all-too-rare occasions to meet and their ongoing friendship; Andréane Morin-Simard and Marc Joly-Corcoran, for their almost daily presence in the office and pleasant exchanges, as well as our academic collaborations; my LUDOV colleagues and friends Hugo Montembeault, Pascale Thériault, Mikaël Julien, and Francis Lavigne; my research assistants of Team INTEGRAE Audrey Larochelle, Pierre-Marc Côté, and Sacha Lebel, who were tremendously helpful, dedicated, and perspicacious and who gave an additional dimension to my initially modest research project; MITP acquisitions editor Douglas Sery for his initial support and ongoing understanding and patience in making this project a reality; series editors Nick Montfort and Ian Bogost for their openness, support, and insightful comments on my initial pitch and first draft (I'd say your comments were pure silver!); the two anonymous peer reviewers, whose excellent and generous work has been incredibly helpful in powering up this book from the initial draft; MITP manuscript workflow assistant Elizabeth Agresta for her keen eyes that saved the figures in chapter 7; Devin Monnens and John Szczepaniak for offering connections and encouragements; Akinori Nakamura and Koichi Hosoi for their kind and positive responses to my probably impolite emails; Dana Plank and Julianne Grasso for revising some of the music-oriented statements in the book (and for headbanging with me to the *Final Fantasy Mystic Quest* soundtrack); David Viens and Hubert Lamontagne of Plogue Art et technologie for revisions on audio technology; the Fonds de Recherche du Québec—Société et Culture (FRQSC) for funding my research project on innovation and graphical technologies in the video game industry; and finally the hordes of anonymous individuals and communities all over the Internet who have provided me innumerable references, trails to follow, and points to argue. I can't retrace all my digital footsteps, but I want to underline in particular the following portals: Wikipedia, the VGSales Wikia, VGchartz, N-Sider, SNES Central, Chris Covell, gamepilgrimage, MobyGames, 1up.com, Kotaku, the Super Nintendo Development Wiki, and the NESDev Forums.

Introduction: Welcome to the Dark Side

This book is about the Super NES—more precisely, it is a book about a certain framing of the Super NES as the technological enforcer of economic and cultural corporate wars in the video game industry. This book is about Nintendo, how it lived the "16-bit console wars" of 1989–1995, and why it went from great to good to bad to worse in the span of 20 years. Ultimately, it is a critical history of Nintendo's fall from grace, from the height of the Golden Age brought by its 8-bit NES console (1985–1990) through a waning Silver Age with its 16-bit Super NES (1990–1996) that ultimately led to a prolonged Dark Age with the Nintendo 64 and Game-Cube consoles (1996–2006). The bulk of the Super NES's lifespan is thus intricately tied to Nintendo's Silver Age, when things began to go wrong for the firm. Figures 0.1 and 0.2 contain some console sales and market share data that easily drive that point home; as can be seen, were it not for the sudden and unexpected "Wiivival" of 2006, Nintendo's long slide downward would have brought them ever farther away from the spotlight and into the darkened margins of home video game consoles.[1]

"But," the gamer who grew up with the console objects when reading this, "the Super NES is routinely hailed as one of the best consoles of all time! It had an incredible library of games!" And this is true. Osamu Inoue's *Nintendo Magic* presents the typically held (if overly positive) view when discussing the belated arrival of the SNES against its rivals: "In the end, the delays in the SNES's development only stoked the fires of fan enthusiasm, and the 16-bit wars ended with the leading brand Nintendo's overwhelming victory" (Inoue 2010, 135). Witness *Retro Gamer*'s hardware profile of the console and its section, "Why the Super Nintendo was great": "Nintendo's 16 bit powerhouse represents the true 'Golden Age' of

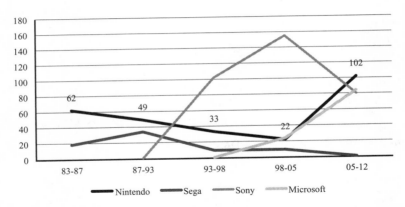

Figure 0.1 Lifetime worldwide Nintendo home console sales, in million units, compared with competitors from 1983 to 2012.

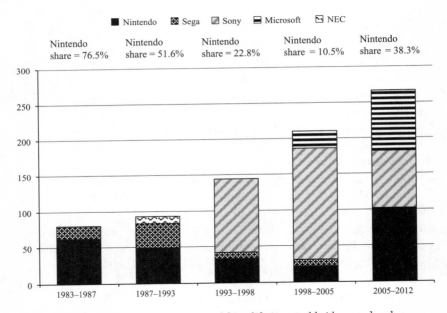

Figure 0.2 Nintendo's market share derived from lifetime worldwide console sales.

videogaming as the likes of Konami, Squaresoft, and even Nintendo itself have arguably never been on better form than when designing games for this machine" (Retro Gamer 2013, "Super Nintendo" entry). Or Don Reisinger from CNet's article, conveniently titled "The SNES Is the Greatest Console of All Time":

> In essence, the NES was the building block of American gaming in the '80s and the SNES was first console to be drastically different (and better) than its predecessor. [...] Instead of releasing a veiled copy of the NES to get in on the fight with Sega earlier, Nintendo created a follow-up that was worthy of the "Super" moniker and gave developers the license they needed to create the legendary titles that we still play today. (Reisinger 2008)

Throughout this book, I will argue the opposite of these accounts on every point mentioned. The Super NES was not a powerhouse, and it does not represent a Golden Age but rather a Silver Age (more on this later). The Super NES was neither drastically different nor better than its predecessor. It was a veiled copy of the NES released too late to play catch-up with Sega. The "Super" moniker was just *markethin*: thin marketing. Nintendo didn't give anything to developers; it was forced to concede some control because they fought for it and went to look elsewhere. The only point I won't dispute is whether game developers have "arguably" never been on better form than at that time.

The Platform With a Thousand Faces

Now, even in the face of the arguments I will develop here, the Super NES still continues to be regarded as a highly successful platform. Why is that? Answering this question requires us to change the way we think about platforms and eschew the traditional question "What is a platform?" for another one: "What is a platform *to whom*?" The Super NES was an incredibly strong platform filled with high-quality games for gamers; it was a one-tracked and short-sighted vision by Nintendo to keep its stranglehold on the market, a strict and intransigent tool of control against independent game developers, a giant leap forward in controller ergonomics, a conservative cement that resisted game genre experimentation, the site of schizophrenic promotional practices, a refuge for concerned parents, flash over substance, and the list could go on. The Super NES asks us to recognize the paradoxical situation where a game console can be recognized as a great platform sporting an extensive library of high-quality titles by gamers, rake in good profits for its owner, and yet simultaneously weaken its overall positioning and long-term success. In short, it asks us to consider for a moment how we evaluate a game platform's success.

Conventional wisdom declares the SNES successful because it sold more units than the Genesis, with reported lifetime worldwide sales of 49.1 million SNESes (Nintendo Co. 2016a) against an often-cited 29 million Geneses.[2] If we take a step back and look at the broader history, however, the SNES period is when Nintendo lost close to half its market share while Sega's tripled. We could thus declare the SNES a failure due to its inability to maintain the status quo. Perhaps we should count the number of games produced for a platform because, after all, gamers buy consoles to play games. Or maybe we should count the total number of software sales because games that don't sell are only unwanted clutter and expenses for their publisher. However, platform owners may not care that third-party developers' games do not sell if their own games are selling and the profit margins are high; maybe the only metric we should measure is the platform owner's hardware and software revenue. But do immediate profits qualify as "winning" when market share has shrunk? After all, conventional economics and business studies describe market share as a valuable long-term strategic advantage. And on and on it goes.

In this light, the Super NES stands as Nintendo's Pyrrhic victory, a symbol of its stubborn and uncompromising conservative nature. This much can be gathered from its name. The Super NES is exactly that: it's the NES, only "Super," whatever that means. The name betrays the console's rushed development, Nintendo's will to capitalize on the NES's success, and the relative emptiness of its proposal to consumers. It almost feels like a newer, improved version of its NES rather than a unique new console. Incidentally, that's exactly what many people gathered back then: the *Economist* claimed Nintendo was set to launch "a professional version of its best-selling 'Famicon'" (The Economist, August 18, 1990, 60). Even in contemporary writings, people make that mistake: When Daniel Sloan reviews the Famicom's success in Japan, he sandwiches a sentence in the middle of the discussion to the effect that "an upgrade came in 1990 with the 16-bit Super Famicom" (Sloan 2010, 70). In other words, the SNES, as a souped-up "Famicom 2.0," is not terribly interesting technologically, encouraging game developers to keep doing what they were doing, only slapping a "Super" on it.

Beyond Technology: The Commercial Platform

To put it as bluntly as I can, the SNES makes a boring case for a platform study, in the usual sense of the term defined by series editors Ian Bogost and Nick Montfort: "Platform studies is about the connection between technical specifics and culture. In one direction, it allows investigation of how particular aspects of a platform's design influenced the work done on that platform" (Bogost and Montfort 2009a). Fortunately, another direction is available: "In the other direction, it looks at how social, economic, cultural, and other factors led platform designers to put together systems in particular ways" (Bogost and Montfort 2009a). Montfort and Consalvo's (2012) piece on the Sega Dreamcast provides an example of the latter by focusing on Sega's development policies with the console. Thomas Apperley and Darshana Jayemanne (2012, 12) situated this approach within the "material turn" of game studies: "the materiality of platforms can be turned [...also] outwards to focus on the organizational structure that allows the platform to be produced."

I want to push this direction further and consider platforms not only as technological objects but also as the embodiments of marketing forces that shape the creative works performed on that platform. This conception of the platform is perfectly suited for Nintendo's stringent controlled environments. The first criterion from which game developers and publishers select a platform is often the business realities of the platform. No one delves into the arcane programming and technical constraints of SNES game development without making sure they will be able to actually release and market their game.

Robert Pelloni found that out when he spent reportedly five years and 15,000 hours making "Bob's game," a one-man project for the Nintendo DS. Nintendo would not send Pelloni a software development kit (SDK) needed to actually produce the game for the platform because Pelloni had no secure office space, staff, or other indicators of him acting as a business rather than an individual. This situation shows how the business practices of platform owners can shape the creative expression of game developers just as much as technological constraints. Platforms are not technology constructs that exist by themselves, with cultural or marketing considerations gravitating somewhere around them; a platform *is* a technology *and* a culture *and* a marketing construct, and these elements are indissociable. Thus, I have consciously named the various economic models described in the book with the same initials as their host platform or corporation, as appropriate; the Nintendo Entertainment System and the Nintendo Economic System, for instance, are flipsides to the same coin.

Thus, although the Super NES may be rather straightforward as a technological platform, it brings a unique opportunity to expand and even redefine how we view game platforms, by putting (perhaps counterintuitively) business and marketing first, culture second, and technology last. In these terms, a platform is a device meant to regulate and protect a firm's market, and platform studies can benefit from a corpus of academic work that has seldom been integrated in game studies: business studies and its neighboring fields of innovation studies, economics, and management studies, which can be seen as forming a second kind of platform studies. Accordingly, one of the central contributions of this book is to articulate the dual nature of platforms as participating in both business-to-consumer (B2C) commerce and business-to-business (B2B) interactions. In Nintendo's case, the discrepancies between the two are so important that the most apt description of the firm becomes "an iron hand in a velvet glove". I will term the need to achieve balance between the fun-loving toy company image and the gravely serious tech firm at heart (Harris 2014, 133–134) the surface-and-core duality, and I will return to it throughout the rest of this book.

Kline, Dyer-Witheford, and de Peuter's framework of *Digital Play* (2003) conceptualizes the games industry as an *Interaction of Technology, Culture, and Marketing*, with three interlocking "circuits" that influence each other and collectively define the three main facets of digital play, along with their actors. The cultural circuit involves cultural texts and meanings, "the practices or activities associated with both designing and playing games," and designers, games, and players. The technology circuit involves digital artifacts, hardware and software infrastructures, and programmers and users. The marketing circuit deals with "research, advertising, and branding practices," commodities, and marketers and consumers (Kline, Dyer-Witheford, and de Peuter 2003, 50–53). Adopting this model, the book presents the interactions of these three circuits to understand the Super NES, which explains the oddities of its title.

Marketing: Nintendo's Super Power

By studying the circuit of marketing, I am pursuing a direction identified by both Consalvo (2006, 134: "Researchers of new media must continue to examine not only cultural products, but also the business practices that lead to the production and circulation of these products") and O'Donnell (2011, 85: "We have not spent enough time looking at the folks who make games or at the broader system that they are a part of"), among others. Too often the various organizations involved in the games business (individual game developers, development studios, publishers, distributors, and retailers) are more or less lumped together in the catch-all category of "the video game industry," whereas in truth their motivations, goals, desires, and responsibilities are often divergent. To say that "the industry wants to sell games and make money" is no more helpful than to declare that "gamers play games to have fun." Just as the important work of game studies scholars has allowed us to go beyond the simple "gamer" term and identify different types of game players, with varying interests and value systems for approaching games, we need to unpack the "industry" and recognize its various actors for what they are: different elements playing unique roles in a larger system.

Considering platforms as part of a business ecosystem allows us to position them as sites of struggle between conflicted and conflicting parties. It provides a unique key to understanding not only some of the technical choices behind the hardware of the system but also some of the aesthetic or design choices that can be found in some of the software on offer on that platform.

A survey of literature from business studies, economics, and management will allow us to further clarify the relationships among gamers, consoles, and games in the game industry, and to highlight the contributions and specificities of Nintendo and other hardware firms. What's a platform to its owner? How can the two traditions of platform studies, from game studies and business studies, respectively, benefit each other and allow us to better understand the complex corporate context in which the Super NES inscribes itself and the restrictions it imposes on game developers and their creative output?

Technology: The Super NES as Silverware

Computers are hardware machines meant to run software programs, and the relationship between the hardware's configuration and the software as expressive practice forms the backbone of platform studies. The "hardware" category, of course, predates computers, and in its original sense, it designates the miscellaneous assemblage of durable goods and tools used in the household to perform various actions, whether by humans or machines—anything from hammers and screws to door handles and window sills, including wires, plumbing, and utensils. It makes sense to think of computer hardware as such, insofar as computers are tools for software developers to make things with.

Sometimes, however, things are not so simple. Think of utensils. Many homes typically use functional flatware (knives, spoons, forks, etc.) in their everyday lives, saving a set of silverware (known as a silver service in Britain or *argenterie* in French) for special occasions. Language comes into play here, as Carolin C. Young writes: "Americans often use the term 'silverware' with casual, democratic optimism to refer to dining utensils of any material. Properly, the word defines any object fashioned from silver, Sheffield plate, or silver electroplate" (Young 2014, 256). Before the 20th century, America put its vast amounts of silver from the West toward producing ever-larger sets of silverware, with different items specially made for everything from lobster forks to potato chip dispensers. Because this specialized equipment required a great deal of care to maintain, it was reserved for the wealthiest strata of society or the most formal occasions, where demonstrating wealth was par for the course.

This analogy describes well a number of the SNES's peculiarities. The SNES, as a technological platform, is a collection of components tailor-made for specific purposes—making the kinds of games Nintendo was making—rather than a flexible all-around hardware solution. Silverware also requires constant polishing, which must be done by someone knowledgeable in the treatment of silver (a silverman or silver butler); likewise, Nintendo's platform required specialized knowledge of the device's operations to yield the right results, the kind of expertise that only the wealthy could afford. Finally (and perhaps obviously), there is no added functionality to silverware over regular flatware, apart from the fact that it looks nicer. Maybe the tool even starts to program its user, like Maslow's Hammer: "I suppose it is tempting, if the only tool you have is a hammer, to treat everything as if it were a nail" (Maslow 1966, 15). As silver shines when polished, it formats people in spending a good deal of time polishing it. This admittedly harsh description applies to the Super NES as well, which formatted game developers in sticking to tried-and-true game formulas, carefully worked on and improved, and coated with the shiny polish of nice graphics throughout its lifetime. Hence, the framing of the SNES as ushering in a silver age, a period of tranquil, easygoing stability that follows the glorious but momentous summits reached during a golden age.[3]

Culture: Spoony Bards

Most people don't get to meet bards nowadays, and if they did, chances are they wouldn't insult them by referencing utensils—unless they happened to play *Final Fantasy II* on the Super NES. The memorable line "You spoony bard!", hurled by the sage Tellah at the poor bard Edward during a dramatic scene, has been circulating over the Internet ever since the Internet took off. Back in 1991, however, it spread around through friends chatting in the schoolyard, video game magazines, and the nascent pre-Internet network culture of Bulletin Board Systems (BBS) and UseNet Groups. The "spoony bard" expression harks back to that estranged time of yore (bardic emphasis intended) when video game culture ebbed and flowed in these distinct channels, Japan was the epicenter of game hardware and software production, and translating and localizing video games from Japan was often an expedited task.

Weird as it may sound, "spoony" is a valid English word (although an archaism), which the Merriam-Webster online dictionary defines as such: "1: silly, foolish; *especially*: unduly sentimental; 2: being sentimentally in love." This is a perfectly accurate way for the sage Tellah to describe (and mildly insult) the bard Edward, with whom his daughter Anna eloped in the game's fiction. But it also perfectly describes the role and attitude that many gamers harbor regarding their preferred video game platform (e.g., what the Internet refers to as "Nintendo fanboys"). I posit that, in effect, gamers too often become spoony bards, foolishly enamored with their video game machines, sentimentally—and unduly—attached to them, and singing their praises far and wide for anyone to hear. The Super NES, the "queen of 16-bits" as the French call it (see Audureau et al. 2013 or *JV Mag* 2015), certainly had its share of spoony bards, in part, because it rode on the success of the NES and its Nintendo Generation. This latter reality highlights the importance of properly situating the SNES among its historical context.

The SNES in Video Game History, Beyond Legendary Luminaries

In a way, the study of any platform is always historical to some degree. But beyond that general sentiment, I feel that Nintendo's home consoles are too important and had too decisive an impact on the games industry and video game history at large to be treated without privileging a historical angle. As it will soon appear when reading the various chapters, to understand the SNES is to understand its situation and the role it played in video game history.

Since Leonard Herman's *Phoenix: The Fall & Rise of Video Games* (1994), a number of books presenting the general history of games have been written by journalists and learned game enthusiasts (Ichbiah 1997, Kent 2001, DeMaria and Wilson 2002, Donovan 2010, etc.). These writings are typically a mix between summaries of factual data and interviews of the key actors who were part of the events. They chronicle the tribulations of companies, consoles, games, and individuals, with a focus on sales data, market penetration rates, major "milestone" game releases, clever advertising campaigns, stunts at trade shows, and social controversies caused by a few games. These general books are complemented by other works that focus on a particular region, historical period, or account.

Given Nintendo's importance in the video game industry, it should come as no surprise that multiple books, papers, and articles have already been written about the firm and its games. A fair portion of these writings can be characterized as positivistic and often admiring narratives, including *Power-Up: How Japanese Video Games Gave the World an Extra Life* (Kohler 2004), *Nintendo Magic* (Inoue 2010), and *Super Mario: How Nintendo Conquered America* (Ryan 2012). Ironically, considering its title, David Sheff's seminal 1993 book *Game Over: How Nintendo Zapped an American Industry, Captured Your Dollars, and Enslaved Your Children* paints a brightly colored picture of Nintendo of America due to the novelistic style and "Nintendo insider" point of view. Among generalist writings, Tristan Donovan's *Replay: The History of Video Games* (2010) and Steven L. Kent's *Ultimate History of Video Games* (2001) also provide good examples of this "celebratory insider view," which is also found in Florent Gorges' otherwise excellent ongoing *History of Nintendo* series (begun in 2008).

Another question is worth asking: What are these histories founded on? Traditionally, Nintendo is as tight-lipped a firm as they come:

> Nintendo prefers not to have its management discussed by outsiders, even eschewing praise. As a result, despite the company's success, opportunities for individual interviews are extremely rare, and there are essentially no publications that deal with Nintendo's management. [...] At the root of that corporate culture is the assumption that even if they were to discuss their management, outsiders wouldn't understand—an eminently Nintendo-like notion. Thus, not seeing any point in such discourses, they practice rigorous information control, consistently keeping exposure to the minimum possible. (Inoue 2010, 8–9)

Hence, Nintendo histories come from a limited number of first-hand interviews, constantly replicated and hinted at, to the point of becoming hearsay, rumors, and "misinformation echo chambers" that ultimately twist and bend video game historiography (Therrien and Picard 2014). When fan website owner "tsr" interviewed Atari programmer Ed Logg about his implication in Tengen and their development of a *Tetris* cartridge for the NES without Nintendo's authorization (a legal saga covered in Sheff's 1993 book *Game Over*), the discussion quickly addressed the issue of historical point of view:

EL [Ed Logg]:   The books are definitely ... They talked to Peter Main and [Howard] Lincoln [from Nintendo of America].

tsr [interviewer]:   Like Game Over.

EL: Yeah, in particular. It's definitely from their side of the story. (tsr, c.2000)

Because our current Nintendo histories are both rare and positivistic, they slip from rumor into legend, becoming alluring, impressive, greater-than-life affairs. They typically present the objectives of key Nintendo personnel and the obstacles they had to tackle, inviting the reader to identify with the protagonists and celebrate the witty and audacious solutions to their problems. The cast of characters may be presented as the *dramatis personae* (word for word in Parish et al. 2015, 12–17; implicit in the "history of NOA" [Nintendo of America] chapter in Harris 2014, 35–59) and typically star Howard Lincoln, Minoru Arakawa, and Hiroshi Yamauchi, with supporting roles by Shigeru Miyamoto, Gunpei Yokoi, and Masayuki Uemura, and the arch-villains Michael Katz and Tom Kalinske of Sega of America, Hayao Nakamura of Sega of Japan, and Senators Joseph Lieberman and Herb Kohl of the US Congress. In the opposite corner, Blake Harris' *Console Wars* (2014) turns the tables to offer Kalinske's point of view, painting Nintendo of America as the tyrannical empire against which the underdog Sega of America rebels and wrests victory.

Whichever side we're on, this case nicely illustrates how much of video game historiography is built on the theory of great men (and here I really mean *males*[4]), exceptional heroes responsible for steering the course of history through their leadership, wisdom, initiative, or daring. I'll have none of it. To riff off Thomas Carlyle's (1841) profession of faith in the impact of great men, I'll note, in the form of a lament rather than an admiring salvo, "The history of the [video game] world is but the biography of great men." Following Carl Therrien (and Paul Ricoeur), these are still "voluntary witnesses," and they deserve to be confronted with "involuntary witnesses"—"other relevant traces that might not be so generous with words, and whose meaning must be deciphered" (Therrien 2015). I don't want to interview and write biographies of individuals; I want to study Nintendo, the faceless corporation, even while it hides behind its reassuring Mario mascot.

To do this, I'll focus on a kind of resource vastly underused, in my opinion, in games history: game magazines from the period, as well as actual game boxes, manuals, and advertisements. This approach allows us to look at the diversified discourses and rhetorics that were used by game publishers, platform owners, game reviewers, and, in some cases, typical players of the time, thus yielding insight on how these games and systems were received by their contemporaries. In a way, this book aims to look past the celebrated plumber and into the plumbing hidden behind, the criss-crossing network of pipes through which the capitals—technological, cultural, and economic—flow.

Against the Techno-Deterministic Narrative: The Issue of Periodization

Video game history faces a problem common to any historical work—that of periodization: "Video game history is usually told as a story of hardware not software: a tale of successive generations of game consoles and their manufacturers' battle for market share" (Donovan 2010, XIII). The "16-bit generation" (or "fourth generation") is thought to start with the release of the Sega Genesis, unfolding through the console wars with Nintendo's Super NES, and ending with Sony's PlayStation. These planets populate the system of home video games, with various asteroids of no consequence, such as the Neo Geo, CD-i, and CDTV erratically bouncing around (and the metaphorically apt Saturn floating somewhere far away, off course). Two problems arise with this orthodox historiographical mapping.

The first and easy-to-find problem is that, although these generations typically last five or six years, late entrants may take years before entering the market, each release may be years apart across different regions of the world, and each console may also take years in each market before achieving success. Hence, the third-generation Nintendo Famicom was released in 1983 in Japan but only in 1987 in Europe—the same year NEC released the fourth-generation PC-Engine in Japan, which also gave it a full three years of lead time on Nintendo's 1990 entry in the 16-bit generation. Coming up with a single timeline of "generations of game consoles" across regions not only distorts the wide spectrum of gaming practices (arcades, computers, and mobile and social network games are all left unaccounted for with the console-based model) but also induces a false sense of synchronicity and teleology in the deeply chaotic nature of video games. This problem ties into the second, more pernicious problem.

At first sight, the "generations" model appears to be a problematic but straightforward form of technodeterminism (the belief that the progress of technology alone is what determines the unfolding future of games). However, things are not so simple: If we were to focus on 16-bit processor technology alone, we'd have to start the 16-bit generation with the Mattel Intellivision in 1979. Instead, we treat the latter as a second-generation console—a rival to Atari's VCS (or 2600). This shows how the classical periodization in video game history really *isn't* technocentrist.

Rather, we define our history according to a number of historical centers determined from market success, and market success comes through corporations brandishing superior technology as a lure to rein in tech-savvy gamers, who flock toward the newest bright machines like moths to a flame. Our history is one of corporate dominions, of game consoles as kings ruling over Kingdom Videoludica. We chronicle who rules and define their competitors as forming one period, until some rival manages to wrest power.

This notion is particularly evident when looking at the transition between the fourth and fifth generations found in usual games historiography. The abundance of consoles that hit the market between 1991 and 1994 are put into either the fourth "Nintendo vs. Sega" generation (the Philips CD-i, Commodore CDTV, SNK Neo Geo, and Pioneer LaserActive) or the fifth "PlayStation" generation (the 3DO Interactive Multiplayer, Atari Jaguar, FM Towns Marty, and Amiga CD32). We could instead recognize all these machines as forming their own "generation 4.5," occupying the interstices between two generations. But we don't build history from the odd attempt or the failed coup; we declare another generation to be opening when the kings Nintendo and Sega announce new consoles, designating potential heirs to the throne. Therefore, generation-driven periodization does not trace technological development: it celebrates market success and popularity by organizing history as a series of rulers and their reign, retroactively structuring conflicts born from their triumphs.

In the context of periodization, this book is not only about the SNES or the console wars of the fourth generation. Rather, I examine the Super NES across three historical continuums. For marketing, I present a history of business models in the video game industry and explain how Nintendo pioneered its own unique business model with the NES, how it clung to and adapted it during the SNES years, and how it lost to the newer network-based model that Sony brought with the PlayStation. For culture, I frame the American Video Game ReNESsance as a cultural period in the history of video games in North America, situating the SNES in its wake and before the "MTV" redefinition of video games that Sony (and Sega) brought. For technology, I posit two larger technological trajectories in video game history and examine how the Super NES negotiated a path through them: the transition from 2-D to 3-D graphics and from cartridge to CD-ROM data storage. Through each of these contexts, the Super NES appears as a transitory object, a stopgap or hinge on the doors of video game history, a sliver of silver between two golden ages.

Overview

The journey into the Super NES will take us on a dive, roughly linearly from marketing to culture and into technology and back to the surface from technology to culture and then marketing. We will also cover the SNES roughly chronologically, from the broader context of video game history and Nintendo's arrival in North America with the NES to the development and marketing of the SNES, its release, and the many alternative technologies and cultural forces that have surrounded or changed it through its later years, until it was dethroned by Sony's PlayStation.

Chapter 1 introduces some of the literature on the games industry in business and management studies and provides a general-level overview of key concepts and frameworks used to discuss it. It traces the historical development of Atari's business model with the 2600/VCS and, in the process, questions and nuances the commonly held assumption that the video game industry follows the "razor and blades" model of giving away the razor to sell the blades. The limits of that analogy are explained as the rest of the chapter focuses on the establishment of Nintendo's business model with the NES in North America, one that I describe as a self-party model and that differs on important points from the orthodox view of the games industry and first-party platform owner models.

Chapter 2 presents the basic conditions that were in place, both internally at Nintendo and more largely in the video game market, when the decision to develop and release a 16-bit system was taken. The marketing, launch, and launch titles of the Super Famicom and Super NES are described, which allows me to challenge the orthodoxies laid out in chapter 1. I argue that platform owners do not sell technology to gamers but rather a ludic promise that needs to be expressed in specific games—launch titles—which become rhetorical moves in larger discourses. I also argue that consoles are heaps of trouble for people rather than desired objects, and system specs are worthless.

Chapter 3 examines the discourses that shaped the anticipation and reception of the Super NES. I study a number of game magazines from the period and consider their varying implications with platforms. By going back to the sources and some later developments of paratext theory, I show how problematic the culture of game magazines in the United States (through *Nintendo Power* and *Electronic Gaming Monthly*) has treated technology, finding three categories of technological discourses: technobabble, buzzwords, and technoliteracy. Ultimately, this shows how the gaming industry's relationship with technology is far from a straightforward affair, and particularly so for Nintendo.

Chapter 4 is dedicated to the technology of the Super NES. It describes the limited processing and memory units, the audio system, controller, and hardware design, before opening an in-depth discussion of graphics in video games through its graphical infrastructure and unique "Mode 7" visuals. I introduce the concept of graphical regimes as a way to discuss the two separate aspects of graphics: the "polish" of special effects and increased graphical complexity and fidelity, and the interactive possibilities that are tied to the visual construction of a game. A discussion of video game genre and innovation dynamics shows how Nintendo's game development and publishing strategy for the SNES enforced a certain conformity to traditional gameplay genres, rather than favoring free-reign experimentation like other platforms, which promoted different technological standards.

Chapter 5 explores the larger technological revolution that video games went through during the SNES's lifespan in the early to mid-1990s: the move from 2-D to 3-D graphics and gameplay. The Super NES's steps in that direction, and how Nintendo negotiated this paradigm shift, further characterize the relative lack of innovation the firm displayed during the 16- and 32-bit eras of video game history. The various meanings of the term "3-D" are described through a number of practices, including technical drawing, geometry, art history, animation, and live-action film. I situate Nintendo's Mode 7 among this landscape of approaches to tridimensionality, as well as the inclusion of polygons in latter games thanks to expansion chips in cartridges. I also discuss some of the planned (or almost complete) games that Nintendo canceled in the waning years of the SNES, projects that highlight the firm's resistant approach to innovation.

Chapter 6 develops the cultural image and identity of Nintendo as a corporation and the trials and tribulations it had to go through during the SNES's life. It briefly covers the corporation's history from playing cards to the NES to identify the focus on family that has remained at the heart of Nintendo. I also present a cultural period of video game history I dub the American Video Game ReNESsance and the cultural redefinitions of video games due to Sega's advertising campaigns and the *Mortal Kombat* and *Night Trap* controversies that led to the creation of the Entertainment Software Rating Board. Nintendo had the rug swept from under its feet and needed to adapt its Super NES, and its entire game library and corporate image, to respond to the changes in demographics brought by the maturing of its "Nintendo Generation."

Chapter 7 chronicles the fall of the SNES by focusing on its failed (and recently surfaced to stardom thanks to a prototype unit being found in

2015) peripheral, the CD-ROM player. The importance of multimedia as a technological trajectory of the late 1980s and early 1990s is established before I chronicle (as best I can) the suite of vague agreements, turnarounds, betrayals, and unholy alliances that were spurred by the secretive corporations Nintendo, Sony, and Philips. I then explain Sony's innovative business model and how it enlisted a high number of game developers and took the market by storm. Although the CD-ROM format is usually described as a technological innovation, I show that it is also a commercial innovation which revolutionized game distribution thanks to specific commercial affordances given to game developers and publishers that favored innovation.

This concludes our overview. Now come ye all! Step up to the gates and hear my song. Spoony as I may be, I will take you on a tour of Nintendo's walled garden, and show you how the alleys were paved and how they decayed, how the young visitors came and were lured away, and the silvery shine to stain gave way. Welcome to the tour. Welcome to the dark side.

Through the Yamauchi and Iwata eras, the lesson has always been the same. It is a simple lesson, but it is something so many video game designers, publishers and hardware manufacturers have missed or messed up. It is a lesson that will always be the Nintendo motto.
  Never relinquish control. (Stuart 2015)

When we think of video games, we usually think of a combination of hardware and software: first we buy a system, and that system is used to play a number of different games. Everything we buy as end users is the result of a five-stage process: development, publishing, manufacturing, distribution, and retail (Williams 2002, 46). Software developers and publishers work together with hardware manufacturers to create a sustainable product ecosystem and market, if not without some disturbances. In 2010, industry analyst Nicholas Lovell described the typical business model of console manufacturers:

The current generation of consoles is predicated on companies subsidizing a very expensive piece of hardware, and recovering their money mainly through a tax on everyone who wants to develop games for their platform. You can make some money selling consoles at the end of their lifecycle, after all the research and development is paid off, but the core of the model is that the console manufacturers have absolute control over their platforms and over who gets to develop games for them. (Lovell cited in Chatfield 2010, 215–216)

This is what Chatfield describes as the "walled garden" model, which traditionally characterizes the video game industry and relies on three conceptual entities. The first-party firm typically is the console manufacturer (or platform provider), who usually doubles as a game publisher and often triples as a game developer. Developers are responsible for producing a game's code and contents in a timely fashion while respecting the allotted budget. The budget for developing the game, marketing, distribution, rights and licensing management, sales, and all financial aspects of the games business is handled by publishers. Third-party licensees are external firms that develop or publish games for the first party's platform. Last, although the "second party" term traditionally refers to the consumer buying the good from the first party, in the video game industry, the word covers the myriad possibilities for hybrid ownership status that results in an external firm having closer ties with the first party than other "regular" third-party licensees. Such cases include independent developers contractually bound to develop games exclusively for a publisher or platform owner, or developers where a significant stake is owned by them. For this reason, it makes sense to think of the parties as positioned over three degrees of distance from the epicenter that the platform constitutes, as illustrated in figure 1.1.

In the figure, "X marks the spot" (the platform), and a square wall is erected outside the first-party internal development studios and publishing divisions. This wall passes right through the second-party publishers and developers, who are contractually bound to the platform owner and yet still have one foot outside the garden. Third-party publishers and developers are sitting outside and are only authorized access under the platform owner's conditions, whose gatekeeping efforts rely on licensing agreements with second- or third-party publishers or on a publishing agreement between the platform owner's in-house publishing and second- or third-party game developers (who are cast in its net, represented by the dashed cone).

The "walled garden" and the three-party structure of the industry, with associated developers, publishers, and platform providers, has become so deeply ingrained in our minds that it may appear to be the only business model that allows a platform to thrive. But that was not always the case. This model had to be developed; it is not a default state of things. Moreover, it does not aptly represent Nintendo's business model, which I term a *self-party* firm. This chapter introduces a vocabulary and concepts from business studies to chronicle the development of Nintendo's business model, situating it in a marketing history of home video games.

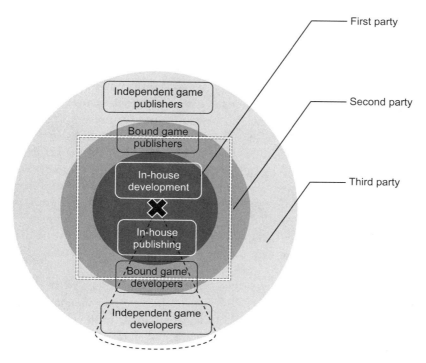

First party

Second party

Third party

Independent game publishers

Bound game publishers

In-house development

In-house publishing

Bound game developers

Independent game developers

Figure 1.1 The walled garden model, regulated by the three-degrees structure.

The Home Video Game Market: A Classical View

Most studies conducted on the home video game market, management, and business treat it as a standard-based industry (Kline, Dyer-Witheford and de Peuter 2003, 110–112; Williams 2002; Schilling 2002), where firms (game developers) must develop products (games) according to the compatibility requirements of a certain standard (a console) over another. This approach is necessary because standards are lowering the investment necessary for game developers to make their products available to their consumers; without standards, developers would have to constantly reinvent (and remarket) the wheel, so to speak. This valuable lesson was learned from the first generation of dedicated home video game consoles (1972–1977), where every game developer manufactured its own machines. It also forced consumers to buy and replace or stockpile systems at home, perhaps successively investing in Coleco's Telstar Classic, Telstar Ranger, Telstar Combat!, and a dozen others. It quickly made more sense to ask the consumer to pay a relatively important fee to gain access to the standard (thanks to a "compatible player," a console) to buy individual titles cheaply afterward in cartridge form, just as with record players or VHS systems.

This move made video games a two-sided market. Some firms develop and sell hardware (consoles, the base good), which make up the first side of the market, whereas other firms develop and sell software (games, the complementary goods) for the second side. Some firms such as Nintendo, of course, cater to both sides of the market. The goals, motives, and obstacles for each of these sides—hardware and software—are not always convergent and can sometimes be at odds. A platform owner wants its platform to be the most successful on the market so that ideally all consumers want to buy it, and the platform's price should be high enough to bring in profit. A game publisher may prefer the industry to have a healthy number of platforms (so that their games do not depend on an all-powerful platform owner who holds the key to the market's one gate), and the platform's price should be low enough to bring in the most consumers with extra cash to spend on games.

Standard-based industries are particularly competitive in nature because their theoretically large market is effectively divided among the various standards, each of them holding a market share; if you're making a Super NES game, it doesn't matter that the global, total video game business is $4 billion big—if the SNES has a 40% share of the home console market, then that's your effective market size. This makes the home video game market hypercompetitive: "competition has flourished as each firm sought (and seeks) the greatest network externalities arising from the largest user base. Without interoperability, it is difficult for firms to see each other as anything besides a threat to their user base" (Williams 2002, 43).

Obviously, barring other strategic factors, firms that produce games will prefer producing their goods for the standard that has seen the widest adoption among consumers (measured as the installed base, i.e., the number of machines that have been sold to consumers and are currently active) to maximize their sales potential. As Gallagher and Park note, "strategy concepts that center around developing market share and mass acceptance of products, such as economies of scale, first mover advantage, and technological innovation, feature greater prominence in the analysis of these [standard-based] industries than they do for others." (Gallagher and Park 2002, 67)

Paradoxically, although conquering market share is the games industry's ever-pressing goal, the industry's conditions preclude firms from developing long-term strategic planning, the usual route that leads to the capture of market share. Kline, Dyer-Witheford, and de Peuter noted this problem in *Digital Play* (2003, 76–77) and offered that the games industry does not proceed through carefully orchestrated plans and a strategic management of innovation insomuch as it is "riding chaos" due to the constant promises of new technology. As Shankar and Bayus write, the 16-bit generation's "console war" did not differ: "The business strategies of Nintendo and Sega centered on their hardware systems, and these firms did not exhibit long-term strategic pricing or advertising behavior." (Shankar and Bayus 2003, 377) These factors may explain the particularly volatile nature of the games industry, which is considered a boom-or-bust, winner-take-all market (Schilling 2002, Grant 2002).

In standard-based industries, market share is a valuable strategic resource in itself, instead of being only a consequence of the firm exploiting its strategic resources to sell its products. Firms expend great effort in building market share because a standard's value is derived directly from its adoption rate. Moreover, market share is traditionally seen as a zero-sum game played out between competing standard bearers. This is why the video game industry typically measures a game console's success by its market share. As a zero-sum game, it means that every gain one firm makes is at the expense of the others. If a gamer that owns an Xbox One decides to spend $400 to buy a PlayStation 4, then that's $400 less for spending on Xbox One games. Hence, standards tend to entrench consumers through an effect known as *lock-in*; after spending $400 on an Xbox One, a gamer is likely to see the need to recoup the hardware's cost by buying games for the system.

Technology Adoption, Lock-In, and Network Externalities
Because an initial investment is required to gain access to the standard, changing standards would require consumers to buy another machine, hence creating important switching costs for them (Katz and Shapiro 1985, Gallagher and Park 2002). Hence, consumers will be reluctant to spend their money up front to gain access to a standard that may not be properly supported—no one wants to be stuck with a machine for a failed standard. This situation is treated in business studies and economics as either the technology adoption problem or the standards race (Schilling 1999, Gallagher and Park 2002), with complex strategies favoring the spread of new technologies among consumers. It is a crucial part of the life of platforms, and I'll cover it extensively in chapter 2.

When all goes well for a new video game console, a core audience of enthusiasts becomes early adopters, some good games are released, and a bandwagon effect takes place as more people adopt the technology and more developers make games. This leads to *network effects* (or *network externalities*), a term that identifies the positive effect that owning a good can bring to other users of the same good, either directly or indirectly, as Clements and Ohashi explain:

> Many high-tech products exhibit network effects, wherein the value of the product to an individual increases with the total number of users. Often these effects operate indirectly through the market for a complementary good. For example, the value of a CD player depends on the variety of CDs available, and this variety increases as the total number of owners of CD players increases. [...] we explicitly characterize the indirect network effect as an interaction between console purchases made by consumers and software supply chosen by game providers. (Clements and Ohashi 2005, 515–516)

Therefore, platform owners will seek to maximize their network because the more users adopt their platform, the more game developers and publishers are going to consider it. In addition, Shankar and Bayus (2003) identified a self-reinforcing dynamic at work when a large network is in place: a number of impromptu consumer-led promotional and circulation practices, such as word-of-mouth discussions and the borrowing and swapping of games. Thanks to the networked play practices of kids who played together and borrowed and exchanged games in the NES era, the games' high cost could be mitigated as each friend contributed his own small library of games to the common pool, reinforcing the network effect through a horizontal consumer-to-consumer axis (or, in other words, a "peer pressure" effect). These kinds of informal networks between peers are seldom discussed but are particularly influential when the main target demographic is composed of children.

On the larger scale of the platform as a whole, new console owners in the home video game market do not typically result in immediate benefits to other console owners.[1] In this situation, the network effects are of the indirect variety: customers buy the console, augmenting its adoption rate, which will hopefully influence game developers to adopt the standard as well and make games for it, which customers will buy, thereby generating revenue for the game's developer and publisher and for the platform owner. This creates a virtuous cycle (or, in cybernetic terms, a positive feedback loop—the changes from the initial state spur further changes in a self-reinforcing effect) of increasing desirability for the platform in both consumers' and game publishers' minds. The whole enterprise hinges on a single common, all-encompassing factor: confidence, from game developers and gamers alike. In this sense, video game platform owners are juggling two businesses at once: conducting business-to-business (B2B) operations with game developers and publishers and business-to-consumer (B2C) sales of consoles and customer support.

This description of the home video game market can be imperfectly applied to describe in general terms a wide range of game consoles thanks to a shared vocabulary. But each platform owner and console must be analyzed to identify its particularities. In the rest of this chapter, I will present the economic models of both Atari and Nintendo, and question some of the basic tenets of video game marketing in the process to refine our understanding of platforms as marketing entities and their impact on the video game business.

Beyond Razors and Blades: A Multiphase Marketing Process

As we saw earlier, the biggest hurdle in achieving platform success is the technology adoption problem. In standard-based industries, gaining market share and a larger installed base is the one condition to building confidence among consumers and producers of complementary goods as well, which are the cornerstones of an expansive standard ecosystem. When Microsoft entered the home video game market in 2001, they were losing more than $100 on every Xbox sold to consumers (Takahashi 2011). This amount was dwarfed by Sony's PlayStation3, whose sales cost Sony between $240 and $300 per machine, depending on hardware configuration (Bangeman 2006). The lesson? Building market share is something to be done at any cost.

The adoption of a standard can be stimulated by this well-known, often-mentioned, but ultimately seldom-discussed strategy: "giving away the razors in order to sell the blades" (Kline, Dyer-Witheford, and de Peuter 2003, 112–113). Although conventional wisdom usually describes the video game market in these terms, the so-called "Gillette model" and razor-and-blades analogy need some thorough recontextualization. The general idea is a sound strategy in economics: sacrifice short-term profit by subsidizing the base good in order to build the largest possible installed base and recoup the losses with the sale of complementary goods over time. However, things are not that simple, as Picker (2010) notes by resorting to video game consoles as an example, because the strategy depends on the firm's ability to lock in the consumer:

You can't lock in anyone with a free razor if someone else can give them another free razor. Indeed, all of this suggests just the opposite: if you want to create switching costs through the razor, the razor needs to have a high price, not a low one. [...] Think of switching from the Xbox to the PlayStation III. In contrast, users of free razors face zero switching costs if the alternative is another free razor. (Picker 2010, 2)

Gillette's razor system was patented in 1904 and thus protected until 1921; during that first period, the cost of a Gillette razor was, in fact, high. Only when the patent expired and competitors started issuing their own cheaper razors and blades did Gillette switch strategies to underprice and effectively subsidize the first stage of the market (the sale of the razor) with a relative overpricing of the second stage (the sale of the disposable blades). In the video game industry, platforms are walled in by the relatively high cost of consoles, which serves as an incentive for consumers to develop loyalty toward the platform they have chosen because they are also investing in it. But platform owners, even when selling consoles at high prices, will forego profit or even incur losses in selling them. This strategy relies on another crucial point of control (over the aftermarket of complementary goods, games) that is often passed over:

> If the razors are actually being sold at a loss—given away for free—then a better strategy seems clear: let the other guy sell the razors at a loss while you sell only the profitable blades. [...] That suggests that low-prices for razors only make sense if customers are loyal or if the razor producer can block other firms from entering the blade market. (Picker 2010, 2)

The modern video game market has, of course, integrated this lesson by erecting a second, legal wall around the platform gardens: that of licensing agreements. But things were not always so. One of the best lessons we can take away from the Gillette model is that pricing and licensing conditions in two-sided markets are not simple, and the dynamics of platform control and openness require delicate compromises and complex models that evolve through a platform's lifecycle—and an industry's history.

Atari, Phase 1: Selling Razors

From their appearance in the arcade business, video games were rather conceived as game machines, like their pinball predecessors. Atari's main line of business was the manufacturing of game machines, for arcades at first and then for the home. When Atari released its *Home Pong* in December 1975, its conception of what home video games should be was in line with the model of board games. When Parker Brothers sells a copy of *Monopoly*, it sells some hardware (a board, pieces, cards, and paper money) for a predestined activity (the game of *Monopoly*, whose rules are printed and included in the boxed goods); if people want to play *Battleship*, then they buy a copy of the *Battleship* game from Milton Bradley instead. The first home video game consoles were likewise dedicated to playing a single game.

This model framed home video games as a perpetual innovation market, where the sustainability of a game-producing firm depends on the continuous creation of new games sold separately, each of them competing against all other games available to a given consumer. Whereas some industries can resort to planned product obsolescence (the nylon stocking and electric lightbulb are quintessential examples) or rely on service, maintenance, replacement parts, or consumables to ensure a certain amount of repeat business and a steady cash-flow to the firm, this is not the case here. In perpetual innovation markets, a firm must constantly create new, desirable products. As competing manufacturers developed and sold their own electronic ping-pong game systems for the home, Atari sought to maintain its lead through constant product innovation, something its founder Nolan Bushnell disturbingly called "eating his own babies," to keep his company ahead of the "jackals," the competing firms feeding on the carcasses of Atari's innovative products by copying them. (Kent 2001)

Atari, Phase 2: Selling Razors and Blades

Although constantly developing new products was working well in the video arcade market, the home market required some means for providing a number of games to people without them having to fill their garages or closets with out-of-flavor (and expensive) machines. The solution came through the development of a game console that would use interchangeable cartridges of Read-Only Memory (ROM), on which programs could be stored and marketed separately. This marked the shift toward home video games as a standard-based industry. As Atari was working on this project (codenamed "Stella") in November 1976, Fairchild Semiconductor released its Video Entertainment System (VES) machine, offering exactly what Atari wanted to. This release forced Atari to move faster and finish Stella before Fairchild could completely corner the market. Atari rushed and in September 1977 released its Video Computer System (VCS), a name chosen to compete directly with the VES. Eventually, both consoles would be renamed the Fairchild Channel F and the Atari 2600, respectively, the latter reigning unchallenged over the home video game market after Fairchild abandoned it.

Because the 2600 featured interchangeable game cartridges, it was a first step toward the idea of a two-stage, two-sided market that would eventually become the dominant structure in contemporary home video games. Fairchild's VES was priced at $169.95 for the console and $19.95 for cartridges, whereas the VCS retailed for $199.95 and between $19.95 and $39.95 for the games (Schilling 2006, 77; also visible in Atari Age magazine's regular mail-order pages). Analysts were quick to describe Atari's and Fairchild's businesses as a transposition of the razor-and-blades model, assuming the firms were selling base durable goods at a low profit margin, so that consumers would then be locked into the long-term purchase of complementary, consumable goods sold at a high profit margin.

It turns out that analysts were too quick in making that judgment. In fact, Atari was slow in embracing that model, and initially remained very much a hardware business of selling game machines. The Atari 2600 had been meant to last 3 years, from 1977 to 1979, and its primary goal was to allow consumers to play arcade games at home (DeCuir 1999, 5). The plan was to have consumers upgrade to the next Atari system afterward; research and development efforts went into the post-2600 future (the eventual Atari 5200, 400 and 800) as soon as the 2600 was released. Bushnell's philosophy of "eating your own babies" meant he didn't want Atari to rest on the 2600's market success. Simply put, Atari never gave its razors away by selling them for just enough to break even while hoping to eventually profit from games after building up a large installed base; it simply sold game hardware for profit and then had an even bigger profit margin from its game software. The longevity of the second-stage software cartridges aftermarket was not strategically planned ahead from the beginning.

An article from InfoWorld in 1983 debunked the already prevalent myth of the razor-and-blades model:

> Industry wisdom has always had it that Atari never made money on the video computer system – it was supposed to be the razor that's all but given away so people will buy razor blades. In fact, it costs about $40 to manufacture a VCS. The average selling price last year [1982] was $125. (Hubner and Kistner 1983, 152)

Although it looks good on paper, the manufacturing cost of $40 per unit took a long time and significant effort to achieve: namely, expanding mass production with larger orders, redesigning the casing and materials for efficiency gains, and offshoring manufacturing to Hong Kong were all specific efforts that added up. But the main natural factor at work is the fact that technology costs tend to go down rapidly in a few years when dealing with computer hardware. The remarkable profit margin from Atari's 2600 hardware is a result of the lack of serious competition it faced from rivals. Without such an incentive, Atari maintained a healthy profit margin on hardware.

In the end, although Atari made great money selling its blades, it never stopped making money selling its razors. One indication that the firm was still attached to hardware sales can be found in the (ultimately misguided) decision to overproduce millions of copies of *Pac-Man*, in the hope the game would sell more systems (Barton and Loguidice 2008, 5). One crucial point to keep in mind, then, is that Atari struggled and attempted mixing strategies to adapt its practices as it went along. On the one hand, it wanted to profit from the gold mine that was the second stage of the 2600 market; on the other hand, it remained conscious of the need to plan the next, more advanced market to follow and not to cave itself in the current market and the 2600's game library. Because the software side of the market proved so much more profitable than the hardware side, however, Atari management shifted the firm's weight increasingly toward the maximization of production and sale of cartridges for the 2600. (Covert 1983, 60)

Atari, Phase 3: The Variegated Candid Software (VCS) Model

The need to control the lucrative aftermarket hit Atari hard in 1981, when some of their best programmers quit to produce 2600 games on their own, forming the independent game publisher Activision. Atari first tried to sue them, but without a technological or legal way to lock the team of rogue programmers out of the 2600 games market, Atari changed strategies, settling on, "If you can't beat them, have them join you instead." Atari signed a royalties agreement with Activision to get a part of their blades' profits, tapping into an unanticipated third revenue stream: third-party publisher royalties. Activision's games could also help Atari sell more razors, enlarging the 2600's installed base and opening the possibility for more game sales.

Following the logic of "more is more," Atari welcomed all kinds of new third-party publishers and signed royalties agreements with them (Barton and Loguidice 2008, 4). The matter now was not to lock competing firms out of its platform, as with Activision at first, but instead to lock them in and ensure they developed games for the 2600 and not for the systems of rivals Mattel or Coleco. The Atari garden had to be the most expansive and lush, with variegated foliage spewing colors in all directions. Diversity of products came from amateur software firms that developed games with candid enthusiasm.

Atari's new business model capitalized on three revenue streams. The first side of the market, hardware, accommodated an elastic profit margin, as high as consumer demand, competition from rivals, and price of components, assembly, distribution, and retailers' cut permitted. That uncertain profit margin was secondary, behind the high profit margin on Atari's cartridge software sales that made up the bulk of the market's second side. A modest royalty fee collected from third-party game publishers complemented software-side revenue. Although the direct amounts were modest, these third-party games played an important role in increasing the software offer for consumers, hence platform desirability, which in turn led Atari to sell more hardware and possibly more of its games.

The economic model's throwaway attitude toward third-party products had important ramifications on the kinds of games developed and sold for the platform. Anyone could hire an ex-Atari programmer (or poach one away) and have him or her single-handedly develop a game, no matter how novel (or bad) of an idea it was. This comparatively low barrier to entry encouraged the proliferation of software and constitutes a creative affordance for game developers who used the platform—arguably, the first affordance (quite literally) that came before any technology or design considerations, which made them able to afford developing and publishing a game for the console.

Crash of the Blades

This economic model was not without faults, however. Two crucial elements were missing from its foundations, both demonstrated by Atari's *Pac-Man* and *E.T. the Extra-Terrestrial* debacles. The first is software quality. An increase in software offer may not translate into increased console desirability if the software is not interesting to consumers. This realization came down hard—but too late—on Atari when shoddy game titles started selling at bargain-bin prices in an attempt to (minimally) recoup the investments of second-rate game development companies that had jumped in the market in a "gold rush" effect. This is because Atari did not create sufficient barriers to entry. The various policies and regulations that platform owners impose on software developers wishing to use their platforms, as well as the financial and logistical conditions required to meet the minimum operating criteria required (teams of employees, office space, equipment, software licenses, etc.), taken as a whole, act as a gating mechanism to protect a market from free-for-all competition. With sufficient barriers to entry, only firms that can successfully over-come the barriers can produce games for the standard and compete in this market.

The second factor missing from Atari's model was software quantity and the resulting peril of market saturation. When most homes likely to buy a 2600 have already done so, the extra desirability conferred to the platform by the third-party games is no longer translating into hardware sales and consequent profits to Atari. Instead, games from third-party publishers are simply cannibalizing Atari's main revenue stream from game sales because the royalty Atari collects from third-party games is significantly less than the profit it makes from selling its own first-party games.

These factors took the Atari Boom to the inevitable next phase of an industry characterized by boom-and-bust cycles: the Atari Bust. Because Atari's competitors Mattel and Coleco had both developed an adapter to play 2600 games on their own consoles, the shared standard's failure brought them down in the spiral as well. The Atari Bust became the North American Video Game Crash. Record losses were posted, firms closed, retailers cleared inventories and saved shelf space for other products, and newspaper titles claimed that video games were dead. Fire and brimstone everywhere.

And then came Nintendo with the NES in 1985.

Controlling With Power: The Nintendo Economic System (NES)

Lo and behold! The world of games was enshrouded in darkness, and Nintendo alone was holding the flame. Or so a common discourse, found in both business-oriented histories and fanboy comments, would have it. Tristan Donovan deftly summarizes the usual position:

> Nintendo's success reconfigured the games industry on a global level. It brought consoles back from the dead with its licensee model, which became the business blueprint for every subsequent console system. It revitalised the US games industry, turning it from a $100 million business in 1986 to a $4 billion one in 1991. Nintendo's zero tolerance of bugs forced major improvements in quality and professionalism, while its content restrictions discouraged the development of violent or controversial games. (Donovan 2010, 177)

Key to Nintendo's approach was a second NES—behind, yet before the Nintendo Entertainment System, laid a Nintendo Economic System. On the surface of business-to-consumer politics, Nintendo presented itself as a family-friendly entertainment provider, a gateway to worlds of imagination that children could safely enter without fearing inappropriate contents—a discourse meant, of course, to reassure parents, the ones with disposable income to buy the NES and games for their children. But this safety net hinged on tight control over the video games produced by third-party developers and publishers. Thus, at the core of business-to-business marketing, Nintendo was an autocratic conqueror who did everything in its economic and legal power to control the chaotic multitude that characterized the video game industry. To be an external game developer or publisher at the time of the NES meant putting up with unprecedented conditions as a software CEO at the time explained:

> We come up with an idea and submit it to Nintendo. Months later, they'll say yea or nay. If it's a go, we spend months and money writing the program. We then send in the final version. Again, they review it. If they decide they don't like it, everything we have done is wasted. If they decide it is only so-so, they will make only a few cartridges and we make no money. We have no say. We are at their mercy. They can make or break any of us overnight. (Palmer 1989, 20)

Just how did Nintendo achieve the position of strength necessary to impose such draconic measures to business partners? They did it by staying true to a central principle, aptly worded by Keith Stuart (2015): "Never relinquish control."

Made in Japan

The NES story begins in Japan in 1983, a world very different from the bust cycle the American market was entering (and known in Japan as the "Atari Shock"). Florent Gorges deflates the somewhat overblown importance of the Crash in United States–centric dominant video game history, noting that, "video arcades remained intensely busy" all around the world, Europe was seeing multiple manufacturers developing "inexpensive micro-computers," and Japan was rather entering a boom cycle: "The console market even hits record activity in the land of the rising sun! Between 1982 and 1983, no less than ten machines are launched to conquer a bustling industry!" (Gorges 2011, 47; freely translated)

In July 1983, Nintendo released its Famicom (Family Computer) console on the Japanese market with a peculiar business model.

Nintendo's history as a toy manufacturer, coupled with its experience with the portable electronic Game and Watch devices (chronicled in Gorges 2010) and the phenomenal distribution and retail networks it had developed (explained later in chapter 6), had convinced the firm it had all that was needed to design, launch, and maintain both the Famicom and its software. It went on sale at the incredibly low price point of 14,800 yen (around $60)—half the price of the competition. How could such a low price be attained?

First, there is the usual technocommercial explanation that Nintendo adopted its engineer Gunpei Yokoi's philosophy of "lateral thinking with seasoned (or withered) technology." Nintendo's Masayuki Uemura implemented a custom software architecture and custom chips to keep the console focused on some key performance issues (great graphical quality at a low manufacturing cost), and Nintendo shopped around for a long time looking for a semiconductor manufacturer willing to supply them with the right processor at a low enough cost. They finally found a willing partner in Ricoh. Nintendo president Hiroshi Yamauchi bet the bank by placing an extremely high (and risky) order, which convinced Ricoh to agree on a very low price per unit thanks to this unprecedented volume.[2]

Although the technocommercial explanation works well to explain the short-term success in developing the Famicom, there is a larger, more important explanation. As we have seen with Atari in the United States, so far in the home video game industry, a platform owner drew substantial revenue from selling the hardware it had designed and produced. The situation for home computers was even more skewed toward the hardware side because computers, in principle, were more open platforms than specialized game consoles. In both cases, hardware firms were concentrating their efforts on the hardware side, and other firms were specialized in the software aftermarket. Not so with Nintendo.

A Software Orientation

Nintendo adopted the Gillette model, minding the two caveats explained earlier. First, the base good, the Famicom, sold for a nontrivial amount, which created switching costs for the consumer to get locked in. An important detail to keep in mind is that even at this phenomenally low cost, the Famicom was not losing Nintendo any money; the firm was making little profit, but the system wasn't subsidized to consumers by selling it below its cost. Second, Nintendo kept all other firms out of the lucrative games aftermarket, thanks to the technological wall of a complicated console architecture that required sustained high-level effort to overcome. They would be the only ones developing and selling Famicom games, which is where they would make the bulk of their money, crystallizing a "software orientation" that has stayed with the corporation ever since (Inoue 2010). This position was antithetical to the principle of a "computer," as various software publishers reproached (Gorges 2011, 49). Still, from its 1983 launch to halfway through 1984, Nintendo produced its games and kept the Famicom gates closed.

However, as the Famicom's success grew, Nintendo could not develop and publish games fast enough to accommodate consumer (and retailer) demand. A choice had to be made: would it hire game developers, expand and substantially grow, or open up its platform to partner firms instead? According to Florent Gorges, the decision to open up the platform to third-party publishers, instead of hiring and training new teams internally, was taken because the latter solution would have taken too much time to fill in the Famicom market's gaps. Nintendo had to open up to other firms by necessity, not by choice. (Gorges 2011, 49)

Drafting licensing agreements for third-party publishers posed a formidable problem. Nintendo's approach, contrary to Atari's and computer manufacturers', was predicated on making almost no money on the hardware to sell it as cheaply as possible; this move would increase installed base, which would then determine the revenue generated from software sales over the console's lifetime. From this point of view, third-party titles could drive hardware sales and technology adoption by consumers, but this ultimately held limited interest because these sales of hardware were not, by themselves, generating much profit. As such, third-party games posed an important threat to Nintendo's true bottom line, game software sales, as Yamauchi explained: "Letting other publishers profit from the Famicom market amounts to sawing off the branch on which Nintendo is sitting!" (Gorges 2011, 50; freely translated)

This statement and position further showcases the need to envision platform economics as dynamic processes that change and adapt over a console's life cycle. The venerable Atari had only accepted third-party games *after* it had taken a considerable lead in the software side of the market. Opening up the platform before achieving such a lead would be self-defeating, and even more so in the Nintendo Economic System. The licensing fees were not just a way to make quick and easy extra income, as they had been for Atari; they had to cover Nintendo's lost revenue because these other publishers' games would cannibalize sales of its own titles.

The Self-Party Firm

In this respect, Nintendo is not a first-party platform provider but rather part of a slightly different category of firms that I propose to call self-party platform owners. Self-party firms follow different strategies and settle on different business models than the classic first-party firms because they are significantly invested in the two sides of the market (hardware and software). First-party firms typically rely on third-party firms to contribute software to the platform hardware and thus tend to view them as partners and cooperators because they don't compete for the same side of the market. Here, I rely on Dikmen, Rhizlane, and Le Roy's aggregated definition of cooperation between firms (2011, 3), which is characterized by two notions. First is reciprocity, which refers to strategies of cooperation and coordination rather than domination, power, and control, favoring the establishment of trust, mutual dependency, and reciprocity. Second is engagement, which can be described as the willingness of partners to expend efforts to make their relationship work, considered in light of long- rather than short-term gains.

A self-party firm, in contrast, does not view third-party game developers and publishers as cooperators because it rules over them with strategies of domination and control. Reciprocity is absent, power relations are one-sided, and dependency is not mutual because the platform owner is also present in the software side of the market and thus can fulfill the core needs of the hardware side by supplying high-quality games. The self-party firm needs the third-party licensees' support to broaden its games library, but it maintains the attitude of domination and forces them into asymmetrical subservience to deny them any competitive advantage. Third-party licensees and the self-party firm, on the software side, are "coopetitors," competitors with whom it is necessary or wise to cooperate for the time being to achieve some particular goal or as long as interests are compatible. In the "walled garden" analogy, they carefully screen developers and publishers massed around their doors and reluctantly open the gate to a select few visitors, confining them to "guests quarters" that are well away from the garden's Tree of Life and Tree of the Knowledge of Good and Evil. The self-party platform owner knows what's good, and its word is law, its power supreme. External firms are to be kept on the fringes, outside the platform's cooperative ecosystem.

When Nintendo of Japan first opened the doors to its garden, it admitted only big, sturdy, reliable firms: Hudson, Namco, Taito, Jaleco, Konami, Capcom, Irem, and Bandai. Nintendo let them publish up to five games per year, which had to be exclusive to the Famicom, reviewed by Nintendo, and free of excessive violence or sexually suggestive content. With minor variations, the licensees typically manufactured and distributed their own cartridges and paid Nintendo a (rather large) 20% royalty that amounted to approximately $6 per cartridge (Hill and Jones 2012, C166). The deal was costly and the conditions strict, but the Famicom's phenomenally low price, combined with Nintendo's strong Famicom games (notably *Donkey Kong* and *Mario Bros.*), had led to such high hardware adoption that the market was huge, making it worthwhile for these firms.

Even those strict conditions were too much control relinquished for Nintendo's taste, once the market had a steady influx of quality games. The Famicom was *their* garden, and if anyone wanted to play on their lawn, then they had to agree to their terms, which on top of everything so far reduced the number of games per year to three and included full control over the manufacturing process:

> Future licensees were required to submit all manufacturing orders for cartridges to Nintendo. Nintendo charged licensees $14 per cartridge [on top of the 20% licensing fee], required that they place a minimum order for 10,000 units (later the minimum order was raised to 30,000), and insisted on cash payment in full when the order was placed. [...] The cartridges were estimated to cost Nintendo between $6 and $8 each. The licensees then picked up the cartridges from Nintendo's loading dock and were responsible for distribution. (Hill and Jones 2012, C167)

This latter combination of restrictions placed high barriers to entry to software developers and publishers. Producing a game on the Famicom meant covering all normal game development expenses but also bringing to the table at least $600,000 ($14 for manufacturing + $6 for licensing per cartridge x 30,000 cartridges minimum order) upfront before the cartridges were manufactured, distributed, and (hopefully) sold. In stark contrast to Atari's VCS model, this was no place for amateurs or risky, unproven game concepts. The rules for software third-party firms were inflexible; as Nintendo would say to consumers years later when marketing the Nintendo 64, "Get N or Get Out." Years later, when European game developers and publishers unaware of the "Famicom Boom" in Japan were introduced to the terms of the Nintendo Economic System, they largely chose to Get Out (Ichbiah 2004 [1997], 50). However, before that came the international breakthrough for Nintendo, which successfully marketed its Famicom in the United States as the Nintendo Entertainment System and in the process kept adding more restrictions to its licensing model.

Marketing the NES in America

Marketing the NES required a different approach, business-wise, to marketing the Famicom. The operation would be taken in charge by Nintendo of America, a subsidiary created in 1980 to take care of arcade games. The first challenge was to convince retailers and consumers to adopt the platform and the business model of selling the system at low profit to benefit from game sales. That could be done initially with the strong library of games the Famicom enjoyed, but eventually more games would be needed, and ideally games that could be more culturally relevant to an American audience. Getting new third-party game developers or publishers was not a challenge; getting them to agree to the exacting terms of the Nintendo Economic System, however, would be. But if the NES succeeded in taking the market in phase 1, firms would line up at the garden's doors and sign to anything for phase 2, so Nintendo first tackled the problem of retailers.

Retailers: "Let's Play Money-Making Game"

Nintendo of America had done everything right to seduce retailers into trying out its "Entertainment System" in 1985 and 1986, after the Crash of 1983. Unlike the old man's proposal from *The Legend of Zelda*, their "money-making game" was a lot less risky (and, presumably, formulated in better grammatical form). A "Nintendo SWAT team" descended on New York retailers (the test market) to set up displays and windows and stock them with systems and games. Retailers would get these free for 90 days, after which they could give Nintendo its due money for their sales and return any unsold inventory to them. (Hill and Jones 2012, C167–C168) In effect, NOA shouldered all the risk. The NES sold progressively more units in subsequent test markets, ramping up to a nationwide release in 1986 and eventually becoming the hottest toy on the market.[3]

Then Nintendo started flexing its newfound leverage muscle. Using its outsider status, it refused to continue playing the retail game according to the rules of the toy industry. (Sheff 1993, 165–169) Reports indicated that "Nintendo threatened to either slow or cut off supplies to retailers who lowered the price of the game as little as 6 cents" (Seattle Times, 1991): "threatened" or gave veiled hints at massive shortages for the future because legally a supplier or manufacturer of goods cannot force a retailer to sell it at a certain price.

Nintendo's overbearing, top-heavy control over retailers came through Nintendo of America's system of "inventory management," as described by its marketing vice-president Peter Main (in Sheff 1993,

165). NOA withheld stocks and always underdelivered on retailers' demands, a feat possible only thanks to its exclusive control over the manufacturing process per licensing agreements with third-party game publishers. Incidentally, this also allowed NOA to undermanufacture its licensees' games and avoid leftover games stuck in warehouses and on retailers' shelves. This in turn avoided the risks of product dumping and games being sold at discounted prices, and it kept game valuation consistently high but of course sometimes created "severe shortages" (Brandenburger and Nalebuff 1997, 113). Retailers were not the only ones to suffer from this system.

Third-Party Developers and Publishers: "Grumble, Grumble..."

The same cocktail of policies found in Japan kept American third-party developers in line and clearly infeodated, begrudging vassals of the Nintendo Empire. Nintendo rapidly developed a reputation for acting as a corporate bully with third-party developers. As Jeff Ryan puts it, "Nintendo was enormous, controlling about 85 percent of the video game marketplace. It raked in billions every year. And it used its heft to insert onerous clauses into business contracts no one with any choice would agree to" (Ryan 2012, 135). Third-party developers and publishers, echoing the Hungry Goriya from *The Legend of Zelda*, would go "Grumble, grumble ..." and take the bait anyway. It would have made no sense to pass up, given Nintendo's market share and the kind of sales their games could obtain, especially with Nintendo's severe micromanaging of inventory:

> Greg Fischbach, founder of Acclaim Entertainment, was one of Nintendo of America's first licensees. He found that his company could sell out every game it produced. And he wasn't alone. "Every company sold out every game no matter how good it was, no matter how well the company was managed," he said. "Anyone with product was able to sell it." (Wesley and Barczak 2010, 21)

Nintendo of America licensees had it even rougher than Nintendo of Japan's second-wave partners. Licensees were limited to five games per year, and all games had to be exclusive to the NES for a period of 2 years. Games were subject to a thorough evaluation process by Nintendo, which controlled them for bugs and general quality, but also to strip any objectionable content from them (see chapter 6). All games were manufactured by Nintendo in the quantities it judged appropriate. Firms had to place an order for at least 30,000 copies and pay the manufacturing fee to Nintendo directly in cash and in advance. Nintendo of America would also handle the distribution of their games. The royalty fee consisted of 30% of the licensee's revenue (Harris 2014, 69).

In addition to the iron terms of the license, Nintendo put an additional technological lock in the NES. Despite its architectural complexity, Nintendo's Famicom in Japan had been cracked by unauthorized game developers, and pirate carts were circulating widely. Never one to relinquish control, Nintendo found a way: It designed a Checking Integrated Circuit (CIC), or lockout chip, that was inserted in the console and cartridges. On power-on, each would send a specific bit of code known as "10NES"; if the cartridge couldn't supply that code (the "key"), then the console would reset and try again. (Altice 2015, 90–91) The "lock and key" mechanism cemented technologically the legal walls of the license: Unauthorized cartridges could not run on the hardware, so licensees had to leave all manufacturing under Nintendo's control.

Due to "inventory management" practices, third-party licensees sometimes received only a fraction of the games they wanted manufactured (and for which they had paid upfront cash) and sometimes months later than intended. As Ed Logg put it when discussing his development of the *Tetris* cartridge for Tengen, "Nintendo the first year was jacking everyone around with 'ROM shortages.' Their contract was very one sided; you paid all the money up front, assume all risk, they tell you how many [cartridges] you're gonna get." (tsr c.2000) In fact, Nintendo was suspected (and accused in a lawsuit) of manipulating order quantities and chip allocations to privilege the manufacturing of cartridges for its own releases while curbing third-party publishers' competing titles. (Kent 2001, 388–390)

Nintendo's level of control over all the vertical stages of the industry was bordering on trust, a technical business term to describe near-monopoly power over a market, and typically anticompetitive business practices to maintain it. Firms stuck outside the garden would attempt to break down or scale the walls of technology by reverse-engineering or bypassing the lockout chip, resulting in lawsuits. Through the NES's golden years (the 1987–1988 "Nintendo Mania"), Nintendo's actions would get them into an investigation by the Federal Trade Commission for anticompetitive practices (Provenzo 1991, 24; Tomasson 1991; Weber 1992).

The five vertical stages of the video game industry identified by Dmitri Williams (2002, 46) were all heavily invested or supervised by the Japanese giant. Nintendo's main activities resided in development and publishing; its licensing agreement with third-party developers made it the world's exclusive manufacturer of cartridges; it was substantially involved in the *Shoshinkai* network of distribution in Japan[4] and distributed licensees' cartridges in America. Finally, it kept retailers in line through overbearing monitoring. The self-party model certainly led to impressive results, as *The Economist* described in 1990:

> Since 1983 its [Nintendo's] pre-tax profits have grown by 30% a year. For the year ending March 1991, Nintendo is expected to make Y110bn [110 billion yen] ($750m) before taxes on sales of Y420bn. It is now making as much money as Sony on a third of the turnover – a sure sign of its control over the market. (*The Economist*, August 18, 1990, 60)

Nintendo had finally become the One firm to rule them all. But the world of video games was set for great transformations, and Nintendo stood to lose Japan to the NEC PC-Engine and America to the Sega Genesis, for the reasons Dmitri Williams notes when assessing the "pattern of market dominance and failure" of the games industry:

> As each firm became dominant, it acquired and then abused its market power. For Atari, it was an issue of hype, poor quality and unreasonable growth expectations. For Nintendo, it was first a lack of innovation in the late 1980s and then an abuse of its relationships with developers in the mid 1990s. (Williams 2002, 43)

Accordingly, many video game fans and publications point out the quality of the game library as the key factor that makes the Super NES one of the best consoles, if not *the* best console, of all time. Part of it came through Nintendo's new rule on the maximum number of allowed publications. Instead of being limited to five titles per year, licensees now had a maximum of three games a year, but if one of their titles scored high enough on Nintendo's review and approval system, it didn't count toward that maximum. The system was perfect for Nintendo's needs: that its own games do not get devalued by low-quality, cheaply sold games.

The system turned out *too* perfect, and the Super NES was soon awash with great high-quality games. This news was certainly good for consumers, but not so much for Nintendo, whose self-party business model relies first and foremost on selling its own games. Although the high licensing fees meant Nintendo collected easy revenue in the short term, they entailed a negative effect for its middle- and long-term positioning: they alienated licensees (on top of the content guidelines censorship issues, detailed in chapter 6) and diminished Nintendo's strength as a provider of games.

Through the SNES years, licensees such as Konami, Capcom, Square, Enix, and Koei rose to fame or increased their already burgeoning reputations (as noted in the introduction, they may arguably be said to have never been in better form before or since then). They carved a larger part of the software sales for themselves, a reality that cut right into the heart of the Nintendo Economic System.

The 1990s loomed over Nintendo like an incoming storm, marking the end of its Golden Age as the firm would gradually slide into its Silver Age.

"If my parents won't get me the new deck," Justin says, "I'll probably sell my old deck and games to get the money to buy the new one. [...] I'll be kind of sad to see the old stuff go," he says, "but the way I look at it is, I'm going to have the same thing back again, only better." (Guinn 1991)

The Nintendo Economic System proved hugely profitable to Nintendo during the Famicom boom in Japan and Nintendo Mania in America, but it would soon get a little toning down. At the dawn of the 1990s, NEC's PC-Engine was seeing a measure of success in Japan, and Sega's Genesis console was also off to a good start in America. Although nothing stellar in themselves, the console sales carried with them the risk of attracting game developers who could produce quality games for these rivals, build up an increasingly interesting game library, and eventually build an increasingly high market share that could spiral out of Nintendo's control and tear down its wall brick by brick. Facing competition from NEC and Sega, Nintendo had to respond quickly. It did so by announcing a new, more powerful console coming in the future: the Super Famicom. Ta-dah! Everything people loved about the Famicom (or the NES) would still be there, only better, so the name hinted at.

This chapter details the context in which the Super Famicom, and eventual Super NES, were conceived and marketed, and the critical process of launching a video game console, a particular case of technology adoption whose importance cannot be overstated. This discussion will lead us to a new understanding of what a platform may be for consumers and how the Super NES managed to take off in America despite the challenges Nintendo faced.

Walled-In and Future-Proof

Content with the Famicom's success, in 1987 Nintendo had no plans to issue a follow-up system and lose its lucrative revenue stream from game sales. Expansion would come from within the garden's walls by releasing the Famicom/NES in Europe and South America. On the development side, the two hardware research and development teams were both at work on different projects. Masayuki Uemura's R&D2 team would add something to the garden thanks to a Famicom Modem, to be released in 1988. The R&D1 team, headed by Gunpei Yokoi, had completed a handheld prototype that would eventually be released as the Game Boy in 1989 to conquer another garden, that of handheld games.

Whereas Nintendo's strategy had allowed it to take over the Japanese and American home game markets, its technological, corporate, legal, and cultural walls made future expansion difficult to achieve. As Sheff notes, "Nintendo had reached relative saturation of its largest group of buyers, households with young boys." (Sheff 1993, 233) Rival firms set their sights further, and soon there were "barbarians at the gates" (Harris 2014, 390) massing just outside their precious garden, building arks and ships that would take them across the seas, across the chasms of new technology, where the greener pastures of new markets sprawled—fields ripe for newer, bigger gardens. When Nintendo squinted hard to look over to the horizon, it realized some of those barbarians were its own guests, who were leaving their garden.

The NEC PC-Engine

Hudson Soft, the first of Nintendo's licensed third-party game developers (of *Bomberman* and *Adventure Island* fame), had approached them with a proposal for expanding the Famicom's graphical capabilities through a custom graphics chip. (Gorges 2011, 65) Nintendo had refused, prompting Hudson to seek out alternatives to the increasingly tight technological quarters the Famicom provided. It found a partner in the Nippon Electric Company (NEC), a general manufacturer of electrical goods and computing equipment that can be described as the Japanese equivalent to the American Telephone & Telegraph Company, AT&T. NEC's technological expertise was doubled by a strong advantage in resources: it was one of the world leaders in semiconductors.

When NEC and Hudson announced the release of a jointly developed console in 1987, the PC-Engine, Nintendo was caught flat-footed. NEC's manufacturing and suppliers, combined with Hudson's graphical technology and game-making expertise, made for a vertically integrated powerhouse in the industry. Together, they would bring to market a technologically superior hardware-and-software proposition, with a CD-ROM drive to boot—a world premiere! In the words of Florent Gorges, Nintendo "freaked out" and announced it was developing a new console—a lie meant to diminish the effect of the PC-Engine's release. In fact, they had nothing in the works because they had intended to keep riding on the success of the Famicom (Gorges et al. 2009).

The PC-Engine was a big success, outselling the Famicom in Japan in 1988 and slowly being imported by some dedicated U.S. gamers. While Nintendo was busy working on a follow-up to the Famicom, Sega released the 16-bit Mega Drive in October 1988 but failed to make any significant headway into the Japanese market. Sega had, however, its sights on the US market and proceeded quickly: It had announced a North American release for January 1989 but revised launch for August of that year.

The Sega Expansive Gillette Attitude (SEGA) Marketing Strategy

Nintendo's long turnaround gave Sega plenty of time to enter the North American market. The one thing necessary for the launch to succeed was for the system to have great games. To achieve this goal, Sega of America would capitalize on home conversions of its arcade hits and endorsements from sports celebrities. However, that wouldn't be enough to compete against the entrenched NES, so Sega had drafted a licensing agreement that was a bit more flexible than Nintendo's while still revolving around high licensing fees and the control over cartridge manufacturing. It soon appeared all but impossible to enlist third-party licensees, however, because all NES developers had agreed to an exclusivity contract under Nintendo's license agreement. Soon the American firm Electronic Arts confronted Sega: It had found a way to bypass Sega's security measures and was able to make Genesis games without any license. With such leverage, Sega of America negotiated with EA and settled on a more favorable deal. It turned out to be a boon to Sega of America because EA contributed to the early success of the Genesis with games such as *John Madden Football*.

Learning from the incident, Sega eased some of the conditions of its licensing agreement and successfully poached developers and publishers who had been working for Nintendo's NES. Like its software library, sales of the console picked up at a steady rate—until the release of *Sonic the*

Hedgehog, which Sega bundled with the Genesis in 1991. This move was, as many historical chronicles pun, "Sega's Sonic Boom," which cut into Nintendo's SNES entry into the market.

Despite the Genesis's success, however, Sega hadn't struck Nintendo-level gold. Because it entered a healthy, occupied market with a strong leader, Sega needed every bit of leverage to maximize its first-mover advantage and followed the first principle of orthodox video game marketing: gain market share at any cost. Sega settled on a "classical" razor-and-blades strategy, which was actually the second-phase, post-patent Gillette strategy, as we saw in chapter 1. That gamble was much riskier than Nintendo's "phase 1" Gillette model, which, like Atari, had it making money on hardware as well as software. Sega would subsidize the hardware and give the razors away to inflate the adoption rate. It would go even further in its expansion strategy and give away its best blade, *Sonic the Hedgehog*, with the razor. Desperate times called for desperate measures. Although the strategy did gain Sega a large share of the American market, it didn't translate into heaps of gold: Nintendo's total net income for all markets, through 1992 to 1996, varied between twice and 12 times as much as Sega's (Grant 2003, 230–231). The focus on market share in discussions of the video game industry, and especially for the 16-bit console wars, too often hides such financial realities. For all its market share increases, Sega would never get to swim in a pool of gold like its rival.

Supering the World in Marketing

When Nintendo caught wind of Hudson and NEC's unholy alliance and upcoming PC-Engine, set for release on October 30, 1987, it knew something had to be done. It was time for the empire to strike back, but the empire had nothing up its sleeves and nothing to do besides praying that its network of fans, consumers, partners, and imperial subjects would stay faithful and not be swayed by other higher forces. Nintendo did more than pray: It started to actively preach about its own Second Coming.

Nintendo summoned the press on September 8 for a shocking announcement: A new 16-bit console, the Super Famicom, would be on sale next year (Audureau et al. 2013, 12–13). Behind the closed doors of Nintendo, no such console was in the works, but the announcement's purpose was to lessen the impact and media coverage of NEC's market entry. Thus, development work on the Super Famicom began under Uemura's lead, and press announcements followed regularly throughout the next months.

Chris Covell's website offers two pages titled "Japanese Secrets!" where he summarizes the Japanese press' coverage of the Super Famicom from its first announcement to its release. The reactions first reported on backward compatibility with the Famicom (September 1987) and then a trade-in program instead (November 1987). Later on, the impending release was the focus instead, with an announced 1988 release in July of that year, then in December, and a revised launch window in 1989; when July 1989 came, the press informed the public that another year of delay was expected. This was quite a wait for the eager Nintendo consumers but within expectations for a game console to be developed from scratch.

Knowing that the Super Famicom was, in fact, a rushed response to competitors rather than a carefully planned project provides an interesting lens for examining some peculiarities around its development and marketing. The first of these aspects is how the Super Famicom's presentation through press announcements revolved around the display (or discourse) of technological supremacy "for the first time in Nintendo's young history" (Audureau et al. 2013, 13). Such a framing of hardware by Nintendo should be noted because it runs against the corporation's usual way of framing virtually every one of its new consoles as an extension or application of Gunpei Yokoi's philosophy of "lateral thinking with seasoned technology." Nintendo's promotional discourse usually downplays the importance of technological performance and argues instead for game quality, fun factor, or game design experience. The Super Famicom and its follow-up, the Nintendo 64, were both uncharacteristically framed as consoles with "more power" than the competition. For instance, *Famicom Hissyoubon*'s report, following the SFC's first demonstration to the press in 1988, frames the official announcement as "high performance beyond imagination" (Covell, "*Super Famicom*: December 1988").

The reason that the Japanese press focused on technical specifications and technological arguments when they covered the Super Famicom is simply because that is what Nintendo focused on in their handouts to the press at the November 21, 1988, conference (reproduced in the December 16 issue of *Famicom Hissyoubon*). The Japanese press' contents trickled down into the US press so that the technological discourse has mostly been relayed uncritically, as I show later in chapter 3.[1] So why did Nintendo forsake its Yokoi principle of lateral thinking with seasoned technology, thus engaging in the arms race for technological power? The simplest explanation is that there was no time to think in the limited time frame they had to conceive, design, and develop the Super Famicom.

In this light, the next console's goal is to be just like the Famicom, only "super," whatever that means. The North American marketing line can be understood entirely differently with this context in mind too. Instead of "Now you're playing with power ... *super power!*" with the ellipsis marking a dramatic pause to create an impactful punchline, we can understand the ellipsis as a marker of uncertainty while the speaker is looking for something more detailed, or more impressive to say, before quickly settling on a vague and ultimately empty epithet: "Now you're playing with power, ... ummm... *super* power!"

Understood in this way, then, the Super NES looks like a more-of-the-same, half-hearted effort at making something "new"; it is in fact a conservative console, a souped-up Famicom—a "Famicom 2," as it was first known internally at Nintendo (Audureau et al. 2013, 11). As I presented in the introduction to this book, it is no coincidence that various publications discussed it as an "upgraded NES" (*EGM* #2, May 1989, 32). It's not just a matter of miscomprehension: During its early development, people believed it would be (and Nintendo tried to make it) backward-compatible in some way with the Famicom/NES. *B-Young Age* reported on November 23, 1987, that Nintendo would take their customers' old Famicom systems in a trade-in program; a year later, *Famicom Hissyoubon* Magazine discussed this on December 16, 1988, with Nintendo's handouts to the press indicating that a trade-in program is "being considered" (Covell, "*Super Famicom*: December 1988"). In the end, the program never materialized.

Still, Nintendo treated the Super Famicom as a Famicom upgrade, most notably in its initial marketing. During the first demonstration to the press on November 21, 1988, Nintendo presented a prototype SFC that could be hooked up to the soon-to-be-released "Famicom Adaptor," a regular Famicom that would have a built-in audiovisual output. When connected to the Super Famicom's audiovisual input, the Famicom Adaptor's signal would pass through the Super Famicom and into the TV, thus allowing both consoles to be plugged into the TV at the same time (and eerily foreshadowing Sega's future Sega-CD and 32X add-ons to the Genesis). The final and most telling sign of this "Famicom upgrade" mentality is that on release day, the Super Famicom was sold in Japan with two controllers and nothing else. By nothing else, I mean no A/C adapter or audiovisual cables. Why? Because the Super Famicom could use the Famicom's, and Nintendo considered that just about anyone who would want an SFC would already own a Famicom. That a consumer product could ship without the cable needed to power it speaks volumes to the manufacturer's noncommitment to pursuing a new, expanded audience. Nintendo's stance when commercializing the Super Famicom is clearly one of promoting continuity from the mindset of a hardware upgrade; the console was intended as a retention tool for keeping Nintendo consumers in the firm's lap.

The Launch in Japan

In July 1989, Nintendo organized a press conference to announce that the Super Famicom would not be released for another year due to shortages in semiconductors, which were tied up by the importance of NES production and the release of the Game Boy in April 1989 in Japan and July 1989 in America. As the next release date of August 1990 loomed by and another target was set for November instead, a Super Famicomania hit Japan with more than 1.5 million pre-orders for the machine. Doubts were expressed on Nintendo's capacity to fulfill these orders, and the Yakuza reportedly (or so Nintendo feared) took an interest in the console in hopes of selling it on the black market. Nintendo launched "Operation Midnight Shipping." "On November 19 at midnight, less than 48 hours before the nationwide launch, a hundred heavyweight trucks went to the company's secret warehouses, each carrying 3,000 Super Famicom destined for Japanese stores." (Audureau et al. 2013, 21, also covered in Sheff 1993, 232–233) The Super NES was put on sale on a chaotic Wednesday. It was chaotic because the 300,000 shipped units could only cover 20% of pre-orders. A store owner reported having registered more than 1,500 pre-orders and getting only 100 packages. Some independent and smaller stores decided not to open at all to avoid the ire of consumers—many of which had taken a day off their job to line up at stores, only to go home empty-handed. Disturbances were enough of a deal to spur the Japanese government to ask console manufacturers to release new hardware on weekends from now on.

An additional 300,000 consoles were put on sale the next week, which depleted Nintendo's stocks for months—including the crucial Christmas period of 1990. This explains the lukewarm results published by Nintendo at the end of the fiscal year in March 1991, with Super Famicom sales of only 600,000 consoles, compared with Sega's 900,000 Mega Drives and NEC's 1.3 million PC-Engines. This slow start dampened analysts' expectations in the United States, which may have hurt the sales of the Super NES when it launched there later in 1991. Unfortunately, the difference between lukewarm sales and a sold-out product that had been underdistributed was lost on the American public to fully appraise the situation. As we will see in chapter 3, this situation was compounded by the fact that the leading Nintendo magazine in the United States did not monitor the anticipation building up in Japan for the console.

Preparing for America

From the retrospective vantage point of the dominant history of games, which claims that the Super NES beat the Sega Genesis after the advertisement-heavy rivalry between the two (ignoring NEC because of a U.S.-centric bias), it might be difficult to envision just how bad things looked for Nintendo at the time. Most analysts reasoned that Nintendo was in a difficult position and that Sega's Genesis had taken over the market. After the Consumer Electronics Show (CES) of June 1991—two months before the American launch of the Super NES in August—*Time* Magazine considered the possibility for Nintendo to crash and burn like Atari:

> At best, say analysts, over the next five years Nintendo will sell about two-thirds as many of the new systems as it sold of the old. At worst, Nintendo could end up like Atari, which in the early 1980s tried to replace a wildly successful video-game player with one that was more powerful but incompatible. Atari ended up with a mountain of unsold game cartridges that got loaded onto dump trucks and used as landfill. (Elmer-DeWitt 1991, 75)

What the American public had in mind was the fact that this new Super NES system would not be compatible with the NES games parents had purchased for their children over the years. (Elmer-DeWitt 1991, Guinn 1991) Japanese consumers had been promised, told, or suggested that there might be adapters or trade-in programs for their soon-to-be-obsolete Famicom, at launch, soon enough, or eventually. In America, one "rumor" reported by *Electronic Gaming Monthly* in October 1990 stated that "The American version of the Super Famicom will supposedly attach to the underside of the Nintendo Entertainment System through the expansion port." But aside from this weird particular mention, there were no discussions of backward compatibility. Most American consumers may have possessed a variety of dedicated first-generation home video game consoles and then an Atari 2600 (and perhaps a home computer for productivity software, bought cheaply after the 1983 home computer price wars). This "Super Nintendo" was their first contact with the cyclical nature of video game consoles and the upgrade logic of noninteroperable successors—in other words, the lack of backward compatibility.

The Atari 2600 game library had been available to both the system's competitors (the Intellivision and Colecovision) in sideward compatibility and its successor, the Atari 5200 Supersystem, in backward compatibility, through adapters. The introduction of the Super NES marked the first time that a platform in good health and with plenty of support was being displaced by a newer, incompatible platform from the same firm. It soon appeared to everybody that contrary to other consumer electronics and entertainment industries, video game consoles were not a standard-based industry, or at least not exactly.

Rethinking Platforms and Standards

In chapter 1, I wrote that standard-based industries are usually viewed as playing a zero-sum game of "capture the market share." This is because standards are usually seen as providing a way for consumers to do something, which is an adequate conception in many technology industries. Users are typically assumed to side with one standard to complete that activity and are not expected to adhere to multiple standards concurrently. For example, having a printer from one manufacturer ties the user to that standard of ink cartridges, and there is typically little reason in having a second printer from another manufacturer, at least in the home consumer market (an office may use a laser printer to print black and white text reports in mass quantities and a color ink printer for occasional graphical elements, of course).

This idea of exclusive choosing is at the heart of a standard, to the point where the cost incurred from "breaking out" of the lock-in created by the standard is called a *switching* cost, implying the idea of moving from one standard to another, instead of adopting one more and using all of them concurrently. Game consoles, however, do not work this way because each console yields access to a different library of games according to exclusive licensing agreements and "signature" products; the printer analogy breaks down because it is as if only Nintendo was manufacturing the red ink and Sony the gray one. Hence, many gamers will own more than one console because they want to play games published by both Sony Computer Entertainment and Nintendo, and each will only appear on their corporation's console because noninteroperability is the name of the game. "Playing games" is not a valid category like "printing documents" (which means choosing between Canon or Epson products) or "listening to music" (which may entail choosing among cassettes, CDs, MP3 players, or smartphones). Platforms grant affordances or present resistances to various game types, genres, audiences, scopes, or publishers, directly or indirectly shaping distinct game libraries. Gamers don't just choose to "play games" when they buy a console, they choose to "play Nintendo games" or "play Sony games," or they choose to "play action games" or "play strategy games", and so on.

The Super NES's coming, like a forecast of dark clouds, had carried a bad surprise for consumers: all that time, they thought they had been investing in "Nintendo games," but in truth they had actually been choosing to "play 8-bit Nintendo games," and now they would have to start anew with 16-bit Nintendo games—and a costly $199 SNES console to get aboard. They knew about switching costs, but now they had to face upgrading costs—a pill all the harder to swallow given that Sega was offering a backward compatibility module for the Genesis to play 8-bit Master System games (Schilling 2006, 78–79).

This situation wasn't like printers and ink, VHS tape decks, or razors and blades (but VHS owners would face a similar situation when the DVD standard picked up). Following Picker (2010), there is a qualitative difference between the complementary goods for razors and game consoles. The razor hinges on disposable blades that are trashed after use, so that no going forward value remains, leaving the consumer free to switch to another razor. On the contrary, abandoning a console means forfeiting an accrued library of games, whose value would otherwise remain for the player to keep enjoying. Because games are not a disposable commodity, the video game market is one where the accumulation of complementary goods (games) creates lasting value for the consumer that can quickly exceed the value of the primary good (the console). This can be measured through the tie ratio of a console, which compares the sales of a main good with the sales of complementary goods, thus expressing in a ratio how many games per system have been sold to consumers. A console that sells for $299 with a tie ratio of 6:1 means that, on average, players owning that console have purchased six games. If those games cost $60 each, then on average, players have accrued a software library valued at $360 for their system, which they would have to forfeit if they switched to a rival.

Having expensive, noninteroperable consoles has an important drawback: consumers tend to adopt a "wait-and-see" approach to ensure that the console will be adopted before gambling on it. This "hold-out" effect can feed back into a vicious cycle and kill a platform's chance of success in the marketplace: a lack of consumers buying the device makes game developers refractory to develop games for the underadopted platform, which makes consumers wait further, and so on. This is the single biggest problem with selling game consoles, expensive technology products that depend almost entirely on complementary goods to convince consumers to spend their money upfront. This is why, in the games industry, the launch window of a new console is absolutely critical. More than anything, a successful launch relies on great games, a notion that merits further discussion before getting to the SNES's launch in particular.

Specs Are Worthless

Although it is admittedly half provocation and half wishful thinking, the idea that consoles' technical specifications could be useless is nevertheless productive—as long as we remember that this book asks, "What's a platform to whom?" This will undoubtedly sound heretical to the economics-oriented literature on the video game industry. When Subramanian, Chai, and Mu (2011), for instance, discuss the collaborative and complementary competencies of Nintendo for the Wii, collaborative competencies exclusively cover the hardware and technology angle of their platform, delving into the interfirm relationships between Nintendo and Datel, Mitsumi Electric, Tabuchi Electric, Analog Devices Inc., and ST Microelectronics Inc, which produce the wired LAN adapter, wireless LAN module and controller parts, AC adapter, and parts and technology for the Wii Remote. The complementary competencies are compared according to a checklist of primary features, determined to be CPU speed, GPU power, RAM, ROM, video resolution, sound channels, and storage media; and secondary features, namely, online capabilities, connectivity, backward compatibility, and controller.

Richard Gretz and Suman Basuroy formulate complex economic calculations based on "console quality," derived from "Graphics processing speed," CPU speed, total RAM, and maximum program size of games designed for the console. (Gretz and Basuroy 2013, table 4) As we'll see in chapter 4, numbers can (and often) lie when it comes to "power" or "quality." For the evaluation of games, they assume consumer homogeneity to compute a "mean utility" value for each published game (287)—an assumption whose limits they recognize (297) but that ignores consumers' preferences and heterogeneity of game content, notably through game genres (Marchand and Hennig-Thureau 2013, 145).

Most humanities scholars would probably balk, chuckle, or roll their eyes at these processes of crunching down the aesthetic pleasures that games and consoles provide into hard data points that contribute to a standardized "quality" metric. Not only is the categorization of these features completely arbitrary, but the games are totally absent from this discussion of a firm's technological and commercial capability. To me, the positions, methodology, and preoccupations of business studies and game studies seem so far apart that we can only stand to gain if we can adopt the other perspective and work at bridging the gap. In this spirit, I will note that, following Ian Bogost's discussion on interfaces and games as experiences (2008), video game consoles are not toasters. We do not buy them based on their technical specifications alone, with the understanding that we will use them for whatever bread we prefer having toasted, because they are gateways to walled gardens, and they enforce technological standards that define the kinds of game experiences we will be able to enjoy. It makes no sense to abstract games away from the competencies and features of a firm that's developing and marketing a games console. It may make sense from a strictly marketing position—hardware and software development depend on different processes, suppliers, distributors, and business models—but it makes no sense from a customer's point of view because the primary reason for investing in a games console is to access a library of games. It makes no sense for Nintendo in particular, given its software orientation.

The case of technical specifications and console launches illustrates the multivalent nature of platforms. As soon as launch titles are published, they make the abstract specs—or at least their effect—concrete and visible for consumers. The role of technology is to attract third-party game developers and publishers and is largely played out by the time the platform reaches consumers. In other words, platform owners never sell technology to consumers. They sell technology to game developers and publishers in a B2B relationship. Game developers use it to create games that they sell to consumers in B2C exchanges. These exchanges feed back into the B2B relationship, with licensing fees returning to the platform owner. Contrary to popular intuition—and to the prevalent paradigm in business studies—platform owners do not sell technology to gamers as a base good; they present technology as a promise of new games to come. In the end, these games are the real base good. As Nintendo of America's Peter Main put it, "the name of the game is the game" (Harris 2014).

The Name of the Game Is the Game
Complementary goods are characterized by the fact that they extend, expand, or otherwise transform the base good's function(s). They are useless without the base good, and the base good's utility or duration is severely hampered by a lack of them. From an industrial standpoint, it may be the case that a platform owner finds itself investing most of its production effort, research and development budget, distribution efforts, and/or capital in the production and sale of its game console, which justifies treating it as the base good—along with the fact that it serves as a cement that brings together all the firm's other goods (games, peripherals, etc.). It may make sense to describe games and peripherals as "complementary" to the platform owner's main line of business then. However, this mental

model is derived from a production-centric view of the industry. Moreover, it runs the risk of firms falling into what Wesley and Barczak have called the performance trap:

> Designers and engineers are often energized by breakthrough technologies that allow them to accomplish tasks they only dreamed were possible. In the process, they often lose sight of the real goal—fulfilling a customer need. They succumb to what we call "the performance trap." [...] (Wesley and Barczak 2010, 5)

The one firm to have remarkably avoided the performance trap through the history of video games is Nintendo. As we have seen in chapter 1, by refraining from the cutting-edge, "next-gen" technology, and instead looking for creative applications in new (lateral) ways for old or outright obsolete technology, Nintendo has kept game development costs low and has sold hardware both cheaply and profitably, without the need to rely on an influx of third-party licensing revenue to offset console subsidizing.

Nintendo understood that technology is not what consumers want. Consumers want games to play. They want *only* games that they want to play—one or two stand-out titles, not a bunch of "alright" games (Clements and Ohashi 2005). Because the console is merely a means to that end (an inevitable means, I might add), consumers only buy a console if and when there are games they want to play on it. As *Electronic Gaming Monthly* stated when discussing the upcoming Game Boy, "The worth of any new system, no matter how versatile or technologically advanced, is in the software that the machine runs. After all, why buy a GameBoy if the system can't play decent games?" (*EGM* #2, July/August 1989, 41) This is often referred to in the business literature as the need to have a "killer app" for the platform, a software title that is so hotly anticipated it creates demand for the hardware. Launch titles are usually tasked with becoming "killer apps" for the up-and-coming platform. They are of the utmost importance in establishing a platform's ludic promise because they function as an interface between the platform's underlying technology, game developers, and gamers.

As such, killer apps are the perfect tool for building the all-important confidence in the new platform across the two target audiences of the platform owner: game developers and publishers, and consumers. In this regard, the Super Famicom's launch provides an exemplary demonstration of the dynamics of "killer apps."

On release, the Super Famicom was sold alone for 25,000Y or with *Super Mario World* for 32,000Y (Sheff 1993, 233; $175 and $220, respectively). This price tag made it an expensive console for the Japanese, who had been paying 15,000Y for the Famicom and less than 10,000Y for the Game Boy. Another sore point was the lack of launch titles: only *Super Mario World* and *F-Zero* were available, although that initial offer was soon complemented with other releases for a total of around 10 titles released by the end of 1990, including notably *ActRaiser*, *Pilotwings*, *Gradius III*, and *Final Fight*. There was, however, no sign of the third *Legend of Zelda* game that had been planned as a launch title for years, ever since the console had been revealed. Sales ramped up following Nintendo's production schedule, and four notable game releases stood out by creating "impressive scenes of hysteria" (Audureau et al. 2013, 22): *Final Fantasy IV* (July 1991), *The Legend of Zelda: A Link to the Past* (November 1991), *Street Fighter II* (June 1992), and *Dragon Quest V* (September 1992). Before getting there, however, it's worth examining closely the contributions of the two launch titles.

Super Mario World

The high-profile launch title for the SFC was *Super Mario World*, fittingly subtitled *Super Mario Bros. 4* in its original Japanese release and widely referred to as such during development, both internally at Nintendo and by the press. The development team, in fact, considered that the game was not different and new enough to be a good showcase for the Super Famicom's increased capabilities, as game director Takashi Tezuka expressed (Audureau et al. 2013, 17). This view is still present today in the Euro-American sphere. When *Retro Gamer* readers voted *Super Mario World* as the greatest game of all time in the magazine's 2015 edition of the yearly poll, the staff's article noted, "In retrospect, *Super Mario World* is surprisingly economical with its resources, given its status as a showcase game for a new console," and "the game makes sparse use of the console's advanced graphical features" (*Retro Gamer* #150, 62).

It may not be surprising to note that *Super Mario World*'s original North American release box does not mention technology at all and is perfectly satisfied with describing the contents and backstory of the game.[2] Contrary to what nostalgia and historical hindsight might lead us to believe, the game was not particularly well received at the time of its release. Florent Gorges notes how in certain magazines in France, the import Super Famicom tests gave *F-Zero* awesome scores, whereas *Super Mario*

World was described as being alright, with a score of around 80%. (Gorges et al. 2009) Sheff, covering the game from a closer historical vantage point of 1993, was critical as well:

> "Super Mario World" wasn't a sufficient departure from its predecessor. "People don't know how to write 16-bit software yet," Greg Fischbach said at the time. "It will be revolutionary, but it will take some time to understand." There would be more lifelike and emotion-filled games because of 16-bit processors. Miyamoto says, "Wait, and I will learn more about the limits of this machine." In the meantime, "Super Mario World" was a disappointment, particularly when it was compared to a new game that was released for Sega's 16-bit system [*Sonic the Hedgehog*]. (Sheff 1993, 231)

Still, although critics and industry pundits lamented *Super Mario Bros. 4*'s underwhelming role in promoting the new console, players bought and enjoyed it immensely. Nintendo's abundance of mosaic effects, scaling and rotation, and scrolling background layers in the game can be read as a means to demonstrate the strengths of the Super NES platform to other developers interested in traditional games. The other launch title, *F-Zero*, showcased the console's unique Mode 7 graphics to stir experimentation in other directions.

F-Zero

A racing game set to a behind-the-car view, everything about *F-Zero*'s concept was perfect to create a convincing illusion. The game relied on a brand-new technology embedded in the Super Famicom, "Mode 7" graphics (detailed later in chapters 4 and 5). This technology allowed game developers to project a playfield (or ground map) in formally correct linear perspective, as if the viewer were standing inside the fictional world with the ground receding away, and distant objects converging up to a horizon line. One of Mode 7's obvious limits was that it could only project flat surfaces, so anything that had to stand up from the ground, such as houses on the side of a race track or mountains, were out of the question. *F-Zero* got around that obstacle by putting the race tracks as elevated highways running atop the surface of planets stretching out below, which we imagine to be far down so everything looks small.

Although perspective wasn't new in the racing genre (various arcades and NES games had used it, including *Pole Position*, *Hang-on*, *OutRun*, and *Rad Racer*), what *F-Zero* offered was an incredible sense of speed with unparalleled smoothness and fluidity. The game's fiction took place in the

26th century, where speeds of hovering cars in the hundreds of kilometers per hour weren't a question of realism. Moreover, because Mode 7 could project static ground maps, the rail guards that border the track consisted of tiny bulbs that formed a line instead of elongated full lines. As the player raced through the stretches and curves of the track, these bulbs (vaguely reminiscent, especially through their pushback/electrical shock behavior, of pinball pegs) zoomed by at fast speed, from the center of the horizon line and all the way down to either side of the screen's bottom edge. It appeared that race cars hit pegs and bounced back, but under the hood, the machine did not register these as material objects, but as painted dots on a flat track, with an "invisible wall" delineated exactly on top of them.

Mode 7 allowed smooth scrolling and perspectival effects on a flat surface; through a clever trick of *trompe-l'oeil*, F-Zero managed to provide the illusion that objects actually existed in the game world and at speeds that defied any other racing game that had been out before—in homes or arcades. Much of that impression came from the simple decision of placing dots on the ground rather than continuous lines. On a macrolevel of video games in general, F-Zero wasn't an innovative game—it wasn't even a particularly feature-rich racing game, with its lack of a two-player mode. Yet on the microscale of racing games in perspective view, its speed, smoothness, and fluidity were impressive achievements. More than anything, however, it proved to be a terrific success for Nintendo as a technical demo to attract developers to the platform. By seeing the game in action, developers knew what could be done with "Mode 7" perspective and the unique strengths of the SFC if they wanted to develop games for it. This led to a wave of games that focused on a similar experience, whether they revolved around piloting and shooting (*Hyperzone*) or racing (*Top Gear, Battle Cars*). Many games integrated "Mode 7" sequences amid their usual gameplay for traveling (*Secret of Mana, Illusion of Gaia, Final Fantasy III*) or for action sequences (the *Super Star Wars* series, *Indiana Jones' Greatest Adventures*).

The Super Famicom's launch illustrates a key but perhaps counterintuitive point: the importance for launch titles to tread in paths familiar to gamers. Both of the SFC's launch titles were an additional entry in a long line of established game genres: platformers and racing games. As such, consumer demand clearly existed for these kinds of games, and it was possible for consumers to evaluate exactly how these games were novel or more sophisticated—in essence, to perceive the added value that the new hardware provided. When a platform is launched with titles that do not easily fit in established generic categories, firms face two challenges at the same time: persuading consumers that the hardware is worth their money (which, as we have seen, they are reluctant to accept), and persuading them that the games are worthy of their time and interest. Launching a console with games from established genres can eliminate the second challenge and provide an indirect effect to alleviate the first one: Consumers can judge how much of an impact the new hardware has on this genre of games.

In the end, the high price of the console, paucity of games offered at launch, and limited available quantities that resulted in a chaotic launch could have all seriously impacted the Super Famicom's initial performance in the Japanese market. But the case illustrates a point made by Clements and Ohashi (2005): The number of software titles on offer during the launch window of a console is only of secondary importance; what matters is for "hit" games to be there.

Consoles Are Trouble

We have seen in the previous section how "killer games" may drive hardware adoption during a console's launch period. According to this logic, consumers never desire or demand consoles: They learn to cope and put up with them. Even after dealing with finances to buy them, consoles remain a hurdle and a liability. They require additional connectors on a TV and occupy additional power outlets in the living room. Cables might be too short and dangle inconveniently. Parents, partners, and roommates may find them bothersome. They take up space, especially with their convex and irregular shapes expressly designed to prevent people from stacking things on top of them. They may break and are costly to repair or replace, as the Xbox 360's "red ring of death" problems have reminded many gamers. Consoles are not a base good; they are a financial hurdle to be overcome for consumers to buy base goods—games.

When consumers exhibit behaviors that may be interpreted as manifesting desire for a platform (e.g., pre-ordering an upcoming console), we should interpret this as a transitional interest in the platform as an inevitable means toward achieving the real desire: getting access to a new game library or specific killer game. Clements and Ohashi wrote in a similar direction (2005, 2): "The console itself does not have any value apart from facilitating the use of software." In other words, the valuation of video game hardware comes from the range of software that is available for it, rather than being an intrinsic valuation like in other industries. Intrinsic valuation includes features such as anti-skip technology on portable CD players, which increases the base good's desirability without providing access to a larger library of audio CDs compared to portable CD players without anti-skip technology. Waterproofing on digital watches, or an increase in speeds on early CD-ROM drives, are some other examples. None has equivalents in the landscape of video game consoles, aside from hard drive storage space options, for instance.[3]

Adopting Technology, Adopting a Ludic Promise

Although the game console as a financial hurdle might be a good way to describe a common mindset, we should be careful not to lump all consumers together as if they were a Borg-like monolithic block of desires. If the utility of a game console is not intrinsic but derived from the games it allows to play, then why are hundreds of thousands of people pre-ordering game consoles as soon as they are announced or buying them as soon as they launch, even with few games available for them?

In fact, a subset of consumers finds genuine value in the console's technology. Such consumers are typically found among industry analysts, reviewers, and other members of the press; game developers or publishers; or people employed in related technology sectors. Like car enthusiasts, racing fans, or mechanics who might collect cars or car pieces, they find intrinsic value in the technology put forth by the platform owner. These I will term *techno-fetishists* and consider that they naturally become early adopters of the platform. The discursive strategies found in the magazines that announced and covered the launch of the Sega Genesis, TurboGrafx-16, and Super NES, to be seen in chapter 3, attempted to shape young and impressionable consumers to become techno-fetishists exactly for this reason: so that they could adopt new gaming technologies by finding intrinsic value in them. As I will show, we would do well not to underestimate the effect of marketing.

These techno-fetishists, however, form a minority within a minority. A sizable portion of early adopters are not techno-fetishists buying cutting-edge technology but rather *gamers* investing in a ludic promise. They invest at the earliest stage rather than adopting a wait-and-see approach for various reasons. They may do so because they desire a particular game, to avoid future expected shortages, to profit from any number of special measures tailored toward early adopters, or simply because they figure out that price cuts won't come anytime soon and they might as well buy it now rather than later. What these consumers actually want are games. They are not buying a base good and waiting for eventual complementary goods to maximize the value they get from their base good because their base good provides them no value to begin with; they are facing the financial hurdle of getting equipped with the proper standard right now so they can buy and use the upcoming games as they are released.

What are the components of a console's ludic promise? I can enumerate a number of them as a starting point and without being exhaustive. The most-often circulated and discussed component is technological innovation, advertised through classic promotional means and demonstrated through the console's launch titles. These launch titles are complemented by a roster of announced upcoming game releases—regardless of whether they actually make it to the market in the end or satisfactorily fulfill these promises. At the periphery of these games sits a much larger (and more diffuse) nebula of unannounced but expected game releases: Buying a Nintendo console always hinges on the expectation of future Mario, Zelda, Pokémon, Donkey Kong, Metroid, and other games in flagship franchises. Beyond direct games, an important component of the ludic promise lies in the third-party firms that have announced support for the platform, even if specific games have not been announced yet. The ludic promise can also benefit from unique distribution or other marketing policies, as when the OUYA announced its principle of providing free demos for any game published on the platform. Finally, other auxiliary ludic services can contribute to the promise, as the game-sharing or streaming play features of the PlayStation 4, or other voice chat and support for network play, specific controller features, or achievements and trophy systems.

In all cases, the base good is largely immaterial and oriented toward the future. Because game consoles function as locked standards, there is no way of separating the value of the platform that could theoretically be attributed to the hardware from the worth derived from its library of games: What the hardware contributes has to be concretely expressed in the form of games and in the form of future games. Therefore, consumers tend to develop irrationally strong loyalty toward their chosen console because the console's success in the marketplace—expressed through market share—will determine whether the platform becomes an attractive standard for developers to support it and whether it will see many games produced for it in a virtuous circle and bandwagon effect or instead slowly wither and die in a vicious cycle of confidence crises from game developers and consumers.

The market logics of locked, noninteroperable platforms make up the conditions that induce high levels of launch pressure and make consumers an indirect part of a console's success. They push consumers to become spoony bards, foolishly enamored with their chosen packs of circuits, metal and plastic, ready to sing their praises to whomever crosses their path. That is, when all goes well. Often console launches devolve into console wars, and the fanatical fervor of devotees turns them into evangelists—or, worse, crusaders bent on fighting in holy wars. The Super Famicom and Super NES managed to overcome the hurdles that lay in front of them, maintaining consumer loyalty and confidence in the firm despite the two-year wait for the hardware's release. This was Nintendo's true Super Power, as deployed through the formidable promotional practices that came through game magazines and used every trick in the book to maintain a phenomenal ludic promise.

The war is about to begin! After successfully invading Japan, we are about to witness the first wave of next generation gaming on these shores. [...] The lines have been drawn and the heavy artillery is about to be revealed to the game playing public. Three gaming superpowers—NEC, Sega, and Nintendo—are flexing their muscles with a variety of products that have to be seen to be believed! (Steve Harris in *EGM* #2, May 1989, 32)

We have seen how the Super Famicom spontaneously emerged as a project to counter the aspirants to the throne of home video games and how its Japanese launch hinged on a strong ludic promise. Here, we get to detail the North American emergence of the Super NES. To push the typical religious metaphor that most historians use when discussing the NES, the idea that it "resurrected" the video game market, we can describe the intense competition between Nintendo and Sega in North America from the late 1980s to the mid 1990s as the holy wars or the Crusades.

In this chapter, I will introduce the Super NES as the general public got to discover it: through the press coverage and announcements from Nintendo and from the video game press prior to the launch. Then I will go over the platform's life cycle and show how the promotional discourses evolved through magazines, with a particular focus on how they addressed technology and shaped the platform's identity for gamers. If the market is the battlefield of Kingdom Videoludica, then the various advertisements and magazines are the war room, where orders are given, plans are established, and strategies are exposed and discussed. Nintendo's discourses on technology and innovation when marketing the Super NES during the early 1990s exemplifies its characteristic surface-and-core duality and was used to marshal its troops in defending the Super NES against the "infidels" that had sworn fealty and loyalty to Sega. As Douglas Crockford (1993) mentioned in closing his account of dealing with Nintendo's content restrictions for porting *Maniac Mansion* to the NES, "Nintendo is a jealous god."

Super Power, *Nintendo Power*

Nintendo's presence in North America came with the establishment of a whole new "World of Nintendo," in the words of Provenzo (1990). One of the strongest ambassadors in pushing this world to the millions of children of the Nintendo Generation was *Nintendo Power* magazine, whose inspiration came from Japan's "Famicom culture," "built gradually with the emergence of numerous video game magazines," including *Beep, Family Computer Magazine* (then *Famimaga*) and *Family Tsuushin* (then *Famitsu*) (Picard 2013). These magazines provided a blueprint for Nintendo of America to create *Nintendo Power*, which played a key role in establishing a Nintendo gamer culture.

    Nintendo Power was dressed up (some would say "masquerading") as a magazine but was actually less of a video game magazine in the now-traditional sense of the term and more of a house organ for the firm (a company catalog or newsletter sent out to employees, when internal, or to customers, when external). Half of *Nintendo Power* stemmed from the Nintendo Fun Club newsletter, an informational brochure discussing (or rather promoting) upcoming games, which evolved into the paid-subscription magazine after seven issues (Wong 2013). *Nintendo Power* was entirely funded by Nintendo of America as a fusion and extension of the Fun Club newsletter and the Powerline (which we'll see next), a customer service expense made necessary by the firm's business model, which stemmed from the hardware limitations of the NES. Framed according to the three circuits of interactivity (Kline, Dyer-Witheford, and de Peuter 2003), technology shaped marketing, which then shaped culture.

Games of Progression and the Longevity Imperative

With *Super Mario Bros.* and *The Legend of Zelda*, games were transitioning into a new type of relationship with their players, according to John Harris (2007): "The older school of thought, which dates back and beyond the days of *Space Invaders* to the era of pinball, is that a game should *measure the player's skill.* [...] The newer concept is that a game should *provide an experience to the player.*" In the words of Jesper Juul, games were moving from open structures of emergence ("simple rules combining, leading to variation") to closed structures of progression ("serially introduced challenges") (Juul 2002). However, as Harris explains, the transition was gradual, and many games exhibited both a steep difficulty curve and scoring mechanisms to evaluate player skill, as well as a narrative or other rewards to be discovered by progressing through the game.

Because progression relies on serially introduced challenges, development costs and memory constraints for games also increased serially. Various game environments had to be constructed, graphics stored, and levels planned to procure interesting challenges and renew the desire for gamers to keep trying to reach the game's end. This led home video games to new and higher equilibrium points between cost to user and expected value; games of progression cost more money to produce, and consumers expected them to last longer and provide an experience of discovery that was different from that of arcade games. This is precisely the reason that Sega of America's Tom Kalinske wanted *Altered Beast* out of the Genesis bundle: It was a great arcade game but not a good home video game (Harris 2014, 98). Because games were sold at relatively high prices to consumers, they had to offer a relatively lengthy life. They couldn't be sold for less, or at least not through the Nintendo Economic System.

This longevity imperative influenced how games were marketed. Arguments that justified video games' resistance to the economic recession of the 1980s centered on the "value" of video games, measured as dollars spent for hours of entertainment received (Terdiman 2009). Deep, rich, and complex games like role-playing games (RPGs) or action-adventures promised—and listed as a selling point—50 or 100 hours of gameplay. This marketing imperative stood for all home video games and would only get questioned with the rise of indie games, sold cheaply via digital distribution, around the second decade of the 21st century. Up until then, the longer the better, and reviews often mentioned the length of a game and its replay value as an important criterion for aesthetic (or budgetary) appreciation.

Manufacturing Difficulty

Marketing constraints informed game design, in a push for longevity and lasting value. Because the limited storage space afforded by ROM cartridge technology restricted the amount of content that game developers could put in their games, other methods of ensuring longevity were needed. A high difficulty level, combined with the need for the player to often restart from the beginning, offered one natural solution. Hard games lasted longer and hence delivered good value to consumers. But hard games could be frustrating, especially for kids. The idea was not to mock or shame them, but to present them with challenges—and ideally provide a customer experience where they would be empowered to acquire skill and eventually triumph (Therrien 2014). From now on, they would be playing with power! (But not too much power; triumph had to come eventually, not right away, for the game to provide lasting value.)

In this business context, Nintendo sued Galoob in 1990. Galoob had released the Game Genie accessory, a pass-through device that latched on any cartridge and could temporarily modify the game's code to allow players to cheat and produce various alterations, glitches, and alternative modes of play. Nintendo (unsuccessfully) claimed the cheating device produced derivative works without their approval, an argument that had no real basis because the modification had no physical support and permanency—it evaporated once power was turned off, leaving the game unaltered—and because, it was ruled, consumers may freely alter a game they purchased for their own enjoyment.[1] Yet this wasn't about creative ownership and copyright. A Game Genie owner could cheat and power through games. In an industry where longevity was a value metric, this significantly lowered a game's value and could result in the owner selling secondhand games back to someone without the incentive to replay at harder levels or top a score. If that player simply rented games—another problem entirely, which led to Nintendo suing the Blockbuster video stores as well (Forman 1989) —they could complete them in a day without a problem and never have to buy any game again.

The Game Genie cut through the first-party lines of support and assistance that Nintendo was offering to gamers and that allowed Nintendo to control gamers' experiences and their relationship with difficulty, just like it controlled the games' contents and the market within which they appeared. With the US release of *The Legend of Zelda* in 1987, Nintendo had launched the Powerline, a phone hotline for players to call when they needed gameplay tips. This ensured that gamers would not get hopelessly lost or confused when playing the game so they could be kept satisfied. The Powerline lasted through five generations of Nintendo home video game consoles and was eventually discontinued on June 1, 2010. *Nintendo Power* thus merged Nintendo's two needs: to promote upcoming games as in the Fun Club Newsletter, and to assist gamers in persevering through games as with the Powerline.

The Self-Party Magazine

Nintendo Power provided access to cheat codes, advice in dealing with hard specific problems in some games, maps and hints of featured games, and previews of upcoming games. A number of other relatively secondary features, such as storyline comics, additional game advice disguised as comics, reader letters, and so on, constituted the building blocks of the magazine. Fake reader letters were also used by the staff to get some messages across, as *Nintendo Power* editor Gail Tilden explains:

> Another thing we used the magazine for was in the letters section with customer service. If they had an issue that they wanted covered in the magazine, we didn't want to be writing preachy customer service articles. One solution for that was to present the customer service problem as a letter, and then respond with the answer. That way, it would have been published. That was the way we at Nintendo Power could get around writing consumer service articles. (Tilden in Cifaldi 2012, 3)

Nintendo Power had privileged and systematic access to the games thanks to a clause in Nintendo's license agreement for third-party developers and publishers. When they signed Nintendo's forceful terms, they agreed to send them the game for review and to make any changes that Nintendo deemed necessary. After *Nintendo Power* was launched, however, they also had to agree to let the magazine's staff access their submission for coverage (Cifaldi 2012, 4). In practice, that was not a hard sell; according to Howard Philips of Nintendo of America, third-party partners were eager to have their games featured in *Nintendo Power* because it meant great exposition directly to the target consumer.

This was especially valuable given *Nintendo Power*'s popularity, which quickly soared to record highs. The first issue was shipped for free to the 3.4 million members of the Nintendo Fun Club, 1 million of which took the paid subscription right away (Harris 2014, 57). Wesley and Barczak comment on a figure of 1.5 million subscribers, making *Nintendo Power* "the most popular youth magazine in America" (Wesley and Barczak 2010, 20). Kline, Dyer-Witheford, and de Peuter mention that *Nintendo Power* "by 1990 had become the biggest-selling magazine for children, with a paid circulation of two million in the US" (Kline, Dyer-Witheford, and de Peuter 2003, 120). Of course, a magazine is not only read by subscribers: Sheff's numbers for 1991 are "about 1.2 million subscribers and 4 million readers" (Sheff 1993, 234). A brief from a 1994 *Billboard* issue mentions that Nintendo has sent 1 million copies of the *Donkey Kong Country* promotional videotape to "a million subscribers of *Nintendo Power* magazine" (*Billboard*, November 12, 1994, 90).

The magazine's sharp success, like that of the NES, was a result of tackling a market without competitors. As the NES gained in popularity through 1986 and 1987, eventually becoming a full-blown success story in 1988, almost no other American video game magazines were in circulation. *Electronic Games* (whose last four issues were rebranded as *Computer Entertainment*), the first video game magazine published in the United States in 1981, ended in August 1985; *Videogaming Illustrated* was briefly published in 1982 and 1983; *Atari Age* and *Electronic Fun with Computers & Games* were both launched in 1982 and terminated in 1984. When *Nintendo Power*'s first issue hit in July 1988, the only other magazine in existence was *Computer Gaming World* (which was dedicated to PC games). The only thing covering game consoles—and Nintendo had the only significantly selling console—was the Nintendo Fun Club Newsletter, given out to consumers who registered their address when they bought a Nintendo game.

Following *Nintendo Power*'s success, *GamePro* appeared in April 1989 and *Electronic Gaming Monthly* in May 1989 (after an initial Buyer's Guide in March). No other magazine appeared in 1990. This shows how little competition *Nintendo Power* faced. Not only was the quantity of opponents limited, but their coverage of Nintendo games was severely limited as well, given Nintendo's contractually negotiated right to coverage for all games that were made for the one platform that controlled more than 80% of the video game market (Provenzo 1991, 13). As the house organ to the biggest house on the block, *Nintendo Power* made the rules and, in large part, contributed to the commercial success of the games it treated. In this sense, the magazine must be seen as an integral part of the Nintendo Economic System that acts as a promotional vehicle for Nintendo and its games, even as it is an important vector in shaping the culture of video games at large.

American Surveillance
It would make sense to turn to *Nintendo Power*, an insider source, to search for the first mention of the Super Famicom and Super NES among American magazines. The first time NP acknowledged the Japanese system was in a single-page feature titled "Super FamiCom announced in Japan" (*Nintendo Power* #16, September/October 1990, 86). We know that Nintendo was in no hurry to promote the system because the NES was selling so well in North America, but if we didn't, we could have inferred so from the backbench position the magazine attributed to the system. There's no

mention of anything related to that article on the magazine's cover, which instead promotes *Maniac Mansion*, previews of some NES games, and a special "Giant Game Boy Feature." The article isn't even referenced in the table of contents but is simply tucked away in the "NES Journal" subsection of the "Player's forum."

In comparison, *Electronic Gaming Monthly* had put the Super Famicom, identified as the "16-Bit Super Nintendo," along with the Genesis, TurboGrafx-16, and Game Boy, on the "Big Bang" cover of its second issue in August 1989—a full year before *Nintendo Power*. The Super Famicom is also the first system mentioned in the "cover story" paragraph in that issue's table of contents. It wasn't even the first time Nintendo's next console was mentioned in the magazine, as the Super Famicom had appeared in a column in the preceding issue of May 1989. Granted, there wasn't much in there other than data on how it was planned for release in the summer in Japan, expected for release in the United States in 1990, and that it was a 16-bit system that had reportedly "been hailed as 'the most incredible game system ever seen' by those who have been privy to the limited exposure that Nintendo Japan has given it" (*EGM* #1, May 1989, 63). *EGM* had, however, caught on Nintendo's savvy marketing delay tactic at the time:

> Continued strong sales for the 8-Bit Nintendo Entertainment System may hamper a stateside release until sometime in 1990. Nintendo simply doesn't need to release their 16-Bit on these shores...they would be doing nothing but cutting in to the sales of existing NES consoles and carts. (*EGM* #1, May 1989, 63)

Nintendo Power's first-ever mention of the Super Famicom described the technical specifications and explained how the "Super FamiCom's new features really wowed those who attended the Nintendo press conference roll-out," before succinctly going over the usual technical specifications: 512 x 448 resolution, 32,768 colors, and "the abilities to twist, rotate, stretch, zoom in on and miniaturize game images." So far it's all standard fare. However, to avoid cannibalizing NES sales, the article ends thus:

> There's still no word on when a Nintendo system like the Super FamiCom will come out in the United States, but you can be sure that you'll read about any plans first in *Nintendo Power*! [...] Look to future issues of Nintendo Power to get hard facts and not wimpy rumors on this hot new development in Nintendo technology! (*Nintendo Power* #16, September/October 1990, 86)

So if we get this right, *Electronic Gaming Monthly*'s coverage of the Super Famicom a full year earlier than *Nintendo Power* should be chalked up as "wimpy rumors." This is somewhat curious considering that *EGM* had simply acted as an echo chamber to Nintendo of Japan's own claims from its 1988 press conference. The staff was visibly piqued by the remark, as a month later in their October 1990 issue, they promised readers an upcoming "complete report with all the hard facts and no wimpy rumors directly from Japan" (*EGM* #15, October 1990, 10).

This certainly highlights the key role that *Nintendo Power* was playing as a formidable promotional engine in the Nintendo Economic System: Readers had to be assured that the magazine was the only trustworthy source of information so that Nintendo could control the flow of information without interference from independent sources in journalism or criticism (however little of those actually transpired). This control over information is an issue that revolves around the concept of paratextuality and merits further discussion.

The Fine Line between Text and Paratext

Video game magazines can be treated as a giant stand-alone text making up a "paratextual industry," which historians can use as documents to understand "what the 'ideal' gamer should know and expect from games" at the time (Consalvo 2007, 20). Consalvo framed them following Lunenfeld (1998) and has provided a certain usage of the term "paratext," which many new media and game studies scholars have used since. As a consequence, "paratext has increasingly become associated as the external elements that shape the experience and reception of video games" (Dunne 2016, 279), including anything from advertisements and reviews to message board discussions and fan fictions. Everything that references a text and influences how it can be received and understood falls under this definition of paratext, which means we are constantly surrounded by paratexts that point toward texts. Indeed, we actually consume more paratexts than texts in our saturated media landscape (Gray 2010).

For Dunne (2016) and Rockenberger (2014), these approaches are too broad because they run the risk of treating everything as a paratext. How can we account for the differences among a promotional trailer, a game review, and a message board discussion for a game if they can all be considered as making up a giant auxiliary text to the main text, a video game? What should constitute a paratext and what should simply be a text that's about another text (in technical terms, partaking in intertextuality)? The debate on paratext may look like academic squabbling over semantics (something like "what is the threshold at which point something is in the threshold?"), but in reality the question is far from trivial. We deal with the nature and status of paratexts whenever we read a product review that turns out to be an advertisement imitating a product review, or when we read articles published on unfamiliar websites that we later find out to be run by corporations providing the goods that are covered in these articles. This proves absolutely crucial when dealing with uncomfortable entities like *Nintendo Power* magazine. Applying the "paratext" label across the board might make us lose sight of the specific practices and relationships behind (para)texts, especially regarding questions of power, control, and agendas.

Genette and the Origins of the Paratext

The notion of paratext was introduced by Gérard Genette in *Palimpsestes* (1982) and subsequently developed in *Seuils* (1987).[2] Originally, it referred to the supplemental text that lies at the periphery of the main text, surrounding and extending it to present it, in the usual sense of the word, and to *make it present*, in the form of a book. Some typical paratextual elements consist of the title, author's name, collection, publisher, epigraph, preface, front and back cover, and packaging. More than a limit or frontier, the paratext is a threshold or an airlock, a zone of transition and transaction where strategies and actions can be deployed by the author or their allies to ensure a better reception and reading of the text ("better" as defined by them, usually meaning to provide the intended experience).

Genette puts forth a key distinction between the *peritext* and the *epitext*: The peritext surrounds the text itself and is not separate from it (it lies at its periphery), whereas the epitext is kept at the surface of the book and circulates independently from it. He also brought a second distinction between authorial paratext, which is produced under the responsibility of the text's author (and on which he focused), and editorial paratext, whose responsibility lies with the publisher. The latter question is, however, pretty straightforward, as the video game industry, for game consoles and AAA productions at least, admits no such thing as an "author" (with a few notable exceptions, such as Shigeru Miyamoto, Hideo Kojima, David Cage, Peter Molyneux, and a select few other); consoles and games are the firm's creation, and the text accompanying it is wholly produced by the "editorial" instance rather than being a polyphonic mixture of the author's and publisher's voices. The more serious problem that paratext theory faces is that Genette originally developed it with written books in mind. This requires adaptation for video games, for both the peritext and epitext.

Accounting for the peritext is easier than the epitext, although more in-depth work on the peritext remains to be done.[3] The Super NES's peritextual documentation, written by Nintendo of America, was adamant about the machine's performance. The Super NES Instruction manual states, "Thank you for purchasing the Super NES™, Nintendo's most advanced video entertainment system, featuring full digital stereo sound and breathtaking graphics!" The back of the system's box was particularly verbose and grandiloquent. This is both unsurprising *and* surprising: On the one hand, the back of the box exists to convince the consumer looking at it in a store to buy it; on the other hand, Nintendo putting technology at the forefront goes against the whole Gunpei Yokoi philosophy of seasoned technology:

> You're about to experience a whole new dimension in home video entertainment—The Super Nintendo Entertainment System®! […] The Super Nintendo Entertainment System will astound you with the most colors, the biggest characters, and the smoothest, most detailed animation imaginable. Cascading sounds echo crisply in super digital stereo. Crystal clear 3-D graphics shrink, expand and spin with amazing speed. Multiple backgrounds allow for complex scrolling, shadowing, and depth like you've never seen in a video game! […] The new Super NES Control Deck features Nintendo's most advanced game technology, with thousands of magnificent colors, huge on-screen characters, stunning 3-D graphics, and digital stereo sound!

Lane and the Criterion of Authorization

When we get into epitext, the limits of Genette's approach are immediately felt because he focused his efforts on the authorial paratext. The authorial epitext, then, is constituted by the author's private correspondence, diary, or preliminary drafts of the final literary work, interviews, conferences, and the like. This is all well and good for the (culturally entrenched) Grand, Profound, and Revered Author but much more marginal for video games. I will rather follow the work of Philippe Lane, who worked on the editorial paratext to supplement Genette's focus on the authorial. Table 3.1, which joins two tables from Lane (1991, 94–96), summarizes some common occurrences of peritext and epitext, both authorial and editorial.

In the Lanean logic of paratextuality, advertisements are considered part of the editorial epitext of games. Contrary to the overinclusive approaches to paratext we have seen earlier, not everything that points

Table 3.1 Typology of the paratext derived from Lane's figures (1991, 94–96).

Paratext	Authorial		Editorial
Peritext	Author name, title, dedication, epigraph, preface, notes.		Front and back covers, packaging, blurbs.
Epitext	Private Correspondences, diary, avant-textes.	Public Mediations, interviews, conferences.	Advertisements, catalogs, publishing press.

toward a text can be considered part of its paratext. Siding with Lane and Genette means that game reviews, previews, feature articles on game consoles, trade show reports, and other such features found in game magazines are excluded from the realm of paratextuality because that conception of the paratext upholds the criterion of authorization (Rockenberger 2014): A paratext has to be produced or authorized by the author and his allies. This definition makes the paratext a question of "Who writes under whose conditions?" rather than "What other text is being written about?"

Hence, although Consalvo (2007) may include game magazines as forming a "paratextual industry" because they affect gamers and help shape their encounters with games, I contend there are many types of texts in magazines that do not qualify for being paratexts that surround and present specific game-texts, such as reviews and articles. Certainly game reviews constitute an important, if not central, mode of engagement with games, and they play a pivotal role in framing games and consoles for gamers. However, we can't simply add two more columns to table 3.1 and attempt to account for "critical paratexts" and "journalistic paratexts." The notions of criticism and journalism imply at least a modicum of distance from the creators or producers of the text, whereas authorial and editorial instances collaborate more or less closely together to provide the paratext. In fact, journalism and criticism, if they are to be credible, most definitely have to *not* be produced or authorized by the author and their allies. Adopting the criterion of authorization to determine the paratextual status of game publications requires us to clarify the sources of writing and the magazine's status of proximity with the article's subject: Whose facts, views, and arguments are being printed out? Whose interests are served by the publication? Quite simply, whose money is being spent in doing so?

Lane's contribution proves invaluable to the study of the paratext in the video game industry, where notions of authorship and editorship are made more tentacular by the specificities of platform technology and economics. In the video game industry, the platform owner has a vested interest in the success of games made for its platform because the more (quality) games there are available for it, the more desirable the platform becomes for consumers. Hence, whereas the Nintendo of America staff working on *Nintendo Power* content may cover games for Nintendo consoles that have not been developed or published by Nintendo, they are never disinterested observers or completely impartial reviewers because promoting these games in the magazine or other product catalogs and television advertisements also promotes the platform.

Because of the market's hardware-software integration and noninteroperability, video game reviews and previews must be understood in completely different fashion depending on where they are published. There are two categories of publications: independent game magazines such as *EDGE* or *Electronic Gaming Monthly*, which have no affiliation with a particular platform owner; and first-party magazines of platform owners, exemplified by *Nintendo Power*, preceded by *Atari Age*, and followed by *Xbox Magazine*, *Official PlayStation Magazine*, and so on.

The Nintendo Power Case

This uneasy proximity and relationship of collaboration between Nintendo and third-party developers and publishers makes *Nintendo Power* a problematic publication in terms of paratext theory: The magazine is offered like a journalistic or critical text but in truth functions as a quasi-editorial epitext, conveying Nintendo's editorial messages and, quite literally at first, spending out its money as a customer service expense (Tilden in Cifaldi 2012). According to Lane, the editorial paratext obeys a specific logic of discourse:

> The linguistic and communicational specificity of the editorial paratext resides in the interlinking of two modes of writing: description and argumentation. Description is the dominant textual mode in this discursive genre; this description however is never neutral, always oriented so as to gain the reader's support; the selected elements are organized, hierarchized according to the editorial goal of producing the most pertinent paratext, accounting for the specific product and the audience. (Lane 1991, 92–93)

Hence, when discussing *Nintendo Power*, "the linguistic and communicational specificity of the editorial paratext" will not only appear in official advertisements for Nintendo products but permeate through what may on the surface appear to be part of video game criticism. That the deeply argumentative nature of the texts was hidden under a veneer of descriptive objectivity (sometimes very thin indeed) explains how the magazine insidiously persuaded children and young teenagers—the magazine's target audience—that they were being given "information" when, in actuality, the magazine was pushing sales arguments and product catalogs, conforming to the surface-and-core duality of Nintendo.

Nintendo Power's coverage of the Super NES perfectly exhibited this dual-level discourse. A four-page feature in 1991 had parts on the SNES's technology that appeared as objective (or at least factual) descriptions but were orchestrated to present the SNES as the logically reasonable option among 16-bit consoles:

> SUPER GRAPHICS. Although graphics aren't the only consideration when comparing games or game systems, they are the most glamorous aspect of video games. Graphics fire the imagination and allow you to roam alternate universes. The first and most obvious aspect of graphics is resolution. Resolution is determined by the number of pixels that can appear on the screen at one time. A greater number of pixels translates into higher resolution pictures. In the case of the Super NES, the resolution is a very impressive 512 x 448. That's almost twice the resolution of most other 16 bit systems. (*Nintendo Power* #25, June 1991, 46)

Independents' Dependencies

Further complicating the question of authorization is the independent magazines' theoretical independence being compromised by the restricted flow of information from platform owners. This leads to magazines such as *Electronic Gaming Monthly* becoming an uncritical relay of Nintendo's discourse when it is describing Nintendo's consoles, which is deeply problematic given that the editorial epitext is predominantly descriptive but "never neutral, always oriented so as to gain the reader's support" (Lane 1991, 92–93). *EGM*'s discussions of Nintendo hardware thus become even more insidious than the editorial content found in *Nintendo Power*, a source that may be more readily pointed out as biased. The *gamepilgrimage* website has extensive studies of the coverage of 16-bit consoles in *EGM* and *GamePro* and highlights how *EGM* had a bias for the SNES from the start. Site owner "sheath" sees in *EGM*'s treatment of the SNES a wider shift from the earlier "wait and see" approach that was in place in video game journalism so far to the "enthusiastic prospective prophecy" (sheath 2010).

In a sense, it would have been hard for independent magazine editors to do anything more than relay, almost verbatim, the inflected descriptions they received from hardware manufacturers for two reasons. First, they often received information on consoles, add-ons, or games that were still in development (and hence impossible to verify) or on technical details and methods that would have required expertise in games programming and design to verify, or been protected as trade secrets by licensing agreements or contractual employment obligations. Second, most game magazines were started by game fans and people working in communications on different subjects. The first American video game magazine, *Electronic Games*, was started in 1981 by Bill Kunkel, Joyce Worley, and Arnie Katz. The trio had met through science-fiction fandom, with Joyce Worley having founded and worked on multiple science-fiction fanzines. Kunkel and Katz had covered pro wrestling in a radio show and then a magazine. Later, they transitioned into a column on video games titled "Arcade Alley" in *Video Magazine*. *Electronic Games* was born out of that endeavor (Fulton 2009).

Had the roots of video game journalism been laid out by ex-industry programmers or other technology-oriented journalists, rather than the Kunkel/Katz/Worley trio's foundations in fandom and general entertainment coverage, the video game magazines might have taken a different (and critical) stance toward the technological promotion discourses of video game console manufacturers. Instead, a magazine such as *Electronic Gaming Monthly* is criticized for basically reading a bunch of Japanese game magazines and translating what they read in there months later for publishing in the United States (Roberts 2009). Tracing the exact provenance of the discourses thus may prove difficult and would require more research to restore the complete chain from Nintendo of Japan's press release to Japanese magazines, which may have been interpreted and translated by American editors and mixed in with other sources as well.

These rhetorical contraptions constituted the first point of contact between the general public and the Super NES. The Super NES's promotion and coverage in game magazines, from its reveal and introduction right up to its displacement by the Nintendo 64, are exemplary of Nintendo's uneasy relationship with technology and of the particular context of the mid-1980s to the mid-1990s. Technology was a discursive Trojan Horse that all video game hardware firms more or less used to push their promotional discourses to the specialized press. The strategy required a careful management of information and a certain cultural context around video game magazines; when successful, it meant writers, reviewers, journalists, and editors of independent magazines could only discuss the game platforms under the platform owner's terms. In effect, technology allowed them to extend their editorial epitext to other, external sources of discourse and information on video games, heightening the simulacrum of information and objective description to reinforce the persuasive technological promotion discourse.

The Turbo-Mega-Super Generation: Between Technobabble and Technoliteracy

Magazines of the Turbo(Grafx)-Mega(Drive)-Super(NES) time routinely discussed which of the consoles was the most powerful or could offer the best games, in a "battle of the bits" or "bit wars" (cf. Therrien and Picard 2015). They featured elaborate comparisons of megahertz, RAM and ROM, number of on-screen colors, number of sprites or background layers, and so on between Nintendo's Super NES and Sega's Genesis consoles. Whole articles were dedicated to the benefits of CD-ROM technology, Full-Motion Video, prerendered 3-D graphics, or some special software technique or hardware configuration that allowed spectacular visual effects. NEC's TurboGrafx-16 was touted as a "16-bit console" in its marketing, although it was knocked off as being "not a true 16-Bit" (EGM #2, May 1989, 32) by competitors and the press. Sega's own Genesis had a "16-BIT" mention centrally embossed in shiny silver letters on the hardware, as can be seen in figure 3.1.

Figure 3.1 Display of "16-BIT" technology on the North American Sega Genesis model 1 (left) and the Japanese Mega Drive (detail, right). In addition to the central "16-BIT," the Japanese has two mentions on the sides: "AV intelligent terminal" and "High grade multi-purpose use." Source: Evan Amos, Wikimedia Commons.

Throughout the mid-1990s, an advertisement by Atari for its Jaguar system encapsulated the technomarketing mindset through a simple equation: more bits = more power = better games. It was a simple matter of counting, as the tagline went:

What makes Jaguar games so awesome? The raw power of 64-bit technology that adds CD-quality stereo sound, 16 million colors, and incredible 3D animation. [...] This is just a preview of what's to come. The Atari Jaguar. 64 bits. Do the Math. (*EGM* #63, October 1994, 40–41)

Technology, it seemed, was everywhere. Or was it? In stark contrast to this assessment, in 2002, Mark Finn wrote:

The marketing of the consoles of this period also seems to confirm the desire to de-emphasise the actual technology underlying the systems. Although some advertisements mentioned the relative performance of each system (a tactic often employed in relation to Sega's Genesis), by far the most prevalent form of advertising avoided emphasizing the technology at all, preferring to focus on brand-recognition through characters. (Finn 2002, 48)

My own research on game magazines from the late 1980s to the mid-1990s, as part of a project on graphical technologies and innovation in the games industry between 1985 and 1995, led me to the exact opposite viewpoint: Technological discourses are omnipresent in the promotion of video games during that period. Part of the conflict between interpretations can be resolved by remembering that advertisements are only a certain type of promotion, and promotion is only a subset of marketing. Yet the matter is not so simple either and will require us to identify the different discursive stances and practices toward technology that have been deployed throughout the press in discussing the Super NES. These can be summarily distributed across three general categories: technobabble, buzzwords, and technoliteracy. As I will show, the promotional discourses and their stance toward technology have transformed quite rapidly from the late 1980s to the mid-1990s due to a cultural change as the promotion of games followed the maturing generation that had been hooked on the NES (detailed later in chapter 6).

In its initial years, the video game press largely relayed the technological details that console manufacturers were supplying them in press releases. These technological arguments were seldom explained in depth, analyzed, or critically weighed by magazine editors; by and large, they simply stated the factual data (in the form of hard numbers) they received from the firms. Table 3.2, which compares systems in *Electronic Gaming Monthly* #2 (July/August 1989, 39) represents this idea.

Table 3.2 Comparison of console specs, reproduced from *Electronic Gaming Monthly* #2 (July/August 1989, 39).

System	Est. Release Date	Est. Price	Processor	Colors	Resolution	Games
NES	Now Available	$99, $30–$50 Carts	6502	52	256 x 240	100s
SEGA Genesis	September	$179–199, $40–60	68000+Z80	512	320 x 224	10
TurboGrafx 16	September	$199, $40 Cards	Hu6502	512	320 x 224	50
Super Famicom	Unknown–1990?	Unknown	65816	32,768	512 x 448	4

In most cases, the articles went beyond the simple list and contextualized some of the data by providing a few examples of these technologies' applications for games. These examples were mostly provided by the platform owner, and magazine editors and writers then speculated more largely on what this could mean for the future of games, as when *Nintendo Power* enthusiastically described the upcoming revolution to be brought by the Super NES's sound system:

> [the Super NES] can reproduce the same digital stereo signals used in CDs with all the tonality and richness that you would expect from a recording of your favorite musical group. This also means that actual voices can be reproduced. Real voices! Imagine a Batman game in which cinema scenes don't have subtitles but the actual voices of Jack Nicholson and Michael Keaton! With the Super NES that sort of realism is possible. (*Nintendo Power* #25, June 1991, 47)

Futurology isn't always right, even when the futurologist is prophesying from their parent corporation's technology. But futurology doesn't have to be right; it has to sell systems.

Technobabble

For a time in the late 1980s and early 1990s, when new consoles and technologies were on the far-off horizon or just around the corner, the technological discourse found in the specialized gaming press functioned more like a dizzying, superficial flash of lights than an inquisitive, thorough searchlight delving into the hardware to illuminate its shadowy secrets. I call such brandishing of factual information and data without context *technobabble*. The word is used in discussions of science fiction literature as a way to describe any pseudoscientific/technological-sounding explanation that is actually a cover-up to dazzle the reader and maintain suspension of disbelief. I find it poetically fitting to see "next-generation" video game consoles described according to the same rhetorical discursive strategies of technology in science fiction.

Two examples from *Electronic Gaming Monthly* will illustrate technobabble. The first citation describes the upcoming Super Famicom console:

> The system uses a 16-Bit CPU (Central Process Unit—the brains of a game system) that is equipped with a CPU utilizing an 8-Bit Data Bus and a 24-Bit Address Bus. [...] The Super Famicom has a built-in math function that uses 8bit x 8bit multiplication and 16bit / 8bit division math that allows the unit to obtain high speed calculations in hardware as opposed to software. (*EGM* #2, July/August 1989, 76)

What are the advantages of calculating in hardware as opposed to software? Savvy readers will know that the hardware can take care of these operations, hence leaving more processing power and time to manage other specific game-related operations in software. Yet what is the advantage conferred by "8-bit x 8-bit multiplication and 16-bit/8-bit division math" in achieving these calculations in hardware? How does it compare with previous technology and rival systems? Is it standard to have built-in math functions or is this an innovation? What exactly is an Address Bus, and how does it relate to the Data Bus? Readers might guess that someone, somewhere, at least, will know. Aside from that, it seems clear that the function served by these sentences in the text is not really to inform the readers but to have them feel that this system is advanced and powerful.

Sometimes trying to go beyond the surface and into more in-depth explanations only manages to show that the surface-level discussion is actually founded on surface-level comprehension. An interesting example of this can be found in the reader letters of the July 1994 issue of *EGM²*. Reader Jason Sootkoos asks, "How can Super Metroid for the Super NES be a 24-Megabit game when the Super NES is only a 16-Megabit system? Is it possible to play a 24-Bit game on a 16-Bit system, and if so, why aren't all games like this?" The question shows gamers' earnest interest in understanding the technicalities of game technologies, and *EGM²*'s choice to feature the letter likewise shows its valuing of this kind of curiosity. The editor's response is just as interesting, as the answer probably caused even more confusion:

The fact that the Super Nintendo is a 16-Bit system doesn't limit the cartridges to 16-Meg. What it does mean is the Super NES can only read 16-Megabits of information at one time. This is also true with the Genesis. Even though Super Street Fighter II will be 40-Meg, the Genesis can only read 16-Meg of the cartridge at one time. (*EGM²* #1, July 1994, 14)

The answer lumps together computational complexity and data storage, as if contemporary discussions attempted to explain modern computers' 64-bit processors by how much of a double layer Blu-Ray Disc's 50 gigabytes of storage space can be processed "at one time." Apparently, the SNES being a 16-bit system allows it to "read 16-megabits of information at one time," hence processing around 66% of *Super Metroid*'s 24-megabit size at any given time. The (more complex) reality is that the 16-bit processor of the SNES can process 16-bit instructions (data points with 2^{16}, or 65,536, possible values), which are stored in the 24-megabit (24,000,000 bits) storage space of these game cartridges. The reply even features a photo of *Super Metroid* whose legend states, "Although the Super NES is 16-Bit, games like Super Metroid are 24-Bit. Confused?" Well, anyone would be too if that kind of technobabble was their only contact with technology.

Buzzwords

Beyond the specialized gaming press, various publications also covered video game consoles in one of two ways. Typically, the general press did not address technological performance at all or did so in superficial terms. A good example can be found in *Newsweek*:

> The new game machines from Sega (Genesis) and NEC (TurboGrafx-16) offer so-called 16-bit processing. That essentially means they move more data more quickly, and it results in noticeably better graphics and sound. Both machines offer power comparable to $2,000 personal computers of the mid-'80s, but are far cheaper and easier to use. (*Newsweek*, June 17, 1990)

In a sense, these kinds of publications are the least problematic because they have (theoretically at least) no link of dependency with game publishers or platform owners, and because they minimize discussion of technology instead of trying to discuss it in more depth than they (or their readers) can understand. However, they can still contribute to technopromotional discourses by relaying made-up words as *buzzwords*. This shows up in the previous examples as "so-called 16-bit processing," which does not attempt to explain what it is at all. In this way, terms can be brandied about without anyone having any idea whatsoever as to what they actually mean. Although this is far from contributing to technical literacy, it is arguably less of a problem than technobabble because the people employing buzz-words to discuss video game technologies at least know that they don't know the technical details behind the word's buzz, placing them in the realm of Socratic ignorance. Technobabble, by contrast, insidiously instills the impression of knowledge in people, hence bringing them into double ignorance—not knowing that they don't know.

Technoliteracy

A more involved discussion of technology could be found in general tech publications, which placed a heavy focus on properly explaining the consoles' specifications. I will give one such example from *Popular Mechanics*, a magazine that has been running since 1902 and that covered the SNES's launch in the context of the console wars:

> First, it's necessary to understand that beneath the plastic exterior and emphasis on entertainment, videogame machines are at heart small, relatively powerful computers. In the same manner that text and graphics are controlled in the PCs we use in our homes or at the office, the on-screen action in videogames is controlled by two tiny but powerful microchips—the Picture Processing Unit (PPU) and Central Processing Unit (CPU). The CPU acts as the brains of the system, interpreting and directing the steady stream of data it receives from the game cartridges. The PPU, in turn, receives information from the CPU and game cartridges, and transforms it into the graphics and video information you see displayed on-screen. (Willcox 1991, 74–75)

In carefully detailing the underpinnings of game technology in an informative rather than a promotional manner, the magazine shows a glimpse of what the specialized gaming press could have been. This way of discussing technology seeks to build *technoliteracy* for readers, that is, to give them access and proficiency in understanding the complexities of technology rather than using technobabble to smash them with complexity and leave them dazzled or beaten senseless. Ultimately, the article from *Popular Mechanics* also shows the limits of discussing proprietary technologies, as even with its informative goal, it couldn't have a discussion of the SNES's sound chip with any more details than "a custom Sony sound chip, complete with its own 8-bit CPU and digital signal processing, provides for impressive digital audio capabilities" (Willcox 1991, 75).

Nintendo Power produced a Q&A about the Super NES in issue #29 (October 1991), with a question and answer that could well be a case of technoliteracy except the explanation conveniently stops at the part that states how much better the SNES is compared with the NES in order to sell it. The general tone and style of writing in the first part are emblematic of technoliteracy, but the description arriving in the second part is ultimately subservient to the overarching goal of persuading the reader to buy it, thus illustrating why these kinds of texts are best understood as editorial paratexts:

> What is a 16 bit machine?
> The term "16 bit" refers to the Central Processing Unit of the Super NES, which is the brain of the system. It means that the Super NES can process 16 bits of information at the same time. That makes the Super NES twice as powerful as the 8 bit NES. The increase in processing speed means that the Super NES can produce spectacular effects such as color layering that allows you to see through objects or to rotate and scale backgrounds. (*Nintendo Power* #29, October 1991, 70)

Another, more insidious case of technobabble advertising from Nintendo disguised as an independent technoliteracy discussion can be found in the "SMASHING the Myth of Speed & Power" campaign. In 1994, Nintendo produced a two-page feature that mimicked the form of regular magazine articles and purported to compare the performance of SNES and Genesis consoles. The description claimed to debunk the "myth about Blast Processing" and present "the cold, hard facts." The article conforms to the strategies of the editorial epitext laid out by Lane: It features description as its main textual mode (for example, "Processing speed can be measured in several ways including CPU clock speed and memory cycle time"), but this description is oriented to garner support ("Mode 7 is a built-in function of the Super NES PPU that has revolutionized home video games").[4]

Table 3.3 summarizes the dominant discursive stances found in various publication types when discussing video game technology.

The end result of these multiple factors and discursive strategies interacting was a certain conception of what the Super Famicom and Super

Table 3.3 Dominant discursive stances on technology found in the press covering video games and their corresponding paratextual status.

Press Category	Specialized Gaming Press			General Press	
Publication type	First-party magazines	Independent magazines (relaying data from platform owners)	Independent magazines (original features and reviews)	Technology publications	General publications
Tech discourse	Technobabble		Technoliteracy		Buzzwords
Paratext status	Editorial epitext Description oriented to garner support		Non-paratext Description is either journalistic or critical		

NES was going to be, a conception that influenced how the platform was framed. It was to be a technological—and more specifically graphical—powerhouse, as the examination of the console's peritext (instruction manual and packaging) earlier has shown. The epitext and other external commentary on the console also underlined graphics as an important part of its identity: "Super Nintendo's main attributes are its brilliant custom chips. ... These are used to create some stunning graphical effects" (*Computer and Video Games* #123, February 1992); "The Super NES feature that has attracted the most attention among game players is a graphics mode the company calls 'Mode 7'" (Willcox 1991). In July 1991, just a month before the North American release, a *Nintendo Power* feature titled "In the Works for the Super Nintendo Entertainment System" (#26, July 1991, 50) provided a general five-sentence blurb to the effect that 29 games were under development or already published in Japan and might be released for the SNES. The rest of the page was filled with screenshots from each of the 29 games, understanding the need for consumers to visually see the difference and pushing the strengths of the console.

"Do the Math": Technological Promotion in Advertising

The discursive stances on technology that I exposed so far have applied to the journalistic and critical contents that appear in game magazines. But game magazines feature another quantitatively important type of communications: advertisements. Advertising discourses differ from journalism and criticism because they can be blatantly honest about their business. Aside from their positioning and motivation, the discursive contents of many ads of the period also revolve around certain framings of technology that are fully compatible, if not without localized differences, with the prior discussion.

A particular two-page *MegaRace* advertisement is something of a piece of anthology. It perfectly embodies the edgy, provocative line of advertisement that characterizes the 1990s in video game promotion, with the entire left page taken up by the mug of a *Mad Max*-esque, pierced, scarred, and tattooed skinhead wearing a chain around his neck and gritting his teeth (the latter adorned with MEGA RACE letterings) under the words "NO COPS. NO LAWS. NO WIMPS." It perfectly exemplifies the competitive mode of address (Therrien 2014) by taunting the player from the typical heavily gendered macho masculinity perspective, the right page titling in all capitals, "ARE YOU A GIRLIE-MAN OR A MEGARACER?"

More to the point of the discussion at hand here, however, the advertisement's text seems to hit up all the right notes, throwing in every buzzword of the time. Two of the three captions that accompany the game's screenshots are particularly strong embodiments of the buzzword mode of technological discourse:

> Spectacular fully rendered animation, amazing 3-D graphics and pulse pounding sound effects make MEGARACE a rowdy, supercharged, one-of-a-kind virtual driving experience. / Over 25 minutes of full-motion digitized video commentary by MEGARACE host Lance Boyle, 15 full rendered tracks, hot rock music track and the virtual ride of your life (or death). (*EGM* #59, June 1994, 26–27)

Rendered 3-D graphics, edgy vocabulary, virtual reality, full-motion live-action video, great sound effects, and CD music: It's all in there (including lame parenthesis jokes).

Tempest 2000's Jaguar port's game box provides a similarly hilarious concentrate of neologisms and buzzwords for the technophiliac:

> Turn out the lights, turn up the volume and prepare for a mind-blowing assault on the senses. Once your neurotransmitters get a taste of the hypnotic rhythms of 100% pure techno-rave, you'll be hooked. ... Unable to escape the rush of blasting Flippers and Demon Heads as enhanced 3D polygons, screaming particle displays and hyperdelic Melt-O-Vision™ graphics warp you into the ultraviolent 64th dimension. ... (Atari Corp. 1994)

Why settle for "virtual reality" and its promises of the 3rd dimension and realism when you can have your neurotransmitters directly hooked up to the 64th dimension and experience hyperpsychedelic graphics that melt your vision? Just Do the Math.

Alongside these over-the-top, orthodox advertisements, in 1994, we find a wholly different stance toward technology present as well. An ad that may appear refreshingly honest is the two-page splash from STD Entertainment, a manufacturer of programmable game controllers for multiple platforms. The opening is strikingly in tune with this discussion:

> Are you into sports games, OR WHAT?! Then you're gonna love this STUFF! We won't bore you with the Techno-Babble, just use our **Advanced Controllers** [...]. **CUSTOM PROGRAMMABLE MICRO-CHIPS!** Now you can handle those Complex Jams and other tough moves! **HIGH PERFORMANCE CIRCUITRY!** Our super-smart engineers have done it again! You'll have the edge in Accuracy, Speed, and Responsiveness! (*EGM* #57, April 1994, 8–9)

They won't bore us with technobabble, but they'll use a lighter version of the strategy by throwing the buzzwords around and not even trying to connect them with explanations. This conscious play on the tensions between technobabble and technoliteracy marks a shift in address and target audience, from the technically savvy and rebellious teenagers dedicated to gaming as their hobby and as a way of expressing their cast-out nature toward a mainstream audience who isn't "into" technology. Technoliteracy is dead, long live the buzzword! Sega's own promotion for the *Virtua Racing* Genesis port presented its chip technology (an attempt to compete with Nintendo's 1993 Super FX chip and its polygons) but didn't discuss it:

> [...] you've been waiting for Virtua Racing on the Genesis. Well, it's here. With all the speed, realism and 3-D graphics of the arcade game. All it took was a quantum leap in processing speed—that's where our SVP chip comes in. Luckily, you don't have to understand the technology to appreciate Virtua Racing. Just drive. (*EGM* #59, June 1994, 54–55)

Nintendo, in its newfound attempt at being cool and hip n'stuff, of course followed suit when promoting *Donkey Kong Country*. Instead of explaining that the game developers modeled and animated polygonal 3-D characters on computers and exported stills and animation frames into the game, the firm created the buzzword "A.C.M." for "Advanced Computer Modeling," which it threw around every possible promotional material. It sounds technological, and it's "Advanced," to boot! A poster from Nintendo of America, dated from 1994 and titled "Want game frenzy? We've got it!!" presents a selection of SNES games and an arrow pointed at a *Donkey Kong Country* screenshot with the words "A.C.M. Advanced Computer Modeling (obviously cool stuff)."

Trademarking technology—or rather, technological-sounding buzzwords—was the way to go if all went well, as Sega's "Blast Processing" campaign had shown. Trying to claim technological superiority over Nintendo, Sega of America promoted the Genesis's "Blast Processing" capabilities, eluding technoliterate explanation until widespread consumer suspicion turned it into ridicule. Unfazed by Sega's humiliation, Atari employed the same tactic to promote *Tempest 2000* for the Jaguar, promising the player will "experience outrageous Melt-O-Vision™ graphics and powerful 3D polygons" (*Video Games: The Ultimate Gaming Magazine* #66, July 1994, 48–49). What's Melt-O-Vision? It may turn out to be nothing more than a trademark (one that was filed in June 1994 and abandoned in May 1996 to be precise),[5] but that's sufficient for the goal of the ad: to instill a sense that there's something graphically unique, "powerful," and advanced in this game, and that makes it worth playing to see what it's all about.

The three discursive strategies of technoliteracy, technobabble, and buzzwords play a vital role in shaping gamers' expectations when new technologies are introduced into the market. They may do so as part of a game or game console's epitext when they appear in ads or as independent journalism and criticism. Regardless of their provenance, they created high expectations toward the Super NES before it even hit the store shelves.

The SNES was an odd combination of a glacially slow 2.58 megahertz (not gigahertz) processor with a tiny 64 kilobytes (not megabytes or gigabytes) of memory coupled with exotic microchips designed to rapidly blast bits onto the screen—if you could figure out the right incantations to make it all work. (Wyatt 2012)

So far, we've seen the technocentrist discourses of Nintendo in promoting its brand-new Super NES. From advertisements to features and previews that made up the SNES's epitext, down to the peritext that accompanied the console as the consumer unboxed the crown jewel of the Nintendo Emperor of Videoludica, a single message was hammered into millions of brains: The Super NES was a powerful system capable of highly polished graphics. Patrick Wyatt, a game developer who was working on the Super NES for Blizzard Entertainment, paints a different picture of the hardware's speed, power, and design in the previous epigraph. It's time to delve into the hardware and examine the technology critically. What will come out of this analysis is how the modular and expansive characteristics that largely defined the Super Famicom/Super NES[1] were also incorporated in the system to serve or push further the typical gameplay experiences of the time—namely, those that made Nintendo's fortunes: side-scrolling platform games and action-adventure titles.

Ex-Centric Architecture

When designing the console, Masayuki Uemura had decided to forego the strategy of putting a strong heart in the middle of the system, which would translate to a state-of-the-art new chip or core, an expensive one that ran counter to the "lateral thinking with seasoned technology" ethos. Instead, the Super Famicom (SFC) would pursue even further another kind of architecture that had been chosen with the Famicom: a decentralized, networked mode of operation, with specialized components dedicated to specific aspects of the process—like specialized silverware, with different spoons for coffee, tea, soup, and dessert. In doing so, the Super Famicom's technological architecture closely mirrored Nintendo's networked organizational structure, as we'll see in chapter 7.

The Super Famicom is made of a central processing unit (CPU), the brain of the system that is in charge of everything. It sends and receives data by storing and retrieving it in 128 KB of random access memory (Work RAM) using address and data buses that are responsible for directing traffic to the right places, and transporting the data itself. This basic infrastructure links the CPU with a second subsystem: the picture processing unit (PPU) dedicated to the game's graphical output. The PPU subsystem actually houses two units: the PPU1 and PPU2. In this we can see an extension of Nintendo's original idea of having a dedicated PPU in the Famicom and of betting on graphics quality. For audio, Nintendo used the 8-bit SPC700 chip, developed by Sony's Ken Kutaragi, and integrated it as the key part of an audio processing unit (APU) that is, physically and logically, highly independent from the rest of the console, contrary to the Famicom's 2A03 chip (Altice 2015, chapter 7). The APU boots by itself and waits for the main CPU's custom sound program (and samples); the code is then executed, and eight channels of digital audio are processed and converted to analog before leaving the APU for output. This technical arrangement maps strangely well onto the exclusionary principle at the heart of the Nintendo Economic System and the "walled garden" model, as seen in chapter 1: Sony's chip, although located inside the console, is still allowed in through a gated access, inside but outside.

The last sign of the SFC's decentralized architecture can be found in the cartridge connector; it provides direct access to one of the PPUs and to the APU, which means cartridges can transfer audiovisual data directly without maneuvering through the CPU and thus play an increased role in shaping the game experience. Once again, this design decision is a refinement of a previous arrangement that had made the Famicom's fortunes: the principle of having cheap baseline hardware open to future expansions, thanks to the possibility of having additional chips added to individual cartridges following their needs. The idea had proved its potential in Japan, with the multi-memory controller (MMC) expansion chips found in many Famicom cartridges. The Super Famicom would repeat this strategy, and as we'll see in chapter 6, expansion chips in cartridges would greatly expand the console's life and reach in its later years.

The Wafer-Thin Edge of CPU and Memory

We have seen in chapter 2 how the console was conceived in a rush and how people at Nintendo and in the press in general perceived it as an extension to the Famicom, or a Famicom 2. The CPU provides the clearest illustration of this, as it was a modest upgrade over the Famicom, to say the least. Initial plans for the SFC revolved around a Motorola 68000 processor—the same used in Sega's Mega Drive/Genesis—but the cost-cutting imperative led to its replacement with something else. Hoping to achieve backward compatibility with the Famicom, Nintendo settled on a custom Ricoh 5A22 processor—a second-source manufacturing of the 65816 processor by Western Design Center—that could emulate the operation of the earlier 6502 (of which the Ricoh 2A03, in the Famicom, was a derivative). Unfortunately, supporting the emulation for the Famicom would prove too costly to get the SFC on the market cheaply, so the backward compatibility plan was axed. The true origin story of the Super Famicom/NES nevertheless remains carved in the silicon of its core: When the Super Famicom is powered on, the processor starts in 6502 emulation mode until a two-instruction sequence shifts it to "native mode" and unlocks its full 16-bit potential (Eyes and Lichty 1992, 44).

In a sense, the 65816 was powerful because it was an upgraded 16-bit microprocessor to the previous 8-bit 6502. The 6502 core had been used and upgraded by Hudson Soft into the HuC6280, which was powering the PC-Engine that had frightened Nintendo. This meant the Super Famicom's CPU was clearly more advanced than at least one competitor. Sega's Mega Drive was another matter entirely, however, because it was powered by the costly Motorola 68000 processor and a secondary Zilog Z80 processor (incidentally, a contributing factor to why Sega never got to dive in a pool of gold like Nintendo, as we've seen earlier in chapter 2). The 68000 and Z80 had been used extensively in arcade games for years. In fact, Sega had more or less ported its System 16 arcade platform for the home with the Sega Mega Drive, whose processors were clocked at 7.6 MHz and 3.58 MHz. Could the Super Famicom best this rival?

The SFC's master clock operated at approximately 21.477 MHz, which looked good for Nintendo on paper—and the firm used that in every side-by-side technical comparison it could publish (or get independent magazines to publish). Nintendo was taking the "bit wars" one step further to claim superiority over another 16-bit competitor with the "megahertz myth"—the valuing of clock speed (measured in megahertz) as the principal indicator of a computer system's performance—like Intel in its war against Apple (Smith 2002). However, the platform's theoretical processing speed was limited by the architecture and configuration of memory at the heart of the system, which demonstrates the complex and sometimes futile nature of evaluating and comparing competing game consoles, as Brian Benchoff remarks:

> The traditional comparison between two consoles is usually presented as a series of specs, a bunch of numbers, and tick marks indicating which system wins in each category. While this does illustrate the strengths and weaknesses of each console, it is a rhetorical technique that is grossly imprecise, given the different architectures. [...] Even the Internet's best console experts fall victim to the trap of comparing specs between different architectures, and it's complete and utter baloney. (Benchoff 2015)

Without delving into technical minutiae and in-depth comparisons of the performance between the SNES and Genesis (which various Internet message boards and wikis can offer),[2] I will identify some of the important architectural features of the SFC and how they express Nintendo's key positions and strategies exposed earlier.

The SFC's roughly 21 MHz master clock means the crystal oscillator vibrates at a frequency of roughly 21 million cycles per second. Contrary to what the "megahertz myth" entertains, the frequency of the crystal oscillator does not automatically translate into faster or more powerful processing power. Each computing instruction handled by the CPU requires a certain number of CPU clock cycles to perform; on the SNES, each CPU cycle in turn required either 6, 8 or 12 master clock cycles to complete, depending on the destination to be accessed. In other words, the master clock's job was not to process instructions as fast as it could, but to keep every destination synchronized by adjusting the variable speed of the system bus, the interface that accessed and transported data across the system's components (namely the central, picture and audio processing units, the hardware registers, the working random access memory or RAM, and the cartridge read-only memory or ROM data itself). Thus, the bus operated at one of three possible speeds: 1.79 MHz, 2.68 MHz, or 3.58 MHz, obtained by dividing the master clock's 21.477 MHz by 12, 8 and 6, respectively. This determines a range of effective operating speed for the SNES from 1.79 to 3.58 MHz — a far cry from the listed master clock speed of 21.477 MHz that shows how meaningless it stands as a performance metric. In fact, the Super Famicom's master clock speed of 21.477 MHz was the same as that found in its 8-bit predecessor, the Famicom, whose CPU likewise ran at 1.79 MHz by dividing the master clock cycles by 12. The SFC's slowest 1.79 MHz speed was used to access the controller port for player input. The middle 2.68 MHz (or "slow") speed regulated most operations requiring RAM and ROM, typically when handling game data from the cartridge and doing most internal system work. Finally, the highest 3.58 MHz speed governed internal hardware registers that dealt with video output to process graphics and sound, as well as cartridges that used faster (but costlier) memory known as "FastROM", opposed to the regular 2.68MHz "SlowROM".

The other main factor limiting the platform's raw operational speed was the architecture of the buses. The SFC featured two address buses responsible for directing the data traffic to the right memory locations: "bus A" (or the "main bus") was 24 bits wide and handled data transfers between the CPU, cartridge ROM, and console RAM; "bus B" was 8 bits wide and had the specialized function of handling hardware registers for the PPU and APU, responsible for the player's audiovisual experience. The address buses were establishing lines of communication between the devices, but the data transport itself was effectuated in a single data bus that was only 8 bits wide, meaning that complex data had to be broken down into multiple, smaller parts and transported in succession, over multiple cycles. This represented an important speed bottleneck, but the settling on an 8-bit data bus appears natural in the context of the console's development as a successor to the Famicom that was to be backward compatible with the 6502 processor's 8-bit data bus.

In the end, the SFC's architecture relied on an unusually high number of different units and processors that handled specific tasks, which cluttered and complicated the programming process just as the accumulation of silverware complicates the dining experience. While all analogies have limits, the situation was akin to having a dinner table laid out with steak, lobster and soup, with tiny matching forks, knives and spoons: each food required using the proper utensils, and a good amount of planning and coordination to get a meal worth one's while. Programming for the SFC/SNES required a good deal of knowledge on how to program for the FC/NES, along with a firm grasp of programming techniques for an esoteric arrangement of additional components. The small step forward the SFC took is echoed nowadays in internet communities dedicated to "homebrew" development and amateur programming. The NES enthusiasts gather on the NESDev portal to find and exchange on NES programming.

At the time of writing, the best place for programmers interested in developing SNES games is the "SNES" subsection of the NESDev community, which illustrates the technological continuity between the 8-bit and 16-bit consoles quite clearly.

Most sources that discuss the technical specifications of systems conclude that the Super Famicom was, at heart, a slow machine, but more important, that its general architecture was a challenge to be overcome compared with the Mega Drive's more familiar 68000 processor environment. The processing power of the SFC's CPU was certainly not favoring Nintendo's console, and it took time for game developers to master the intricacies of the system, as René Boutin from Sunsoft summarized:

> You needed very good programmers to make use of these resources, since the central processor was pretty weak compared to the rest, and the system architecture was extremely complex. [...] We used to call it a "fake 16-bit"; fundamentally, it was a custom 8-bit, with a few 16-bit functionalities. (Boutin in Audureau et al. 2013, 19)

From Sony with Love: The Audio Subsystem

The Super Famicom's sound was praised by the press and fans for two reasons. The first is essentially technological: the SFC marked a transition or turn for game console music hardware by being based on sound samples, whereas previous consoles had used tone generators and frequency modulation (FM) synthesis (Collins 2008, 45–47). Each SFC game could feature its own sound samples to build distinct soundscapes in 8-channel stereo, a notable improvement over the Famicom's monophonic channels with limited variance.

The second reason that the SFC's audio was celebrated were the early published games for the system. *Super Mario World* and *F-Zero*, the two launch titles, provided a good demonstration of the variety that the audio subsystem allowed, from piano to electric guitars, trumpets to bongos. *ActRaiser*, released within weeks of the console's launch, featured a soundtrack that stood out with its orchestral style, a rarity at the time. It utilized many different sound samples, all eight sound channels, and echo audio effects that widened the sound, giving the impression that a large number of instruments were used; with enough echo, a couple of string instruments could produce an impact similar to a whole string section instead. Compositionally, it explored a wide range of styles and moods, ranging from the dramatic film score to the epic brass-heavy orchestra, taking detours through soothing harps, peaceful village themes, and a variety of ethnic music.

Soon Super Famicom games pushed in all kinds of directions. *Super Castlevania IV's* soundtrack took the famed series' direction of dark upbeat rock flirting with metal to a graver, more serious level, just like Konami did for the graphics, with a more subdued color palette and away from the cartoonish style of previous Famicom iterations. The SFC sequel's choices of samples and compositional direction ("baroque with jazzy flavors"; Mecheri 2014, 36) goes further in the dark and brooding direction, in what could be called "pop-gothic dark ambient." Dark strings, ominous reeds, and church organs coexist with upbeat drums, bass grooves, and echo. Lots of echo, as if one were listening in a cathedral on the eve of Judgment Day.

Not all composers followed in the atmospheric or orchestral directions, however; building on the strength of samples, the SFC soundtracks were varied in their explorations. Melodic/symphonic epics appeared through *The Legend of Zelda: A Link to the Past*, *Final Fantasy II* and *III*, *Secret of Mana* and *Chrono Trigger*; broody, foreboding atmospheric music in *Super Ghouls 'n Ghosts* and *Super Metroid*; playfully eclectic dance beats and synth-pop fused in *Teenage Mutant Ninja Turtles IV: Turtles in Time* and *Street Fighter II*, while hard rock and heavy metal/pop hybrids burned through *Ys III: Wanderers from Ys*, *Battletoads in Battlemaniacs*, *Mega Man X*, *Final Fantasy Mystic Quest*, and *Rock n'Roll Racing*, among others. Many SFC games had their soundtracks released in Japan, some of them becoming best sellers or seeing rearranged versions with rock bands or orchestras.

Advanced as it was, the audio took a back seat to the real priority targeted by the SFC/SNES: the graphics. Before getting to the *pièce de résistance*, however, we must first lay our hands on the silverware and discuss the Super Famicom and Super NES's case and controller.

Hardware Design, from Console to Controllers

The Japanese and American consoles, like their predecessors, both featured an expansion port on their bottom. Nintendo had plans for a CD-ROM add-on and other peripherals, likely developments given the impending trajectory of multimedia devices that lay ahead (to be detailed in chapter 7) and in keeping with the prior Famicom Disk System. As can be seen in figure 4.1, the Super NES differed in shape from the Super Famicom, but not as much as the NES had differed from the Famicom.

Nintendo of America's designer Lance Barr gave the Super NES harder, more angular lines to give the console a look closer to a domestic VCR and to give it some volume, as he found the Super Famicom looked like a bag of bread (Margetts and Ward 2012),[3] a solution that also would better

Figure 4.1 Left: the Japanese Super Famicom; right: the Super NES. Source: Evan Amos, Wikimedia Commons

accommodate the sure-to-come expansions that would plug in from under the console. The angled top of the North American SNES also prevented people from leaving drinks on the machine, thus avoiding damaging spills. The light gray body and dark gray faceplate found on the Japanese system were also simplified into a uniform light gray body, except for the small, recessed dark gray eject switch and the two bright purple Power and Reset sliding switches.

Arguably, the most important departure from the original Japanese hardware is the replacement of the Super Famicom's "colors of the rainbow" logo (visible on all marketing materials but also in-game in bright lights in *Super Mario World*'s Special World). The green, blue, red, and yellow circles deployed like the petals of a flower were replaced by a more sober, serious, and discrete purple-and-gray two-tone scheme. Unfortunately for technofetishists and purist aesthetes, these color palette changes weren't the only ones: The SNES's plastic casing contained a chemical flame retardant additive that causes unseemly yellowing discoloration in normal aging conditions—a modern form of tarnish for modern-day silverware.

Barr's most important contribution, however, lies in the Super NES's controller. The Super Famicom controllers had the SFC logo printed on them, which obviously had to go for the North American adaptation, but they also had the "colors of the rainbow" visually encoded in their buttons, as each of them took on one of the four colors. Barr replaced the red, yellow, blue, and green button colors with purple and lavender to go with the redesigned console's sober light gray and purple theme. More important, however, he followed a conceptual trail that appeared in the SFC controllers by turning their shapes into two pairs of matching buttons. As can be seen in figure 4.2, the original SFC buttons were organized in pairs

Figure 4.2 Left: Super Famicom (top) and Super NES (bottom) controllers. (The L and R shoulder buttons are hidden by the photo's angle.) Right: Famicom (top) and Genesis (bottom) controllers. Source: Evan Amos, Wikimedia Commons

by two light gray diagonal oblongs, which visually defined the A/B and X/Y duets (in addition to their alphabetical split). The SNES controllers would match the buttons by their colors and shapes: X and Y would be concave and lavender, whereas A and B would be convex and purple.

The decision was important because it made it easier for people to learn how to deal with this new four-button material interface. The buttons could be told apart by the touch only, rather than having to take the eyes away from the screen to look at the controller. Moreover, for people not quite used to the handling of video game controllers, the arrangement and shape of the buttons indicated the common way to place one's fingers; the end of the thumb could be laid to rest gently into the concave groove of the X or Y button, with the convex shape of the A and B buttons making them easy to depress by flexing the thumb's joint without moving it back and forth between buttons (a handling that had been necessary from the Famicom days of the *Super Mario Bros.* series, if one wanted to hold the run button while pressing the jump one). Together with the larger size and "dogbone" shape, the Super Famicom (and particularly the Super NES) provided a great improvement in video game controller ergonomics.

As for the controller's functionality, Nintendo's software orientation had led it to develop hardware according to the needs of its software. Just like the Famicom had been designed to play *Donkey Kong* (Altice 2015), the Super Famicom had been designed to play *F-Zero*, *Pilotwings*, and *Super Mario Bros. 4*, which in its earliest stages looked more like *Super Mario Bros. 3–2*, as can be seen in the Japanese press following Nintendo's second SFC demonstration (Covell, "*Super Famicom*," July 1989). The L and R shoulder buttons offered finer controls for turning left and right in addition to the directional pad's four-way movement scheme, a forward-thinking innovation that mapped perfectly to tridimensional spaces. As *Pilotwings* (and later on *Contra III: The Alien Wars* and the *Super Star Wars* trilogy) exemplify, the direction of facing could be controlled with L and R rotations, whereas movement through translations was independently controlled by the directional pad. In this sense, the SNES prefigures the twin-joystick or mouse-and-keyboard control schemes that separate the "move" and "look" functions, which allows strafing in modern games.

The shoulder buttons would become a standard in video game controllers that persists to this day (with the PlayStation having expanded on it by featuring four shoulder buttons). More important, it further increased the total count of available buttons on the controller. Together with the four face buttons (twice as many as the Famicom and PC-Engine and one more than the Mega Drive), the Super Famicom gave opportunities for gamers and game developers alike to develop more complex games, a feature that would prove crucial in the platform's success.

Controller Complexity: *The Street Fighter II* Lesson

One key game for which the controller made a significant difference was *Street Fighter II*. The 1991 smash-hit arcade game from Capcom caused a revival of the arcade market, which was slumping along after the glory days of the early 1980s. *Street Fighter II* was as popular in Japan as it was in North America and Europe, and it was so successful it spawned a whole genre of likewise fighting games. One reason for this success is that it was a technically accomplished game as far as controls went. Capcom's programmers and engineers perfected programming routines and button wiring that made it possible to execute complex multibutton and joystick manipulations for special moves that differed for each character. The arcade game, like its predecessor, had six different attacks (quick, medium, and strong punch and quick, medium, and strong kick), which together formed the nexus of strategy and skill that players had to develop and master in their quest to become the World Warrior. Moreover, the three-level grading of attacks affected the characters' all-important special moves: Executing the same maneuver using the strong punch or strong kick instead of their quick or medium grades resulted in a Hadoken fireball traveling faster across the screen or a spinning kick reaching farther. The complexity of mechanics and control system, along with a delicate balance among the game's characters that prevented one of them from overpowering the rest, made it an intensely competitive game.

The popularity of the game of course demanded ports for home video game consoles. The 16-bit Nintendo version was the first to reach the market in the summer of 1992 and featured a 16-megabit cartridge, which still wasn't enough to guarantee an integral replication of the arcade experience. Bonus stages were modified, some background elements in the levels were abandoned or simplified, some voices were cut out, and some script and storyline changes were made. But these features were all auxiliary to the game's main interest. The most important things about *Street Fighter II*, those that defined its identity and made it interesting, were the characters, their special moves, and the game's controls and three-grade attacks. In this respect, the SFC/SNES had it all.

Although the Super Famicom had been selling well in Japan, in North America, the Super NES was still slumping against the Sega Genesis, and many consumers were holding out on the upgrade cycle. *Street Fighter II* functioned as a killer app for the SNES, selling 6.3 million units worldwide (in no small part thanks to Nintendo creating a SNES *Street Fighter II* bundle), compared with 1.65 million for the later September 1993 Sega Genesis version, superlatively titled *Street Fighter II': Special Champion Edition*. By then the SFC/SNES had also received a follow-up, *Street Fighter II Turbo* (July/August 1993), based on the arcades *Street Fighter II' Turbo: Hyper Fighting* and *Street Fighter II': Champion Edition*. The latter was soon superseded by *Super Street Fighter II* (June 1994), just in time for the game's two-year anniversary. Aside from looking like a creativity contest for Capcom's marketers, the titles show that the "turbo-mega-super generation" logic wasn't restricted to platform owners. In the end, the three SFC/SNES releases reached a combined total of more than 12 million copies, against 1.65 million for the Mega Drive/Genesis.

The extreme discrepancy in sales is partly explained by the fact that the SFC/SNES benefitted from a long first-mover advantage. However, the impact of the consoles' controllers is what truly made the difference. The Sega Genesis controllers had three regular face buttons and a fourth "Start" one, which cut right into the core premise of the game's three-graded punch and kick attacks. Playing on the Sega Genesis meant using the A, B, and C buttons to make quick, medium, and strong attacks, with the Start button toggling between punches and kicks. The awkward toggling mechanism completely broke the flow of the game by making it impossible to rapidly alternate between punches and kicks. A veteran

Guile player hurling Sonic Booms with his punches would furiously reach for the Start button if the opponent jumped over them and most likely would never switch to kicks in time to fire off a Flash Kick against the airborne attacker. Genesis owners looking for the authentic arcade experience had to buy a special six-button controller—or two of them if they wanted to play against a family member or a friend, which is the main point in playing these kinds of games. Instead, they could get an SNES and the game, which netted them access to a whole other game library—another sign that consumers desire games, not technology in itself, as we have seen in chapter 2.

Now, with our silverware interface in hand, we are almost ready to get to the Super Famicom's main course—the graphics. First, we must get through the *entrée*, the smaller course that will prepare us to fully appreciate the main course: the conflicting role of graphics in video games.

The Graphics Matter

The importance given to graphics in video games predates Nintendo's 16-bit system. It also predates its 8-bit predecessor. A two-page advertisement for the Intellivision titled "two pictures are worth a thousand words" had used the "graphics argument" in the early 1980s, claiming that the Intellivision's advanced graphics clearly showed how advanced the system was compared with the Atari 2600. Focusing on graphics has always been a good strategy, one that Nintendo had simply followed with the Famicom. The console's distinguishing architectural feature had been the creation of a separate processor to manage graphics (the PPU), a "major design innovation" that "improved and simplified the way graphics were stored and delivered to the screen. It also allowed the CPU of the console to spend more time doing game-related operations and less time doing graphics-related operations" (O'Donnell 2011, 94). Altice (2015, 29–30), however, explains that this "contribution" to game hardware design was in all likelihood lifted from Coleco's Colecovision machine.

In any case, this architecture is a substantial turning point in the history of game platforms and has been a constant in video game hardware since the Famicom. By dedicating special resources to graphics instead of treating them as part of the CPU's workload just like every other computing operation (artificial intelligence routines, storage and retrieval of data values, management of controller input, and so on), the Famicom/NES's hardware architecture had singled them out as an area that merited more care and attention. That the PC-Engine would feature a 16-bit coprocessor dedicated to graphics—and, even more clearly, that the entire platform was built from Hudson's initial project of developing a graphics chip to extend the Famicom's graphical capabilities in the first place—demonstrate how influential Nintendo's success with the Famicom and NES was and how engineers understood it as a demonstration of the supremacy of graphics in video game technology.

Indeed, as we have seen in chapter 2, graphical technologies are of paramount importance when considering the launch of a platform because they can spur technological adoption and start the virtuous cycle of confidence by developers and consumers. Hence, graphics, when envisioned in the context of technological innovation, act as a conceptual interface that allows consumers and third-party developers to get a glimpse of the underlying, invisible technologies. Launch and early titles (as well as other flagship titles, such as Sega's *Sonic the Hedgehog* or id Software's *Doom* and *Quake*) cannot be thought of as simply providing entertainment to consumers. Instead, these games become rhetorical devices in themselves, parts of a wider discourse from a platform owner that attempts to seduce and convince third-party game developers and consumers to choose their own technology over that of competitors.

Although graphics have always been leveraged into rhetorics of persuasion from console manufacturers, the fourth generation of game consoles made it particularly evident. *Electronic Gaming Monthly*, as part of their feature on the coming 16-Bit consoles, offered a preview of the Sega Genesis. A frame titled "8-Bit VS. 16-Bit...a difference you can see" presents side-by-side screenshots of *Altered Beast* for the 8-bit Sega Master System and what could either be a screenshot from the arcade version or a preview of the upcoming Sega Genesis version. As much as the article praises graphics, it also frames them critically, the second title reading, "The Genesis games—only good looks?" and the text, "The first Genesis games are spectacular in appearance, but fall flat in some important areas of game play" (*EGM* #2, July/August 1989, 37).

This article crystallizes the gaming community's love/hate relationship with graphics. On the one hand, gaming culture manages a special place for graphics and endlessly discusses them as part of the never-ending quest toward realism, photorealism, or visual aesthetics in general, making graphics and visual style an argument for the artistry of video games. On the other hand, gaming culture's dominant discourse has adopted a critical stance toward graphics as well, urging gamers to go beyond "eye candy" in search of wholesome, nutritive food and to avoid flash and style and go for the real meat and substance: "gameplay," however it's defined (and most often isn't). A crass term even exists (indicative of the historical gender politics of gamer culture) to dismiss people who value graphics over gameplay: "graphics whore." This shows how graphics were sometimes positioned at one end of an axis, opposed to gameplay: The games were either pretty and shallow or ugly and deep. Although caricatural, this framing still accounts for ambivalent sentiments toward video game graphics.

Beyond "Eye Candy": Graphical Regimes

To resolve this tension, Pierre-Marc Côté and I have proposed the concept of *graphical regime*. Inspired by the concept of technological regime (Nelson and Winter 1982, Winter 1984), which is the set of particular knowledge environments where firms engage in problem-solving activities, the graphical regime is defined as "the junction point between gameplay and graphics" and "*the imaging of gameplay and the gameplay of the image*, independently of the technological graphical capabilities or limitations" (Arsenault and Côté 2013). The idea is that in video games, graphics are both something nice to look at (an aesthetic object) *and* something that is interacted with (a functional object). Thus, graphical innovations may be cases of *radical innovation* (Norman and Verganti 2012) when they open new graphical regimes (i.e., new ways of playing with the image or new ways to set in images the gameplay). Those that do not demonstrate new modes of gameplay and are simply regarded as upgrading the fidelity, resolution, or "polish effect" that graphics can provide are instead instances of *incremental innovation* and may be rejected as simple "eye candy" for impressionable consumers who don't know better.

In a later publication (Arsenault, Côté, and Larochelle 2015), we detailed the various components that make up a graphical regime by developing the unified Framework for the Analysis of Visual Representation, the game FAVR. Although I won't go into details for every component, generally, a graphical regime includes a certain interface and disposition of elements across the screen (the composition); a certain point of view, such as first-person, third-person, cinematic camera, and so on (the ocularization); a framing mechanism (implying an anchor; i.e., what is being targeted by the view, and a mobility range, or what triggers the viewpoint's movement); and a configuration of in-game space that involves the type of graphical projection method (perspective, isometric, etc.), viewing angle (bird's eye view, top-down, horizontal, etc.), and pictorial materials (pixels, vectors, polygons, etc.).[4]

What this means is that we can describe a graphical regime like the "side-scroller" in *Super Mario Bros. 3* and *Super Mario World* (by no means exclusive to these two games) by noting it has a full-screen game space (complemented by a data interface ribbon), displaying a world in external ocularization with a horizontal angle, with the view anchored on Mario with a connected mobility (moving Mario makes the frame move along with him), and where every element of characters and backgrounds is represented in raster graphics (grids of colored pixels). When we turn to *New Super Mario Bros.*, we find that the side-scrolling 2-D game can be implemented in a 3-D engine. The only difference between *SMW* and *NSMB* is the visual materials, which evolved from raster graphics to 3-D polygons. At heart, however, these different technologies partake in the same graphical regime, the same gameplay/image relationship, making them squarely part of a process of incremental innovation.

The concept of graphical regime is useful in theorizing the role of technological innovation for platforms and, as such, will form the backbone of my discussion of the SFC's graphical innovations. In general, the Super Famicom's graphics can be understood in two broad categories. Incremental innovations include the colors, sprites, and multilayered backgrounds the platform offers, which have facilitated a number of graphical programming and design techniques that were in use at the time. The SFC's unique contribution to video game graphics, "Mode 7," is a mixed item, offering both incremental innovation through matrix transformations and radical innovation in perspective projection.

The SFC's Graphical Infrastructure

In conservative logic, the Super Famicom would iterate on the Famicom's contributions to video game hardware and simply "go for more" with a careful balance of finely tuned innovation; the console would excel at doing better what the Famicom was doing before. The main substance of gameplay rested on sprites, the moving and animated on-screen objects and characters, and tiles, the blocks that made up a game's background. Both of these could be handled for the Super Famicom in the same way as for the Famicom, allowing developers to transfer their expertise to the new system.

The common programming logic for both systems was that, given memory limitations, graphical elements had to be broken down in tiles of 8 x 8 pixels, which could be organized in larger sets (metatiles or metasprites) by supplying a tilemap, a list of which tiles should go where. The PPU sorted through all the elements to be displayed and hierarchized them, drawing sprites on top of backgrounds. To achieve scrolling, the system prepared extra columns or rows of (meta)tiles beyond what the screen could display. With proper timing and (very) efficient coding, the fragile illusion of a cohesive world filled with characters, scrolling by in a smooth movement, could be maintained. Efficiency was mandatory because the console needed to output the entire screen's graphics 60 times per second. If any part of the computations wasn't ready in time, then a frame had to be skipped while the processing finished the job, which resulted in slowdowns.[5]

SFC (meta)sprites could have sizes ranging from 8 x 8 to 64 x 64 pixels, but the console could only display sprites of two different sizes at once; it was 8 x 8 and 16 x 16 sprites, 8 x 8 and 32 x 32 ones, and so on. Up to 128 of them could appear at once—at least theoretically. In practice, the SFC's limitations in processing speed, as well as a limit of 32 sprites on a single horizontal line, proved severe and caused problems of sprite flickering. If more than 32 sprites were to appear on a single line, then the PPU could render them on alternate frames, making them rapidly flicker between visible and invisible in a ghostlike fashion.

The issues of flicker and slowdown would plague most Super Famicom games in any sprite-heavy action sequence and remained a constant issue for the platform. Early shooters (shoot'em ups) such as *Gradius III* (1990)—a launch title for the U.S. release of the Super NES—*Super R-Type* (1991), *Earth Defense Force* (1991), or *Thunder Spirits* (1991) were beset with slowdowns and flicker. This outcome is rather unsurprising considering the typical hails of bullets, missiles, rockets, and ships that fly around in every direction in this game genre. Nevertheless, the issues crept across all kinds of games and in all kinds of moments. In the Landspeeder piloting stage in the Tatooine desert of *Super Star Wars*, sprites accumulate as the screen gets filled with Jawas, Sandtroopers, hopping creatures, explosions, bullets, health power-ups, cacti, and rocks, causing noticeable slowdown. In *Contra III: The Alien Wars*, a car must be blown up right at the beginning of the game, and the explosion uses too many sprites, which causes noticeable slowdown. Level bosses explode when they are defeated, causing noticeable slowdown. In stage 3, the Tri-Transforming Mecha Wall Walker traps the player(s) between its legs—which are made of rotating sprites—and launches rockets, causing noticeable slowdown. Slowdown was so present that it sometimes came to be not only noticeable but desirable; some players (like me) purposely sprayed bullets around during this sequence to exploit the added slowdown, which helped with fallible human reflexes.[6]

The SFC lagged behind its competitors when dealing with sprites and scrolling, but one of its strongest advantages was its phenomenal range of colors. The Genesis and TurboGrafx-16 had 9-bit palettes that offered

512 colors; the SFC's 15-bit palette had a whopping 32,768 colors available to choose from. Yet that spectacular number (once again repeated *ad nauseam* in Nintendo's promotion practices and specs comparisons in magazines) didn't translate directly on the screen at once. Sprites could each have 16 colors, which was a lot more than the Famicom's three-color sprites,[7] but the total number of on-screen colors depended on the background. The SFC featured multiple graphics modes that specified a number of background layers and a color palette for them, ranging from 16 to 256 colors. The system's quirk is that overlapping background colors could be mixed in together through limited, but at the time impressive, transparency options and color averaging algorithms. The average value between two overlapping colors could be computed and rendered on-screen, which increased the effective color count and perceived visual richness. In the end, however, advertising 32,768 colors was more of a marketing ploy than an account of the visual experience because most games would end up with somewhere between 90 and 150 on-screen colors at a time.[8]

Colors, Resolution, and Backgrounds

The most determining visual feature of the Super Famicom was its eight graphics modes, hard-set combinations of certain numbers of background layers, with varying trade-offs between color palettes and resolution. This choice in designing the hardware indicates a first kind of form-setting on Nintendo's part, as it meant the platform was expressly designed to support some kinds of imaging, according to what the firm felt could be "standard" or useful. Modes 0 through 4 offered two to four background layers, with 4 to 256 colors. Modes 5 and 6 offered a higher resolution of 512 horizontal pixels but did so at a heavy price for colors, a price that few developers were willing to pay. Seeing the notable exception *RPM Racing* is enough to understand why; although the game was made for the same platform and by the same team than the later *Rock n' Roll Racing*, the limited amount of on-screen colors makes it look closer to its 8-bit predecessor *R.C. Pro-Am*.

The "Hi-Res" modes weren't supposed to make SFC games play in 512 x 448 resolution, although Nintendo's promotional discourse and even the specs comparisons in magazines listed that impressively high number everywhere. The real reason for this particular graphical mode was to allow Japanese games to display *kanji*. It had made a strong impression on the press during the 1989 Nintendo conference that unveiled the Super Famicom. A screenshot of a 16-bit remake of *Zelda II: The Adventure of Link* was shown, with a dialogue box displaying *kanji*. That moment was a technical achievement for console game graphics, a strong cultural signifier of Japan, and a promise of richer, fuller game dialogues and storylines—a promise that dating sims and visual novels, chiefly *Tokimeki Memorial*, would fulfill, along with RPGs.

Many games produced for the Super Famicom used the Hi-Res mode to display Japanese characters, considerably increasing the mileage of the limited screen estate. *Secret of Mana* and its Japan-exclusive sequel, *Seiken Densetsu 3*, are perhaps the most well-known games to have used the hi-res mode for the full-screen menus and dialogue boxes, but they were not the only ones; various games used it for menus, title screens, and credit rolls, from *Final Fantasy III* and *Lufia II: Rise of the Sinistrals* to *Kirby's Dream Land 3* and *Jurassic Park*, as well as *Smash Tennis* and *Donkey Kong Country*.

Mode 7, the last of these graphics modes, will get its own separate discussion later. For now, it is worth reflecting on the possibilities and logic behind the multiple backgrounds in modes 0 to 6.

The evolution of video game graphics can be framed as an accelerated re-creation of the evolution of traditional animation film. Early arcade games and home consoles had to completely redraw the picture every frame, just as some early pioneers of animation. As a result, backgrounds were either completely absent, which justifies the many early games taking place in space or against empty backgrounds, as well as the Magnavox Odyssey's plastic overlays to be fixed on the TV screen. Likewise, many of the earliest animated films featured an artist drawing on an easel (*The Enchanted Drawing* by James Stuart Blackton) or a chalkboard (Blackton's *Humorous Phases of Funny Faces*, Émile Cohl's *Fantasmagorie*), with no complementary scenery. This strategy eliminated the hundreds of tedious background recopyings that would have been required—one for each frame of film (Winsor McCay's 1914 film *Gertie the Dinosaur* provides a nice example).[9]

Animators, however, thought of ways to speed up the laborious process. The easiest solution was to separate the animated characters from the largely static backgrounds so they would not have to be redrawn every time. In the 1910s, Raoul Barré devised a "slash system." A pile of papers would be stacked and fixed in place through perforations and pegs. Because a detailed drawing of a scene would have animated characters or objects only in a certain part of the picture, the artist would tear away that region and draw the next phase of movement, keeping the remainder of the scene's drawing for the next frames. This technique was eventually superseded by Earl Hurd's celluloid sheet (or "cel"), invented in 1914 but patented and expensive. This system allowed artists to draw characters on transparent sheets that could be stacked on top of detailed background pictures. Here, we see the sprite-and-background structure that video games have quickly adopted and that characterized the Famicom.

Multiplane Cameras, Animetic Space, and Parallax Effects

The next step in film animation had been the multiplication of background layers, a logical extension because transparent cels could be stacked over each other. The Super Famicom (and the Sega Genesis before it) would follow the path of animation film and develop their own software equivalent of the multiplane camera. German animator Lotte Reiniger had developed a multiplane camera for her 1926 film *The Adventures of Prince Achmed*, the world's first feature-length animated film, besting the Walt Disney Studios on both counts by 10 years. But while she invented it, Disney exhibited and popularized the invention by discussing the studio's own multiplane camera in trailers and previews for its upcoming 1937 *Snow White and the Seven Dwarfs* feature film—a promotional philosophy of foregrounding technology that is not unlike Nintendo's own practices, a fact that strangely resonates with the shared history between the two firms, as we'll see in chapter 6.

The multiplane camera was a technical infrastructure designed to hold several cels on transparent glass layers, fixed in front of a film camera that would photograph one frame at a time and with independent controls to manipulate them. Cels with characters ("sprites") could be sandwiched between a background cel and a cel with foreground elements ("backgrounds"), giving a sense of depth to the picture. Figure 4.3 presents an

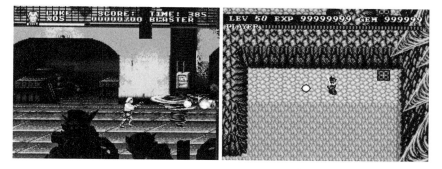

Figure 4.3 The *Super Star Wars* cantina stage (left) and the mountain cave in *Soul Blazer* (right) both resort to foreground elements to induce a sense of spatial depth, whether in side view with nearer patrons or in top-down view with hanging icicles. Emulated on Higan v0.95.

example of this impression of depth resulting from a flat drawing being superimposed over the main plane where the player-character runs and fights.

The kind of depth achieved here, however, is markedly different from that which can be reached through traditional cameras and our own embodied experience of space in everyday life. This "layered space" (Picard 2010, 252–264) is made up of flat bidimensional planes separated by an "animetic interval" (Lamarre 2009); in short, an animetic space, which is different from cinematic space. As Côté, Larochelle, and I wrote earlier, "To a large degree, this difference can be attributed to the difference between 3D and 2D graphics" (Arsenault, Côté, and Larochelle 2015, 98). The Super Famicom's built-in capacity to display up to four background layers brought it into the realm of the animetic. In this the platform is part of a larger conceptual transition toward the key technique used in film animation: compositing. No multiplication of 2-D planes, however, would ever bring it into the 3-D, cinematic space that polygons would eventually provide.

Just like the multiplane camera allowed individual cels to be displaced left or right in front of the camera, so could each SFC background layer be moved at different speeds, thus achieving a parallax effect. Motion parallax is a depth cue by which the closer an object lies in front of us, the faster it scrolls by as we move—and, conversely, the farther away it stands, the slower it will move. Up until the Mega Drive and Super Famicom, the parallax effect had been implemented in select video games such as *Jungle Hunt* and *Star Wars: The Empire Strikes Back* for the Atari VCS or *Bucky O'Hare* and *Joe & Mac* for the Famicom. The effect had been difficult to pull off with a single mass of undifferentiated background graphics; the Super Famicom and its multiple backgrounds in most graphics modes would make this easy. Consequently, a great number of games featured motion parallax effects.

Certainly the most egregious case is found in *Jim Power: The Lost Dimension in 3-D* (Loriciel 1993), where the background layers move in *increased* speed the farther away they are from the viewpoint, in addition to moving in opposite directions and lacking proper color-shading to approximate atmospheric perspective[10]; these combined factors make the game disorienting if not sickening. *U.N. Squadron* made good (if somewhat straightforward) use of multilayered parallax. More inspired uses could be found in *Ys III: Wanderers from Ys*, where the town of Redmont was given a more lifelike feel thanks to another street scrolling by as a secondary background glimpsed between buildings; in *ActRaiser*'s Bloodpool-1 action level, the titular pool stretching out in the background has distinct currents flowing at different speeds, thereby attracting visual attention and gaining volume.

The addition of scrolling background layers was an incremental step up in the current paradigm of 2-D games. Although it was often used as little more than a cosmetic upgrade,[11] it sometimes impacted gameplay and offered slight novelty effects. In *Super Mario World*'s "Forest of Illusion 1" and "Outrageous" levels, trees are displayed on a background layer that's actually placed in the foreground, hiding the sprites and game terrain, creating occlusion and potentially hiding traps or secrets. More interesting, in Iggy's Castle, Mario can leap onto a giant grating suspended in mid-air, punch through revolving grates to find himself behind the grate, and give chase to koopas that are clinging on either side.

Exploring the intervals between layered space was not new in itself, of course; *Super Mario Bros. 3* had famously hidden a warp flute behind the exit to level 1–3, which could be reached if Mario ducked for several seconds on a white block, getting him behind the scenery. However, the fact that the Super Famicom could manage multiple background layers in hardware, by itself, as opposed to necessitating hand-programming techniques, greatly facilitated a widespread usage of such visual and gameplay motifs. This constitutes a genuine case of incremental innovation, albeit one on which Sega had already focused with its Mega Drive/Genesis, which allowed three background layers and enough on-screen sprites that some developers built a whole additional background layer out of sprite tiles (MacDonald 2000). Once more, Nintendo was incrementing on past innovations to catch up.

The Special Effects of Mode 7

The most notable graphical contribution of the Super Famicom was graphics Mode 7. As the SFC's slowdown problems were more and more acknowledged by the press (and experienced by gamers), Sega seized the opportunity and positioned itself (and its cool Sonic mascot) as being all about speed, thanks to the Genesis's mysteriously unique "Blast Processing" programming. In retaliation, Nintendo focused on its own unique asset for the SNES: "Mode 7." Much touted in discourse, the eighth graphics mode (counting from 0) allowed a single background layer—but one with up to 256 colors—that could be subjected to geometric matrix transformations: rotation, scaling, translation, reflection, and shearing. All of these, except for shearing, were incidentally possible for animated film: rotation of one or multiple cels was always possible, translation was controlled by rotary levers that could slide cels left or right (into or out of the camera's frame), scaling worked by having the camera travel in or zoom in on the cels, and reflection could be handled with mirrors or other post-filming duplication techniques.

One particularly popular use for scaling, rotation, and translation of backgrounds was the title screens. By and large, SFC games have title screens that practically dislocated their letters trying to outperform their rivals in generating a spontaneous "wow factor". Titles zoomed in (or out) dramatically, spiraled around into view, crashed into the screen, and basically spare no effort in maximizing Mode 7 effects to impress players.[12] Although we often forget or minimize the importance of title screens, they deserve our attention as possibly the one part of the peritext (see chapter 3) that has the greatest impact in shaping our expectations and preparing us for the text we are about to experience. Game manuals could be left in the box, and the game box often featured art that had little or no relation to game graphics; the text on its back could be forgotten, misremembered, or simply unavailable (as when a friend lent a cartridge or when contemporary players use an emulator), but there was no avoiding the title screen. Collectively, they indicate a crucial direction in which the Super Famicom's graphics hardware was pushing: toward the implementation of special effects. Indeed, *Electronic Gaming Monthly* reported in October 1990 that "the current working title of the new Nintendo super machine is the NES-SFX (for Nintendo Entertainment System-Special Effects)" (*EGM* #15, October 1990, 30), and many reader letters from the same issue confirm that the name had caught on already. The Super Famicom's architectural philosophy could be summarized as incremental improvements over familiar games and graphical special effects to dazzle viewers.

Moving toward in-game content, the Mode 7 dramatic zoom was a popular special effect. *Contra III: The Alien Wars* had a bomber plane flying toward the screen and bombing the ground in the first level, similar to when Bowser flies through the screen in the final fight of *Super Mario World*. *Super Metroid* used the same device when Ridley kidnaps the Metroid hatchling in the introduction taking place in the Ceres space colony. These effects were all implemented through Mode 7, which is only applied on backgrounds not sprites. In all of these cases, the characters had been rendered on screen as backgrounds, making them unable to collide with the player or otherwise interact with the in-game sprites. In other words, it was all for show. When Bowser rushes toward the screen until he passes right through the player's face during the final fight of *Super Mario World*, he obeys the logic of the special effect much more than that of gameplay innovation; Bowser could have just as well went offscreen by a lateral translation toward the screen's edge.

Game environments, being always backgrounds, were more naturally subjected to matrix transformations than characters or vehicles. In a large number of cases, though, the visual effects had little direct impact on the gameplay. When discussing the Mode 7 effects and multiplane scrolling in *Axelay*, whose box promises "graphically shocking 3-D levels," Kurt Kalata (2009, 6) dismisses them as "gimmicky effects." The same could be said of *Super Castlevania IV*'s stage 4–3, where the background wall is stretched and scrolled with an effect that gives the illusion that Simon Belmont is progressing through a tubelike environment. It makes for spectacular scenery, but the background graphics could be ripped out without altering the gameplay of this stage, which still consists of jumping across platforms and whipping enemies in a side-scrolling graphical regime. (Arguably, the background may be said to impact gameplay because it distracts the player, but if this is so, then any kind of distracting background, Mode 7 or not, would perform the same function.)

A number of games used a "mirage" effect by setting a back-and-forth shearing transformation across the lines of the picture. Quintet's "Soul" conceptual series uses the mirage effect for different purposes throughout its games. In *ActRaiser*, it creates a blizzard during the boss battle in the Northwall region's second stage. In *Soul Blazer*, it is used to represent "dazzling space" in the final World of Evil and for an aurora borealis when standing atop the Mountain of Souls. Extreme heat is another common use for Mode 7 shearing, as in the Natives' Village in *Illusion of Gaia* or the background buildings in the burning village at the start of *Castlevania: Dracula X*. In *Breath of Fire*, the mirage effect appears in underwater environments to simulate the distortion caused by water ripples.

Sometimes, game environments had matrix transformations applied to them that went beyond graphical "eye candy" effects and impacted gameplay. In *Super Metroid*, after the Ceres space station's self-destruct sequence has been activated, the vertical shaft through which the player must climb swings erratically from side to side, thanks to a Mode 7 rotation that's carefully engineered to appear out of control, as the surroundings stray out of the screen's surface and complicate the player's escape. In *Super Mario World 2: Yoshi's Island*, when Yoshi eats or touches the spiky Fuzzy clouds in level 1–7 ("Touch Fuzzy, Get Dizzy!"), the ground starts to rise and fall in a wavy pattern as backgrounds get distorted and saturated colors and pitch-shifted music create an effect that gamers on the Internet often compare to hallucinations provoked by LSD.

The idea of environmental rotation is pushed even further in *Super Castlevania IV*'s stage 4–2. Here the player progresses through a set of rooms where some of the walls, ceiling, and floor are covered in lethal spikes. Rings laid out in mid-air can be activated, making the room revolve 90 degrees around the player and effectively turning open ceilings into corridors and gravity into a guide for the player to progress forward. Here, the graphical effect of rotation is exploited in service of an innovative gameplay proposition, even if it is only a one-time gameplay effect. This idea was elevated to become the key game mechanic in *SOS* (Human Entertainment, 1994), a game where a side-scrolling game environment literally revolves around the player-character to open or block possibilities for spatial navigation. As the ship sinks, tosses, and turns, the player must walk on the walls and ceilings that have become floors to access new areas. Currently labeled by Wikipedia as a "survival adventure," a term that aptly describes the game, it stands as one of the truly original titles for the SNES.

The independently scrolling background layers and rotation, scaling, translation, and reflection Mode 7 transformations were the Super Famicom's central incremental innovations, contributing to perfect the already well-established graphical regimes of the side-scroller and top-down view, and their related genres: the platformer, the action-adventure, and the shoot'em up, among others.

Beyond Graphics and into Genre Innovation

Although often stated in retrospective articles dedicated to the console, the strength of the SNES' (and SFC's) game library requires serious attention from the perspective of genre because it highlights the two modalities of generic evolution, which I introduced in an earlier journal article: reiteration and innovation (Arsenault 2009). The importance of generic templates in game design, which Ernest Adams (2009) attributes to Nintendo's draconian publishing policies with the NES platform, reaches its apex during the 1990s on the Super NES, where the many incremental technology advances favor reiteration.

The industrialization process that took over Japan and the United States, and the resulting lack of game diversity that resulted from it, is easily demonstrated if we look at the context of Europe, where microcomputers ruled the roost in the 1980s. The Sinclair ZX Spectrum, for instance, held a position in the United Kingdom similar to Nintendo's NES and Famicom—an inexpensive game machine that met with success amid the masses, except for the heavy industrialization. Instead, a "proto-industrial push" happened, thanks to a direction of "homebrew" development, spurred by game magazines that printed code for Sinclair owners to type in their own games. In the words of Skot Deeming, curator of an exhibit on homebrew development on the ZX Spectrum at the Université de

Montréal, this amateur development culture was free from the imperatives of profitability, which resulted in a lot of formal explorations away from conventions.[13]

As a design practice, video games are always, at least somewhat, about innovation and problem solving, a reality that lends itself relatively well to an evolutionary conception of game genres (Arsenault 2009). A game is often produced following model games, genres, or design features that are blended together with some unique new propositions. As Alastair Fowler noted when discussing literary genres, "What produces generic resemblances, reflection soon shows, is tradition: a sequence of influence and imitation and inherited codes connecting works in the genre" (Fowler 1982, 42). These series of influences trace certain trajectories of innovation, nondeterministic paths that offer enough leeway or the freedom to go in another direction entirely but that favor some experimentations over others (especially in the video game business, where the industrial risk is high given the "hit-driven" nature of the market, and where innovation may not translate into accrued sales).

Games may be labeled as "belonging" to any number of genres, defined according to multiple criteria, and this labeling may differ from one community to another. Ultimately, genre does not correspond, as in biology, to innate features that some games would have in common in any objective or positivist manner; genre labeling is a discursive act that frames an existing game in a certain way, and genres are such linguistic codifications, shifting, imprecise, and always culturally situated (Arsenault 2009). That is why Thomas Schatz described genre in Hollywood as "a *range of expression* for filmmakers and a *range of experience* for viewers" (Schatz 1981, 22). This framing of how genre operates is not restricted to Hollywood but also functions in other industrial and heavily marketed entertainment sectors. What distinguishes games from literature and film, from a generic standpoint, is that sometimes trajectories of innovation in gameplay stem from or otherwise interact with technological trajectories.

Erwan Cario (2013) refers to the 1990–1995 period as "the Age of Genres," a time where, aided by the relative stability of technology between the third and fourth generation of game consoles (as we've seen in the discussion of the Super Famicom's architecture), game developers experimented with original controls, interfaces, and ways to play. Successes were copied fast, and "practically all major genres of the modern video game have their origin (or their confirmation) in these early 1990s" (Cario 2013). If we try to chart out the genres that find their origin in this period (through processes of innovation) and those that find their confirmation (through the process of reiteration), the question of platforms inevitably surfaces, as innovation was unequally distributed. Nintendo's platform favors reiteration across already proven genres (mainly platform games, turn-based role-playing games, and 2-D action/adventures) and largely integrates its graphical technical innovations into these gameplay reiterations.

Although 2-D platformers and action/adventure games with spectacular visual effects were all the rage on the SNES, the personal computer, bolstered by new technologies (chiefly CD-ROM storage and real-time 3-D polygon rendering), engaged in experimentation through a number of new genres: full-motion video (FMV) games with digitized footage, 3-D action/adventures, the ubiquitous first-person shooter, and the real-time strategy genres. The Sega Genesis and TurboGrafx-16 were situated somewhere in between these two poles, with an abundance of classic games but also CD-ROM add-ons (and the 32X for Sega's machine) to engage with these new genres. In contrast, the SNES genre *par excellence* was the platform game (a legacy inherited from the NES) and its corresponding subgenres: the run-and-gun, the cinematic platformer, and the puzzle platformer. The fighting game and top-down action-adventure complemented the platformer and made up the bulk of the SNES library.

Sega cultivated a risk-taking approach that was compatible with its general philosophy of letting the consumer decide in the end (Harris 2014, 280). The Sega Activator, for instance, took motion gaming further than Bandai's PowerPad accessory for the NES. Contrast this to Nintendo's Super Scope accessory, a light gun turned light bazooka, whose main innovations over the preceding NES Zapper were being wireless and bigger (and, I suppose, not being named "Super Zapper"). Third-party developer Code Masters created the J-Cart, an oversized Genesis cartridge standard that also included two additional controller ports on the cartridge to allow four-player gameplay—an idea simply infeasible under Nintendo's manufacturing stranglehold over their platform.

All of this isn't to say that Super Famicom games never experimented with innovative control schemes, gameplay mechanics, or spatial treatment. *E.V.O.: Search for Eden* presented an audacious mixing of adventure and RPG elements that enriched the platformer genre by making the player spend "experience points" to upgrade body parts, evolving into different life forms throughout the adventure. *Nosferatu* offered a synthesis of cinematic platformer *à la Prince of Persia* and beat-them-all game with a variety of fighting moves and dynamic combat. In *Dragon View*, the player gains experience, levels, and inventory in nonlinear exploration, like in most RPGs, but fights enemies in a real-time, beat-them-all formula.

These examples show that innovation could creep in through genre-crossing features, as long as they revolved around established genres.

Innovation often manifested itself in a different way: New gameplay possibilities were first integrated as specific parts or alternative modes in the context of a larger, more traditional game type. *ActRaiser*, for one, combined two wildly different game genres—the side-scrolling action platformer and city-building simulation—into an integrated ludic proposal. Overhead levels were interspersed between classic run and gun levels in *Contra III: The Alien Wars* just like the Mode 7 vehicle levels in the *Super Star Wars* trilogy broke the usual platforming structure. Although the canceled SNES-CD would rule out any FMV game on the SNES, the SNES mouse peripheral did yield access to one thing that PC gamers had: the strategy, puzzle, and CRPG genres that were all the rage on there and couldn't be found in arcades or at friends' houses with other consoles. A good range of titles were ported to the SNES: *SimCity*, *Lemmings 2: The Tribes*, *Cannon Fodder*, *Sid Meier's Civilization*, *Might & Magic III: Isles of Terra*, *Eye of the Beholder*, *SimAnt*, *Utopia*, *Populous II*, and *Nobunaga's Ambition*, one of the earliest examples of complex grand strategy war games. There are few original strategy titles to balance out this slew of ported games, however, *King Arthur's World* being one—although originality, here as elsewhere in the SFC's library, is a contentious descriptor, seeing how *King Arthur's World* was basically *Lemmings* in swords and chainmail.

Super Castlevania IV is a great example of the SFC's graphical technologies being designed to support "special effects" for classically proven gameplay ideas. The game's first level is pretty much a guided tour to special effects on the SNES. The first gameplay screen features parallax scrolling backgrounds, as the skull-shaped mountain range in the background layer, scrolling slower than the walls immediately around the player, are designed just high enough to occlude the moon in the high sky. The drawbridge closes (through Mode 7 rotation) as soon as the player steps on it. Coming into the next screen, an iron fence is raised, and the player must pass through a door to cross behind it, navigating through different background layers like the revolving doors in *Super Mario World*'s Iggy's castle. Then the map in between levels is rendered in Mode 7 so that we may get the zoom on it, and in later levels we find the previously mentioned revolving room and the spinning tube background.

Still later in *Super Castlevania IV*, Simon fights the oversized Stone Golem Koronot, who gets wracked with a mosaic tiling effect and shrinks in size every time it is hit. These Mode 7 effects can work because the golem is rendered as a background rather than sprites. Unfortunately, as Mode 7 could only support a single background layer, the actual scenery had to be sacrificed, making the boss encounter appear against a pitch black background. Here the Super Famicom is incrementing on a familiar design pattern born out of necessity on the Famicom (Altice 2015, 232–237), promoting continuity in succession through the special effects. Still later on, Simon jumps on giant swinging chandeliers—once again, Mode 7 backgrounds, this time in rotation and translation across the screen.

Even with all these dazzling effects, fundamentally, *Super Castlevania IV* remains all about walking, jumping, whipping enemies, and collecting power-ups. Even the soundtrack reprises all the classic songs from the first three Famicom episodes. The game plays like the simpler 1986 *Castlevania* (and covers the same story of Simon Belmont's quest to defeat Dracula in 1691) rather than picking up after the gameplay experiments that had been going on in *Castlevania II: Simon's Quest*, which featured nonlinear trajectories through the game, an inventory system, and puzzles to solve. It may be considered as a remake of the original, at least to an extent, according to the game's director Masahiro Ueno (Szczepaniak 2013). However much of a remake we consider it to be, it definitely lies on the conservative side of the innovation spectrum with incremental improvements rather than radical innovation.

Super Castlevania IV, along with *Super Mario World*, stands as perhaps the clearest example to demonstrate Nintendo's 16-bit console's stance on innovation. All this shiny new silverware had been designed to accommodate a number of same old familiar dishes. It was "back to basics… Super basics!" Nintendo would go even further down the path of reiteration by releasing a buffet of remakes (this time indisputably so): *Super Mario All-Stars*, a graphically and sonically revamped combination cartridge that let gamers play the NES *Super Mario Bros.* titles. As if we needed additional arguments that showed the Super Famicom to be, in the end, a "Super" version of the Famicom, a conservative console bent on providing the same game experiences with nicer graphics and sound.

Well, at least they didn't call it *Super Super Mario Bros.*

> So the grand dimensionalization project began, at Nintendo and everywhere else in the game world. Every 2-D franchise would, via trial and error, see what it would play like when placed in a virtual world. Just about every game franchise would have a stumble or two making this move. They were fundamentally different types of game play, and therefore resulted in different types of games. [...] The move to 3-D would be the biggest single design change games had ever seen. (Ryan 2012, 188, 178)

In the previous chapter, we saw how the Super Famicom's Mode 7 graphics could stand as a shiny piece of silverware, capable of putting twinkles in the eyes of guests at the grand table and enhancing usual meals with a little *je ne sais quoi*—some spicy rotation here, a pinch of scaling there, the occasional dash of reflection, and a helping of translation. The SFC's graphics capabilities, however, also sported a more radical innovation, one that was nested in the Mode 7 shearing transformation. To fully appreciate this contribution and properly situate it among the technological landscape of the 1990s requires us to tackle the larger question of 3-D graphics and technological innovation. In this chapter, we will see how the SFC's Mode 7 infrastructure allowed the console to attain a free-roaming perspective view typically held as the goal of 3-D graphics, even as it remained at heart a 2-D or "2.5-D" system. The chapter will close with a review of how Nintendo's business decisions kept the firm away from the forward momentum in the later years of the platform.

Techniques and Technologies for 3-D Graphics[1]

The late 1980s and 1990s in video games can be seen as globally driven by a common goal: the race toward 3-D. As Carl Therrien's etymological inquiry into the origins of the first-person shooter as a genre reveals, "3-D" was one of the quintessential buzzwords of the decade, present in post-id Software shooters but primarily in role-playing, action, simulation, and racing games alike. Reflecting on his study of video game promotion and reviews (including but not limited to the epitext and peritext of games), he remarks, "Most of the games under scrutiny in this paper have been discussed and/or sold as a three dimensional experience; '3-D' appears to be the most pervasive textual element in our network" (Therrien 2015). Although the drive toward 3-D and its use as a buzzword have almost always been present in video game discourses and marketing (it can be traced back to the 1970s, as we will see in this chapter), there is an intensification of the efforts to pierce the third dimension from the late 1980s and into the late 1990s.

In a way, this was the third frontier to be overcome in video game spatiality, after the first frontier, which had been the move from fixed- to multiscreen games in the 1970s (think of *Berzerk*, *Robotron: 2084*, *Adventure* for the Atari VCS, *Pitfall!*, etc.), and the second frontier: scrolling screens, first unidirectional (horizontal in *Defender* and *Super Mario Bros.*, vertical in *Xevious* and *Kid Icarus*), then multidirectional (*Rally-X*, *Metroid*). A few early pioneers had tackled the third dimension, with some success (*Night Driver*, *Pole Position*, *Hang-On*), but the occasional foray would only become a full-scale offensive push in the late 1980s. This "three-frontier" description, however convenient, faces a bit of irksome counterfactual history: In truth, 3-D had been present for quite some time already within certain video game genres. Indeed, computer games had been having 3-D ever since the 1970s, well before arcades had scrolling. Why? (or how?) Because they weren't going for the same kind of 3-D—or, more precisely, the same graphical regimes—than arcade and console games were.

As we will see, 3-D in itself is not a technology or a "thing" with substance. 3-D is an idea and a problem. To say that a game (or a film or picture) "is 3-D" is to say that the visual qualities of the object are organized in a way that accurately represents or simulates the three dimensions of spatial perception (width, height, and depth, technically abstracted into the x, y, and z axes), although they are, in truth, 2-D objects. Put more bluntly, the goal of "going 3-D" is to take a bidimensional surface (screen, canvas, or paper) and somehow "stick a third dimension in there." The reason that video game developers strived to make 3-D games (and why video game marketers insisted on it) is that it contributed to a sentiment of "being there" for the gamer, as Therrien (2015) writes—of being more "immersed" (another powerful buzzword) in the virtual world depicted. Achieving 3-D can be done through a variety of graphical techniques or technologies, which can be partitioned into five groups: axonometric projection, stereoscopy, linear perspective, prerendered polygons, and real-time polygons.

Axonometric Projection

Many games sought to achieve 3-D through axonometric graphics, a form of parallel projection that dates back to *Zaxxon*, *Q*Bert*, *Ant Attack*, *Knight Lore*, and dozens more games. These games present the in-game space (and characters) from an angled "three-quarter view" as 3-D, unlike the side view from *Super Mario Bros.*, which hides width, or the top-down view in *The Legend of Zelda*, which renders height difficult to assess. Axonometric games can appropriately render all three dimensions but not according to human perception; objects, buildings, ships, and anything else do not appear smaller to the eye the farther away they are or distorted in their proportions because they recede toward the horizon at the back (a practice in art known as foreshortening). Lines that are parallel in an object (e.g., paved floor tiles, as in figure 5.1) stay parallel in the picture and do not converge toward the horizon. In fact, games rendered with axonometric projection do not feature a horizon at all: Tiles of ground fill the screen as far as the player can see, as if looking down at a chessboard.

Usually called "isometric" through popular usage and tradition, although the term is technically inaccurate,[2] these games can be seen as the ludic legacy to practices focused on spatial measurement, planning,

Figure 5.1 Axonometric ("isometric") graphics in the SNES titles *Shadowrun* and *Equinox*. Emulated on Higan v0.95.

and accounting, including descriptive geometry, technical and architectural drawing, and industrial design and engineering. Because they favor a more rigorous, intellectual, and strategic approach to space, it is no surprise to find many strategy or management games using the view (*Age of Empires*, *Final Fantasy Tactics*, *SimCity 2000*, *FarmVille*, etc.). These games output the fictional world as a grid of angled square tiles, and they don't attempt to simulate someone's gaze from a specific (and human) point of view; they construct space as an abstraction, a map for players to manage, like interactive animated graph paper. Thus, although the graphical technique is indeed a way of achieving tridimensional space, it is not done in the tradition of illusionism in art—the long-sought ideal of *mimesis*, the imitation of natural phenomena. As such, though axonometric projection is different from the other kinds of 3-D that we will see in the chapter, it is worth keeping in mind that the relationship between 3-D and illusionism is not automatic.

Stereoscopy

Stereoscopy is another case of 3-D that has been experimented with at various stages of video game history, as a constant but always marginal movement. The principle behind stereoscopy relies on the optic phenomenon of convergence in human vision. The human visual system is a set of two eyes, each of which perceives the world separately. When we focus our visual attention on objects situated in the large overlapping area covered by both eyes, they converge toward the point of visual attention. This results in two slightly different images, a few degrees of angle apart, that are mixed in and analytically composed by our brain into a total, unified image. The averaging of disparities between the two images, however small they may seem, allows us to indirectly perceive depth and the volume of objects. The recent surge of 3-D films and video games that have swept movie theaters, home televisions, and even handheld game systems (with the Nintendo 3DS) may use a number of varying technical protocols to achieve the effect, but they always share the same basic principle: two slightly different images are emitted, and our eyes perceive them as one global image with a depth interval.

The 8-bit Sega Master System had its SegaScope 3-D glasses, which were used for games like *Space Harrier 3-D*. On the 8-bit NES, *Rad Racer* also used some glasses, as did *Jim Power: The Lost Dimension in 3-D* on the Super NES. Nintendo went the extra mile in this direction, basing a whole system on the premise of stereoscopy: the Virtual Boy, symptomatically marketed with the slogan "A 3-D Game for a 3-D World." The Virtual Boy's failure was unequivocal: Nintendo pulled it from the market within six months, with fewer than 800,000 units sold between the summer of 1995 and the spring of 1996. A monochrome red display on black backgrounds was a difficult sell, even if the binoculars offered working stereoscopic graphics. Ergonomics were a definite issue because the system proved too bulky to be "headheld" or really "portable"; it had to become a "transportable" system to be used as a tabletop device, supported by a tripod (with users typically suffering from back pain, on top of eye strain). In the end, however, the games failed to impress because they did not offer new modes of gameplay. The stereoscopic effect enhanced the depth impression, but ultimately it was the same graphical regime as the 2-D games, with added backgrounds and parallax scrolling seen in chapter 4. The stereoscopic layering of pictures could not produce authentic tridimensionality but rather resulted in an animetic interval between two bidimensional pictures.

In this sense, there is something even more 3-D to be found inside the fabric of stereoscopic (and nonstereoscopic) pictures, something so common that it is often overlooked: the organization of a drawing (or of computer graphics) according to the rules of linear perspective.

Linear Perspective

A long and rich tradition of illusionism exists in the history of Western art, one that revolves heavily around the principles of linear perspective put forth by Leon Batista Alberti in the 1435 treatise *De Pictura*. Alberti proposed a set of techniques that relied on geometrical and mathematical principles, which artists could use to construct a space on their canvas that accurately represented depth as perceived by humans. The essence of linear perspective lies in a vanishing point, a central focus of visual attention toward which all the lines of objects that stretch in the depth axis should converge. Unlike axonometric projection, this method does not accurately render the dimensions of objects or of the space but rather imitates the view a human subject would have of them. What is rendered is a subjective gaze rather than an objective space. Objects that are farther away from the viewer will be visually situated higher, closer to the horizon line. They will diminish in size as well and appear smaller than they really are, unlike in axonometric projection, where tiles and objects keep their absolute size regardless of where they are on the visual surface. Their shapes and lines will be distorted, with their depth being increasingly compressed through foreshortening. The objects' colors will progressively lose their saturation and blend together with the background earth and sky into successive strata of green and then blue haze (a technique called atmospheric perspective).

The techniques forming linear perspective have been widely adopted by artists throughout the centuries, making it something like a "default" system of representation (Damisch 1987). The earliest video games to have integrated 3-D graphics were, in fact, simply showing game environments according to a system of predefined views made of static pictures that followed (more or less closely) the rules of linear perspective. This method can be found in the 1974 *Maze War* and the following RPGs that later came to be grouped as the "dungeon crawler" subgenre: *Akalabeth: World of Doom*, *Tunnels of Doom*, the *Ultima*, *Wizardry*, and *Might & Magic* series, *Dungeon Master*, and so on, including the *Eye of the Beholder* series shown in figure 5.2, next to *F-Zero*. Because the graphics were structured with lines receding toward a vanishing point and a horizon line, the impression of having a tridimensional space functioned to create maze-like experiences and a type of spatial immersion unlike any other. Gamers could move into a fictional world, turn around and explore other directions, and in general found themselves in the middle of a game-world space, rather than occupying a privileged position of viewing separate from the world (either above it and looking down, in top-down view, or outside a glass window or transparent wall and looking at it from the side, in side-scrolling view).

These games instilled a specific graphical regime: the step-based slideshow of linear perspective pictures. Environments were not scrolling by in real time and fluid space but were rather a predetermined set of postcards that provided a fixed "hard space." As a result, this graphical regime offers 3-D *views* of game space but do not feature a 3-D space; the pictures result from a tile-based construction of the game world, with player movement limited to going either forward or backward one tile or making 90-degree turns around. Logically, the game is partitioned as a

Figure 5.2 Linear perspective in the SNES port of *Eye of the Beholder* and *F-Zero*. Emulated on Higan v0.95.

grid of x-y coordinates (like graph paper), but visually each time the gamer moves, the game displays a picture of the scene according to the rules of linear perspective, creating the illusion of exploring a tridimensional world. This illusion is easily underestimated nowadays, used as we are to seeing video games rendered in technically correct linear perspective, and can make us forget how impressive it is. *Electronic Gaming Monthly* reviewer "Major Mike," discussing the Super NES port of *Eye of the Beholder*, noted, "A highlight of this one is 3-D graphics" (*EGM* #59, June 1994, 33). It is easy to understand here that 3-D means "a succession of views organized according to the principles of linear perspective," for which *Eye of the Beholder* is not particularly notable. But by 1994, 3-D was all the rage and everywhere to be found in the post-*Doom* glut of first-person shooters, 3-D graphics cards, and polygons.

Although linear perspective provided an adequate sense of depth in constructing a 3-D portrait of space, it had to come in static pictures. The next step was to find ways to make 3-D worlds compatible with action gameplay to eliminate the hard spaces of fixed tile distances and make it fluid.

Mode 7 and Perspective

Beyond the special effects it could sprinkle over 2-D worlds, what really set the SFC's Mode 7 apart was the ability to generate pseudo–3-D experiences through an impressive perspective effect. In this, Nintendo's innovative contribution to graphical technologies took inspiration from Sega's Super Scaler Engine. Yu Suzuki of Sega developed the influential arcades *Hang-On*, *Space Harrier*, and *OutRun* using sprite scaling to have objects smoothly zoom in toward the player in real time as the ground rolled forward underneath. The functioning of Mode 7 differed on a crucial principle: It would apply to a background map (the "ground") rather than sprites, stretching, twisting, and rotating it as a flexible surface and scrolling it smoothly at high speeds. It functioned by changing the transformation matrix across scanlines: As the picture was processed and displayed line by line on the screen, the PPU could be instructed to draw the next line according to a different transformation. Accordingly, Mode 7 gave game developers the possibility of taking a detailed image of a landscape seen from a bird's eye view and display that "map" by slightly stretching the image more and more as the lines got drawn on the screen, successively widening the ground so that features seemed to recede in the distance and converge toward the horizon, as with a perspective drawing.

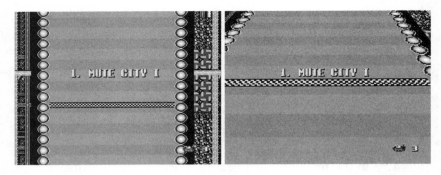

Figure 5.3 Illustration of a line-by-line transformation to simulate perspective in Mode 7, exported from *F-Zero*. Left: top-down view of the ground map. Right: progressive angling to reach the perspective shearing. Emulated on Higan v0.95.

Figure 5.4 *F-Zero*'s playfield without the background skyline (left), and without the playfield (right). Emulated on Snes9X v1.53 for Windows.

A second background plane, representing a skyline as seen when looking over the horizon line, is drawn in the top portion of the screen to create the illusion of a total unified space. Over the Mode 7 "playfield," the 2-D sprites (individual movable objects) were superimposed and positioned according to distance (higher toward the horizon the farther away they are). This technique was demonstrated by Nintendo's *F-Zero*, and the fragile illusion can be broken down by disabling select background layers in emulators, as I've done in figure 5.4.

Although the tentative move toward 3-D was important in establishing the Super Famicom's identity—"Mode 7" was a term thrown around by everyone and understood as "that special thing the SFC can do"—the bulk of the SFC's specs were designed with 2-D games in mind, which was a perfectly reasonable thing to do back in 1988. Nintendo's teams were "thinking in 2-D," contrary to Yu Suzuki (at least if we believe his claims from Mielke 2010, 3); Mode 7 was a way to render visually what was logically computed as a top-down 2-D map, as can be seen in figure 5.3. Because Mode 7 can only project flat surfaces, everything on which cars should bump or race around had to be included as a sprite. In fact, anything meant to stick out of the ground needed to be represented as a sprite laid on top of the right coordinates.

The fragility of Mode 7's illusion is perhaps best captured if we try to imagine it in physical space instead of in the digital realm. To achieve the Mode 7 effect, we would need a sheet of paper with a detailed ground map in bird's eye view drawn on it. We would take that sheet and lay it on an angled 45-degree table, one that had been fitted with a special lever-operated treadmill that somehow folded and stretched the sheet of paper, one line at a time from the bottom, until the vertical parallel lines converged toward the center top of the sheet, through an ingenious system of mechanical pegs perhaps—the most difficult operation to realize without a computer to do matrix transformations. With our "background plane" in place, we would then take some characters and objects (drawn in profile view from the side, front, or back) glued on upright cardboard stands and carefully place our cardboard cut-outs on the exact spots they should occupy on our ground map.

Then, finally, we would take a *real* background picture—a postcard of the sky with a nice mountain range, for instance—and pin it to the wall or corkboard behind our angled table. We would place ourselves in front of the table, in the middle, get down on our knees to have our sight down at the right level, and we'd be graced with an illusionary projected world in perspective. Then, if we turned the lever, our table's treadmill would have our ground map scroll by (and loop back), but we'd need an assistant with wires or such to move our cardboard cut-outs in synchronicity (and pull them away from the scene if we scroll the "background plane" too much). If we did all this, then we'd have a projected world in perspective and smooth motion—no small feat.

There is still one more problem with Mode 7's perspective trick: As elements (sprites) got closer to the player, they needed to be enlarged. Unfortunately, sprites could not be scaled, rotated, or otherwise affected by the matrix transformations that Mode 7 permitted because Mode 7 was applied to backgrounds, not sprites (contrary to Sega's Super Scaler engine). Game developers had to include predetermined renditions of every sprite in multiple "distance copies"; the game checked every object's distance away on the projected landscape and pulled the necessary smaller or larger presupplied version of the sprite as necessary to simulate their

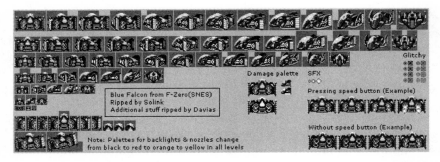

Figure 5.5 Racing against the Blue Falcon in *F-Zero* means seeing the car at various predrawn sizes and angles as the player overtakes it. There are more angles of view when the car is up close (in the top three rows) and a lot less as it is farther away. Spritesheet built by Solink, with contributions from Davias, downloaded from Spriters Resource (http://www. spriters-resource.com/).

growing or shrinking. This made for weird "pop-ins" during the play experience as sprites crossed their distance threshold and grew in size (and sometimes crossed it back as the player slowed down or backpedaled in a dance of jittery metamorphoses). Combined with the SFC's restriction of having only sprites of two sizes at once, this drastically limited both the raw number of sprites and the quality of the depth illusion in pseudo–3-D Mode 7 environments because the copies of different-sized sprites could tie up precious visual memory. Figure 5.5 illustrates how a single race car in *F-Zero* could require multiple distance (and angle) copies for the illusion to work satisfactorily.

The Earth Was Flat

The perspective effect, although fragile and with obvious limitations, was a convincing step in the direction of representing 3-D worlds, thanks to the smoothness and speed at which the ground scrolled and the 360 degrees of freedom of movement afforded to players. This distinguished Mode 7 from the previous depth-scrolling racing games of Sega's Super Scaler system, which only offered forward movement along a predetermined race track. However, it came with an important and absolute limitation: the flatness of the terrain. Because Mode 7 was, at heart, a trick of 2-D, it presented ground maps with width and depth but not height. The illusion was made salient whenever a player, floating high in the air, like in *Final Fantasy III*, came closer down to ground level, revealing the mountains below to be just pictures of mountains painted on a flat carpet or map (see figure 5.6). Anything that would normally stand upright had to be represented as a 2-D sprite, carefully positioned on top of the Mode 7 floor

Figure 5.6 Flatness of mountains revealed when flying low in *Final Fantasy III*. Emulated on Higan v0.95.

map and scaled appropriately using different distance copies to maintain the illusion as the player moved nearer or farther away.

An equally jarring example of Mode 7's limits often occurs in *The 7th Saga*. As the player travels through the overworld in a top-down view, enemy encounters are played out through an impressive and dramatic Mode 7 spiraling zoom, bringing a perspective view down to the exact tile where the player-character was standing. The player's detailed battle character sprite is shown, and enemies appear in front of them— somewhere along the adjacent north tile. This works wonders when the player is traveling in a plain or another flat surface, but when the player is walking alongside a mountain range, the Mode 7 perspective illusion breaks down as the player-character and enemies battle back and forth over grass and some flat, distorted mountain pictures on the ground. Far from creating an effect of immersion in the game-world, in these cases, the perspective rendering of the background only heightens the artificial- ity of the game's visual representation, confirming that what the player is traveling on is a schematic map rather than an actual world. In this respect, *Illusion of Gaia* had a more adapted use of the perspective effect because it presented the characters in "travel sequences" that displayed an old and stylized map acknowledged as such, instead of going for a convincing illusion of a world.

A more serious issue *The 7th Saga* would face is when the player is traveling in an indoor environment. These environments depend on the 2-D top-down tiles that make up the background "floor" being carefully crafted with angles and colors that attempt to depict walls and create the illusion of castle halls, or cave and dungeon walls. If encounters in these tight quarters used the same perspectival effect than on the overworld,

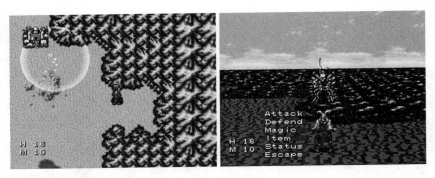

Figure 5.7 *The 7th Saga*'s transition from top-down overworld traveling (left) and perspectival fight scene (right) reveals the artificial construction of height as the mountains are reduced to a flat picture on the ground. Emulated on Higan v0.95.

Figure 5.8 Inspired alternating between perspective and top-down views in *Secret of Mana* means the flatness of mountains is deemphasized by the top-down view. Emulated on Higan v0.95.

then the illusion of walls and ceilings would be shattered as the player's character and monsters would fight atop flat wall pictures spread on the ground. Instead, the game simply has the map fade out to a generic fight scene with the background completely dark, an arrangement that works regardless of the actual location where monsters are encountered, and that preserves the fragile illusion of space.

One game that solved the height issue elegantly was *Secret of Mana*, pictured in figure 5.8. When riding the dragon Flammie high over the world, the game offered the perspective view, but when the player went too low in altitude in preparing for landing, it switched dynamically to a top-down view of the ground map. Presenting the top-down view allowed the player to aim more precisely at the spot on which to land but also helped to mask the artificial flatness of the Mode 7 plane.

Many sports games went with the Mode 7 perspective effect: They had to represent a finite number of players on the playing field (often well within the sprite limits of the console), a ball, and two nets or goals, and that was it. The rest was just lines on the ground, drawn on a 2-D plane, an ideal fit exacerbated by the convenient fact that just about any sports needs to be practiced on flat ground. The audience, rink, walls, and any large number (or large size) of upright objects were, however, problematic. Figure 5.9 demonstrates two approaches to the issue. *NHL Stanley Cup* went for an uneasy mash-up by plastering rows of fans seated in a fixed frontal view at the top of the screen (as a background skyline) while the hockey rink rotated around, suspended in empty space. *NCAA Basketball* resolved the problem by doing away with the audience altogether, and the playing field just floated among a background of blue Nether.

Many SFC/SNES games included a Mode 7 effect that wasn't offering full 360-degree movement but kept to a graphical regime of top-down or side-scrolling view, enhanced by a slight angle to give some additional volume to the graphics. *Brett Hull Hockey '95* offered some Mode 7 shearing that significantly angled the view, as well as *Super Soccer* and other sports games. Many games from other genres offered such aesthetic Mode 7 treatments. In *Final Fantasy II*, when the player pilots the Big Whale, the world map is angled further back from the usual top-down view to give a sense of majestic scale to the Lunar spaceship. In *Final Fantasy III*, the overworld map is slightly angled to give the illusion of a round earth receding away, on a larger scale than the typical top-down view for the villages and dungeons players must explore.

The crucial difference between the top-down or side-view graphical regime with Mode 7 angling sprinkled on top, and the newer graphical regime of 360-degree freedom of movement, was whether the viewpoint was mobile. A mobile viewpoint, as in *NHL Stanley Cup*, meant objects had

Figure 5.9 *NHL Stanley Cup* and *NCAA Basketball*. Emulated on Higan v0.95.

to be redrawn dynamically to have their size and angle of view consistent with the viewpoint's potentially new position every step of the way—they needed to be sprites, but Mode 7 applied only to backgrounds, and the SNES had more trouble handling a high number of sprites simultaneously than its rival Genesis, let alone keeping multiple copies of sprites for different sizes and different angles of view as well. Mode 7 couldn't represent indoor environments because walls would have been made of sprites— enormous sprites that would have exceeded any limit, of visual memory, metatiles, or sprite per scanline. Even the outdoor environments suffered from the lack of a properly simulated height dimension, as the flat mountains of *The 7th Saga* and *Final Fantasy III* have shown.

The *Super Star Wars* trilogy should be noted for going beyond the call of duty, especially *Super Star Wars: The Empire Strikes Back*, in the Battle of Hoth level. The game managed to offer hills and slopes to players as they flew their snowspeeder around in Mode 7, which was no small feat, as *Nintendo Power* described the stage: "Now the action takes to the air in some of the coolest flight combat in any video game as you fly over 360° of 3-D terrain" (*Nintendo Power* #53, October 1993, 11). This impressive technical achievement was hyped to gamers in *Nintendo Power*'s "making of" article dedicated to the game, which described the functioning of Mode 7 in a refreshing display of technoliteracy among the realm of technobabble and buzzwords:

> Other technical wonders are found in the speeder stages and when the X-wing flies over the clouds. The sense of speed is imparted from splitting the screen and scrolling two different images. The background (above the horizon) scrolls conventionally left and right. The foreground (below the horizon) is created from a topographical map. Using Mode 7, the map is tilted sideways and the 3-D textures look like surface features as it scrolls beneath you. In Empire, these maps also rise and fall, giving the illusion of passing over hills and valleys. (*Nintendo Power* #52, September 1993, 85)

Super Empire was pushing against the limits of "faking" 3-D space in a platform made for 2-D games. But to the discerning gamer (or to any gamer, really), something was off. Its impressive hills and valleys were, in fact, randomly generated (more accurately, rhythmically generated) as the player went forward, instead of being located in certain defined spots to make up a virtual topography. Players needed only drive in a certain direction, see how the landscape's height rose and fell, and then reverse course and drive back the same way to realize the game had no memory of the slopes and valleys they had just passed, and that the hills were generated in a rhythmically regular but spatially inconsistent way. Further compounding the problem was the level's objectives: Because players had to circle three or four times around the legs of AT-AT walkers, they were bound to see hills, flat lands, and valleys generated successively while circling around the same spot.

All in all, the idea of generating varying height slopes was great, but the impossibility of tying the variations in elevation to specific coordinates on the map means it would have been perfect for generating waves on the sea rather than an illusory pseudo-topography sure to break down under scrutiny. Still, Sculptured Software's creative take on the limits of Mode 7 testifies to both the developer's technical skill and the increasingly tight technological quarters that Mode 7 was growing into—not at all unlike the Famicom a few years before. 3-D was making headway into video games through a much more powerful yet disarmingly new way: polygons.

And Then There Were Polygons

The computation of polygons in real time had appeared in video games through a plurality of entryways. *I, Robot*, developed in 1983, is often credited as the first game to have used 3-D polygonal graphics. Five years later, in 1988, Namco's System 21 and Taito's Air System were released in the arcades, and polygons were showcased in the former's *Winning Run* and the latter's *Top Landing*. Flight simulators were perfect candidates for polygonization after all, given that they relied on the accurate simulation of all three dimensions. In the early 1990s, polygons made up the hallways and "sectors" of *Doom*, into which 2-D sprites would move and shoot each other, not unlike the cardboard cut-out sprites of Mode 7, with an important addition that Mode 7 could never do: walls. *Alone in the Dark* reversed the concept, placing characters and objects made of 3-D polygons over backgrounds that were fixed graphics. Sports games also got their polygons, with *Stunts* and then the hyperbolically named *4D Sports Boxing*. Strategy games, but most of all the multiple descendants of *Doom* that crystallized the first-person shooter genre and ultimately everything else, would eventually follow suit.

Polygons were here to stay, and many PC gamers invested in a new technology for their computer: 3-D accelerated graphics cards, an additional piece of hardware solely dedicated to the specialized function of calculating and rendering polygons. A convergence in marketing united games and 3-D accelerated graphics cards; personal computers were on the road to technological supremacy and brought complex, intricate gaming experiences with them. The hard spaces of discrete tiles in dungeon crawlers evolved into fluid tridimensional worlds, a transition perfectly seen in DreamForge Intertainment's RPGs *Ravenloft: Strahd's Possession*, *Ravenloft: Stone Prophet*, and *Menzoberranzan*. These games let the player toggle between the two graphical regimes of step-based and 360-degrees free-form movement. Players could travel through most of the games in steps, which accelerated movement, but occasionally activate the fluid 3-D engine and gain finer, smoother control, instead of being locked into the tiles' discrete spatial organization.

Many games did not use real-time polygons, that is, polygons rendered on the fly by the host computer and that could be dynamically redrawn to accommodate movement of the viewpoint by the player. Aided by the extra storage capacity of CD-ROM drives, many of them used pre-rendered polygons to present impressively detailed, sprawling virtual worlds to their players, stirring immersion. By rendering the views of polygons ahead of time, powerful computers could work for an extensive amount of time to produce high-quality visuals, which would then be recorded and played back as movies. The method was essentially what the animation industry used to render 3-D animated movies, with the same drawback: Once the images and movements had been computed, they could not be altered.

Myst reprised the postcard-style static screens that rendered in perspective drawing the 2-D "graph paper" corridors of dungeon crawlers, this time organizing the visualizations in an irregular suite of creative, "cinematic" (or more accurately "photographic") views. *The 7th Guest* provided the same postcard type of views but articulated transitions between postcards with an animated traveling sequence, linking together the static screens by dynamic movement. These transitory animated sequences, however, were not enough to alter the graphical regime of the step-based slideshow that was common to both of them, because players did not interact with the transition to explore or perform other actions. *Star Wars: Rebel Assault* pushed movement as its strategy: Every level had been constructed as virtual scenes in 3-D polygons, and LucasArts had predefined a path of movement through the level they rendered as a movie. The gamer steered a starship or aimed at targets on the screen while the movie of forward movement through the set of polygons played on, thus bringing the game in the same graphical regime of on-rail shooters than the Sega-CD live-action games *Sewer Shark* and *Tomcat Alley*.

The Super Nintendo was ill equipped to deal with polygons. Its slow CPU and limited data buses left it with little raw power to work with things that did not fall neatly into the corporation's predefined graphics modes.

Multiple scrolling backgrounds and parallax effects, high-resolution graphics modes, or matrix transformations applied to 2-D backgrounds couldn't do a thing for polygons. Lots of flashy 2-D would never result in 3-D—it could at most give "2.5-D," as Nintendo liked to describe *Super Mario World 2: Yoshi's Island*.

A number of games managed to create polygons (or derivatives, such as vectors with color fill-ins) on the Super NES, but they all did so at the expense of plodding frame rate, reduced number of colors, or by windowing the screen's surface to limit the display area. *Dragon View* is a good example of the latter technique because its impressive real-time 3-D polygonal overworld traveling mode is confined to a window roughly half the size of the screen—and even then it has important slowdowns when multiple objects appear on screen. *Another World* was made of filled vectors (2-D polygons, such as the *Drakkhen* overworld) and, as a result, is one of the few SNES games to have loading times between areas, on top of a choppy frame rate during action sequences (although the introduction cut scene to *Flashback: The Quest for Identity* makes anything seem silky smooth by comparison, really).

That polygons could appear in 2-D games under controlled conditions wasn't a particularly shining achievement. Nintendo would not sit by on its flat Mode 7 background plane and watch polygons take off from the sidelines. The specialized silverware and decentralized architecture of the SFC/SNES could accommodate an additional coprocessor dedicated to managing polygons. Instead of marketing that additional computing power in a risky add-on, with the associated problems of installed base and submarket segmentation that Sega was wrestling with thanks to its CD-ROM and 32X expansions, Nintendo would follow the way it had charted out with the Famicom and rely on expansion chips set in game cartridges.

Expansion Chips: "Now they're playing with effects ... Super FX!"

Although every platform offers a set of possibilities to game developers by facilitating certain aspects of game making, each of them also has an internal history: the early days and years of a system see a lot of software experimentation from designers trying to maximize the console's potential and go beyond the original hardware limitations, which is gradually accomplished throughout the platform's life. Although this applies to all platforms, it takes on a whole new dimension with Nintendo's cartridge-based consoles because new technology is also added into cartridges as the platform advances through time.

One of the defining features that had made the Famicom and NES so adaptable to the ever-shifting nature of the games business, as well as keeping the initial cost of the system down, was the concept of having special enhancement chips inserted in particular cartridges to expand on the system's base specifications. Masayuki Uemura's expandable and flexible engineering solution was repeated and taken to a new level with the Super Famicom, as the number of cartridge chips and the impact they had in shaping their games really pushed beyond the limits of the platform.

Some of the earlier expansion chips had modest effects because it wasn't visually clear how the chip contributed to the game, and so many gamers did not even know about these expansion chips. *Pilotwings* and *Super Mario Kart*, for instance, are usually presented as strong examples of Mode 7 graphics, but they actually benefitted from an onboard digital signal processor (DSP) chip, the DSP-1, which assisted with various math functions to accurately track coordinates in space, render images, and scale or rotate them in Mode 7 perspective view. What the chip was doing was assumed to be the working of regular Mode 7 technology, and Nintendo of course focused *Super Mario Kart* advertisements in pushing Mode 7, so that the SNES as a whole would look all the better (Harris 2014, 312).

The early DSP-1 still wasn't enough for Nintendo's ambitions, however. Therefore, in 1990, the venerable Japanese giant consulted a team of hotshot British programmers known as Argonaut Software. They had managed to perform two equally impressive feats: getting 3-D polygons in a functional NES prototype version of their computer game *Starglider* (renamed *NesGlider*), and getting 3-D polygons in a functional Game Boy prototype for a game that Nintendo picked up, produced, and published in 1992 under the name *X*. When Nintendo called them in, they needed a way to make the *Pilotwings* plane rotate in real-time 3-D instead of displaying multiple versions of its sprite that had been predrawn for a selection of predefined angles. Although the allotted three-month delay was too short for that, the Argonauts set to work on a powerful graphical accelerator expansion chip that would eventually become the Super FX chip, to be demonstrated with great fanfare in Nintendo's 1993 original game property (the first since the SNES launch in 1990): *Star Fox*, a game jointly developed by the Argonaut team from an SNES prototype of *NesGlider*, and Nintendo developers led by Shigeru Miyamoto. Thanks to the chip, the game would play out almost entirely in real-time 3-D polygons.

The Super FX chip would be the one to bring chips in the spotlight, getting mentions in magazine previews and articles left and right, and even appearing on *Star Fox*'s game box: "Revolutionary Super FX Micro Chip Creates Special Effects Like Never Before!" This short text, as well as the chip's name itself (FX for Effects, with the Super that had practically become a Nintendo trademark by then), embody the logic of "special effects" that I positioned as Nintendo's approach to graphical technologies in the 16-bit era.

Chips became a technological argument for developers; Capcom promoted its CX4 chip (specially designed to integrate 3-D wireframe meshes in their 2-D platformer) on the back of the *Mega Man X2* box: "Enhanced realism and 3-D effects with the new CAPCOM C4 graphics chip!" Square's *Super Mario RPG: Legend of the Seven Stars* and Nintendo's *Kirby Super Star* used another chip, the SA-1 (for Super Accelerator-1), which housed a 65C816 microprocessor with a clock speed of 10.74 MHz (three times the SNES's 65C816 "quick access" speed of 3.58 MHz or four times the 2.68 MHz "slow access") and an array of enhancements, including faster and additional RAM, memory mapping, and math functions. Essentially, this made the SNES hardware little more than a box to house the real brains behind the game: the chip nested in the cartridge.

Nintendo's commercial push for the chip was of course taken up by the games press. The Super FX chip was revealed by Nintendo on August 26, 1992, at the *Shoshinkai* trade show. *Electronic Gaming Monthly* covered it in a one-page article titled "Super-FX Chip Brings 3-D to Super NES" (*EGM* #40, November 1992, 48). It is worth noting that *EGM* partitioned the article's page with a text box explaining that Nintendo wouldn't be releasing a CD-ROM attachment for the Super NES anytime soon, the project having been seemingly abandoned. *EGM* causally links the two events, seeing in the Super FX chip a way for Nintendo to skip CD-ROM technology and have the SNES compete favorably against its competitors—and, most notably, the threatening Atari Jaguar (cue chuckle from contemporary readers who know from their retrospective vantage point how the roaring Jaguar fizzled away in the end).

The linking of the two news in the *EGM* feature encapsulates the interplay between technological trajectories that took place over the late 1980s and early 1990s: FMV proved to be a dead end because it sacrificed interactivity in trying to achieve photorealism. What the gaming world needed was not more graphical fidelity but more graphical regimes; polygons provided a way to achieve realism in building a fully realized virtual world while also creating new gameplay possibilities and situations for gamers to enjoy. The Super FX chip could do so, to an extent, but was merely a ticket to the defining technological trajectory for the future of games, a preview of things to come. The train would be Nintendo's next console, announced during the 1993 *Shoshinkai*, code-named "Project Reality," and codeveloped with Silicon Graphics—the firm that was on everyone's minds for computer-generated special effects, responsible for the T-1000 in *Terminator 2* and T-Rex in *Jurassic Park*. Even as it had the ticket in hand and the train coming up, however, Nintendo was working on a different tangent in the trajectory of 3-D: the previously mentioned monochromatic, stereoscopic wireframe graphics "headheld" system, the Virtual Boy. However, Nintendo had bet on the wrong horse, and the Virtual Boy died before the train even got to the station. Stereoscopic wireframe graphics were tied to the old (graphical) regimes and weren't the way to go; the brave new world of polygons lay ahead.

Like any king or emperor facing newfound expanses of democracy, Nintendo wasn't in a hurry to jump into tridimensional polygonal games, a new way of making games that required "thinking in 3-D" (Mielke 2010, 3) and could topple the established order by invalidating competent game developers' expertise in 2-D games overnight. Many histories of the period claim that Shigeru Miyamoto was developing a 3-D Mario game at the time of *Star Fox*, a project referred to as "Mario FX" (cf. Ryan 2012, 165). This is incorrect. As Evan Gowan (2012) shows, Miyamoto had the *idea* of making a 3-D Mario game, but nothing was materializing at the time. "Super Mario FX" was the codename given to the Super FX chip during development by Argonaut Games (Mathematical Argonaut Rotation I/O). There never was a question of producing a 3-D Mario game on the SNES. Instead, Nintendo was actively fighting against the inclusion of 3-D games on its 16-bit console.

A Stubborn Gorilla Goes 3-D: *Donkey Kong Country*

True to itself, Nintendo adopted polygonal 3-D for its surface-level graphics and treated it as a way to up-end graphical fidelity while pursuing games that conformed to traditional graphical regimes and gameplay genres. It was as if Nintendo, the giant gorilla of video game business, was too stubborn to adapt to the changing reality of video games. Another technically strong British developer was going to help Nintendo push further in the polygonal 3-D trajectory. Rare had been developing games for the NES since 1986, contributing more than 45 titles to the platform's library, including original series like *Battletoads* and *Wizards & Warriors*. It was one of the only developers to have invested a substantial amount of money in getting equipped with Silicon Graphics workstations to model 3-D characters or environments. 3-D graphics had an instantly recognizable aesthetic—one that was *au goût du jour* at a time when society was obsessed with dinosaurs thanks to the computer-generated imagery in

Jurassic Park. In 1994, Nintendo purchased a 49% participation in the studio, making it a second-party developer.

Rare married technological innovation with conservative design, which would result in *Donkey Kong Country* and *Killer Instinct.* Both featured 3-D graphics in the clear, familiar frame of well-known 2-D genres (the platformer and fighting game, respectively): graphical upgrades within familiar graphical regimes. When Nintendo presented footage from its upcoming game at the Summer 1994 CES, the press assumed it was a preview of a game for the firm's announced Project Reality, a dual arcade-and-home all-encompassing system. Everyone was taken by surprise when it was revealed to be a game coming out for the baseline Super NES. 3-D characters—and way better looking than Sega's *Virtua Fighter* blocky humans that had impressed people the world over in arcades—running and jumping in perfectly fluid framerates on a 16-bit console? What was this new devilry?

There was a secret: The polygonal characters had their animations prerendered and stored as individual frames in the game's memory. Technically, they were played out exactly like any other game's character animations, highlighting the fundamental difference between modeling and animating that constituted the foundation of polygonal 3-D graphics. Modeling the character could be done with any materials: The classic case of digital pictorials in pixel-drawing, hand-drawn pictures scanned into still images, individual photographs of people who had been filmed and then digitized (as we will see in the next chapter), clay models hand-animated with stop motion techniques (as in *Clay Fighter*), or characters modeled with 3-D polygons and then animated frame by frame were all equal in the animation process executed by the SNES's PPU; it was simply a matter of displaying individual frames one after the other. In that way, the grain and visual signature of 3-D computer-generated polygonal graphics was present, but it was all surface; the deep functioning of these graphics was still prerendered, inflexible 2-D sprites.

Donkey Kong's comeback (which I covered in chapter 3) wasn't only a cultural statement by Nintendo (which, always reiterating, christened the Japanese game *Super Donkey Kong*); it was also, and more bluntly so, a technological statement. Promotion around *Donkey Kong Country* revolved heavily around the technological advancements it was bringing to the table, in a notable departure from the typical technology-avoiding trend that characterized promotional discourses from 1994 onward. Hence, *Donkey Kong Country* represents an interesting site of tension between the two approaches of technological promotion. The Advanced Computer Modeling (ACM), listed as "obviously cool stuff" in a Nintendo promotional poster that downplayed the technological discourse, was flanked by "old-fashioned" technological flaunting in another untitled two-page spread by Rare for United Kingdom magazines of the time:

> It's taken 22 man years, **32 megs**, 32,768 colours and 1 super computer to make him look this **gruesome**. You've never seen anything like this before. Donkey Kong Country is the world's first fully-rendered video game. To produce it took 22 years work on 6 SGI work stations and one XL Super Computer. The graphics are 3-D. The playing arena is 32 megabit. The levels number 111. (No, that's not a misprint—one hundred and eleven). But the most amazing aspect of Donkey Kong Country is that you don't need a 32 bit machine or a CD-ROM system to play it. Because Donkey Kong Country is only on the Super NES. So go and grab one now. You'll go absolutely ape.

Donkey Kong Country sold a whopping 6 million copies in the first 45 days from launch, proving that something worked somewhere along the way, whether it was the popularity of the classic video game character, the technological marketing, or simply—and regretfully—the amazing surface-level graphics. Shigeru Miyamoto, who had helped Rare finish *Donkey Kong Country* by making various design touch-ups to improve the gameplay, reportedly said, "*Donkey Kong Country* proves that players will put up with mediocre gameplay as long as the art is good" (Kent 2001, 518). It did more than sell 6 million copies over the 1994 holidays (Buchanan 2009), however: It helped Nintendo seize back the market lead from Sega's Genesis (Schilling 2003a, 11). Miyamoto's answer to that would come with the next flagship game for Nintendo: *Super Mario World 2: Yoshi's Island.* When he proposed the game to Nintendo's marketing, they turned it down, asking for projects that featured impressive visuals, like the 3-D prerendered graphics of *DKC*. Miyamoto retaliated by pushing further *Yoshi's Island* child-crayon art style, which gave the game a distinctive visual signature that satisfied marketing.

As child-like and innocent as it may have looked on the surface, however, *Yoshi's Island* was an impressive technological beast at its core, in a new spin on Nintendo's characteristic duality. It was equipped with Argonaut's latest version of the Super FX coprocessor, astutely dubbed the Super FX-2 (having letter-and-number combinations was always a sign of technological complexity and an easy way for the public to perceive something as improved). That chip provided advanced sprite manipulation possibilities, advertised by Nintendo as "morphmation" technology: Sprites of enormous sizes were one option, but more important, the chip allowed sprites to be scaled and rotated, effectively rendering the Mode 7 operations available to be performed on sprites rather than background planes.

Aside from technology, there also was creative evolution. As we've seen in chapter 2, when the SFC was launched, Miyamoto had promised, "Wait, and I will learn more about the limits of this machine" (Sheff 1993, 231). The more inspired techniques found in later SFC games, such as *Secret of Mana*'s point of view switch to alleviate Mode 7 flatness, *Chrono Trigger*'s time-traveling Mode 7 sequence, and finely tuned *Yoshi's Island* moments—the Fuzzy-dizzy LSD trips, the rotation of the entire sky when running across a small moon to battle Raphael the Raven, the gigantic Baby Bowser walking forward in the background—all fulfilled the promise and show how platform mastery increases over time thanks to both technological advances and creative experience.

Nintendo's choice in sticking with 2-D sprites and classic gameplay is representative of its cautious treading on the grounds of innovation. It wasn't for lack of polygons and 3-D games with new types of gameplay around Nintendo. Argonaut had developed a Super FX game of its own, *Vortex* (1994), and assisted Nintendo in creating *Stunt Race FX*—granted, a conventional racing game in its gameplay, but still one made of polygons. Sadly, the more innovative games on which Argonaut worked had their release canceled by Nintendo after substantial development effort.

Inches Away from the Finish

Star Fox 2 was not only "fully completed," according to Argonaut programmer Dylan Cuthbert (in Gowan 2010), it had even been promoted by Nintendo, who disclosed screenshots and ran previews in *Nintendo Power* (cf. #69 in February 1995 and #76 in September 1995), as well as having the prototype on display at the Winter 1995 Consumer Electronics Show (Gowan 2010). Nintendo's decision to cancel its release may be explained by the recent release of the PlayStation and its more advanced polygonal 3-D graphics, which would have made the game look crude by comparison. Most accounts, however, link that decision with the impending release of the Nintendo 64 and the choice to have 3-D games coming out only on the N64 (in the end, as Cuthbert notes, the N64 would get delayed for so long that *Star Fox 2* wouldn't have hurt anything). Gowan's assessment of the game contextualizes Nintendo's resistance to innovation: "The final beta of *Star Fox 2* is the culmination of a nearly two and a half year development process to take the game from an on-the-rails shooter to a fully 3-D experience" (Gowan 2010). In other words, it was not simply a change in graphical technology but a more significant change in graphical regime.

Many unique elements in *Star Fox 2* can be characterized as full innovations in terms of genre conventions, bringing together the genres of real-time strategy and shoot'em up. A main map screen displays units advancing toward each base, and the player must chart a course to intercept them, somewhat like *Ogre Battle: The March of the Black Queen* or the older 1979 *Space Battle* for the Intellivision—or, more troublingly, like Argonaut's 1992 Game Boy game *X*, with which *Star Fox* (and especially the *Star Fox 2* prototype) bears more than passing resemblance. Planet and battleship levels offer mazes that the player must navigate, in addition to things to be shot. None of these features would make it into the next Star Fox game, *Star Fox 64*, which in comparison looks like an enhanced remake of the original *Star Fox* that conforms to the logic of reiteration rather than innovation. Dylan Cuthbert expressed it so: "*Star Fox 64* incorporated a lot of the newer ideas we created in *Star Fox 2* but it didn't, in my view, take the genre a full step forward. *Star Fox 2* really was a different direction of gameplay" (Cuthbert in Gowan 2010).

The other missed opportunity to innovate was *FX Fighter*, a 3-D fighting game Argonaut was developing to compete with Sega's *Virtua Fighter* that had been making a killing in the arcades since its release in late 1993. However, the game had been dethroned by *Killer Instinct*, an arcade game released in late 1994, jointly published by Nintendo and Williams and developed by Rare. The game was announced to be running off Project Reality hardware, and a port for the Nintendo 64 would come; the home version would use the same technology, bridging the gap that separated home and arcade hardware, as the Neo Geo had attempted to do. However, as the N64 was delayed, *Killer Instinct* was ported for the Super NES instead, hitting store shelves in August 1995. It is hard not to consider the implications this had for *FX Fighter*. Like *Star Fox 2*, the polygonal fighting game was presented at the January 1995 Winter Consumer Electronics Show and previewed in *Nintendo Power* #69 in February. Like *Star Fox 2*, it was canceled by Nintendo.

Piecing together these different events gives a clear and easy line of reasoning for Nintendo to have acted in such a way: Rare's *Donkey Kong Country* had received enormous praise and sold millions of copies in record time, thanks to prerendered 3-D graphics integrated in tried-and-true 2-D platformer gameplay. Sega's *Virtua Fighter* had made a splash in the arcade, but Rare's *Killer Instinct* had taken up the mantle by integrating 3-D prerendered graphics in tried-and-true 2-D fighter gameplay; ergo, there was no need for *FX Fighter*. Gamers were satisfied with games that had novel and impressive graphics in refined and familiar gameplay situations. That approach would prove its worth with *Yoshi's Island* as well.

Known formulas allowed Nintendo to leverage its accumulated expertise in game crafting, rather than risking ventures in new game genres that slipped outside its control. It was a simple restating of what the platform had been about all along: The Super Famicom was, after all, a "Super" version of its Famicom that favored incremental improvements on known genres and special effects. Likewise, the additional hardware chips in late Super Famicom games would provide "Super" effects that tied into the same game experiences in a renewed display of "lateral thinking." Sega might have kept repeating its slogan, "Welcome to the Next Level," but Nintendo would insist on sticking to the basics—super basics—as if enough polish could make the Silver Age last forever.

> The world of Nintendo is not simply involved in manufacturing video game players and controllers but is interconnected with larger media and communication systems which have an enormous potential to shape and define our culture. (Provenzo 1991, 27)

Understanding the Super NES's role, position, and importance in video game history—North American video game history, to be specific—requires us to first understand how Nintendo came to be such a household name piercing the heart of children's popular culture. To do that, we must take a step back and contextualize the corporation's presence in the video game industry, and as it was established through the NES in North America. Nintendo's first 95 years as a company (1889–1984) will provide us with some of Nintendo's DNA and *modus operandi.* As we will see in this chapter, the NES's release and success opened a cultural period in video game history, the American Video Game ReNESsance. Accordingly, the Super NES as a cultural platform articulated a transition in Nintendo's positioning among the changing landscape of gaming from the late 1980s to the mid- to late 1990s. Spurred in part by the *Mortal Kombat* fiasco (and more generally by Sega's successful promotional campaigns), Nintendo erred away from its long history as a family-oriented entertainment provider, as well as its shorter history as a kid-centered firm, and stumbled through the mid-1990s before the great Fall at the dawn of the millennium.

Nintendo started operating in 1889 as a manufacturer of *hanafuda*, traditional Japanese playing cards, and progressively cemented its reputation for quality. In 1949, Hiroshi Yamauchi was appointed president of the company at age 21 to replace his dying grandfather. He modernized the production by manufacturing Western plastic-coated playing cards in 1953. However, in mid-century Japan, playing cards had a bad reputation for being associated with illegal gambling controlled by the *yakuza*.[1] Nintendo's reputation would have been seriously endangered if not for a timely licensing deal that Hiroshi Yamauchi signed with Walt Disney in 1959 to produce playing cards backed with pictures of Mickey Mouse and other Disney characters. These successfully expanded Nintendo's market to include young people and families, even getting advertised on television. To reach these new customers, Yamauchi structured a new distribution system that would get the cards into larger department and toy stores. Yamauchi's initiative yielded a doubly positive outcome for Nintendo: Its sales exploded and brought immediate financial benefits, but through the long-term shift in perception for playing cards it instilled, the firm earned a positive image as a provider of domestic family entertainment, as well as some all-important business connections in the toy industry.

From there, Nintendo specialized in developing technological toys. The Ultra Hand (1966), designed by Gunpei Yokoi, was its one early success. A second notable invention was the Nintendo Beam Gun, a light gun developed by Yokoi and a collaborator from Sharp Corporation, Masayuki Uemura. That invention allowed Nintendo to enter the electronic entertainment industry by installing shooting galleries operated by optoelectronic devices all around Japan. The Nintendo Beam Gun project proved to be pivotal for two reasons: First, it led Uemura from Sharp to Nintendo, where he would design the Famicom and Super Famicom. Second, it gave Nintendo expertise in the light gun and electronic entertainment industry, which prompted Magnavox to contact them for the development of its own light gun to be included in the Odyssey home video game console (Gorges 2008, Picard 2013).

Light guns and playing cards provide the technological and cultural blueprints to how Nintendo would go about entering the Japanese and American home video game markets with the Famicom and NES in the 1980s. At the time, Japan's video arcades ("game centers") were confronted with a problem of cultural image: High school boys would lurk there and bully younger kids, forcing parents to patrol game centers

(DeWinter 2014, 333). For concerned families, investing in a home video game console was a way to avoid these issues. Hiroshi Yamauchi, having already dealt with the negative image associated with playing cards in the past, understood that well. Nintendo responded in the same way it had done for gambling in the 1950s: by featuring contents and styles appropriate for children and the whole family and redefining the product for them in the domestic space. Nintendo games would enter Japanese homes like Nintendo cards had done some 25 years earlier.

It is not surprising that Hiroshi Yamauchi found the name "Family Computer" to be "in logical continuity" with Nintendo's tradition of "developing products that can be used by the whole family" (Gorges 2011, 34). As Florent Gorges writes, Nintendo took every effort to present its Famicom as a family product:

> The very first television advertisement for the Family Computer, airing in September 1983, did not begin with images from *Donkey Kong* or *Mario Bros.*, but rather with *Mah-Jong* and *Gonarabe*! The message is then extremely clear: the 30-second spot launches a campaign aimed at winning over the breadwinning fathers. The slogan goes in the same direction: "The whole family together, around the Family Computer." (Gorges 2011, 41–42; freely translated)

Although the machine was publicly advertised with a focus on the family, behind the scenes Nintendo was targeting its simple and cheap machine to a core audience of kids. This aim was present from the inception of the system: Yamauchi had set the target retail price of the console, which Uemura strived to meet in designing the hardware, at 10,000 yen, an impossible command that ended up at a still impressive price of 14,800 yen (around $65). That price was based on the usual allowance money of children in Japan at the time, which according to polls amounted to 24,000 yen per year. Yamauchi figured that left them enough money to buy cartridges (Gorges 2011, 23, 32). In short, the marketing was aiming broadly at the family but targeting in priority children; as their parents owned the disposable income and control over the domestic space, Nintendo had to get them interested as well. The Famicom's success gained Nintendo a 90% share of the 8-bit market in one year and 30% of the Japanese toy market during the mid-1980s (Picard 2013).

After successfully breaking through the arcade market of the United States with *Donkey Kong* and with the success of the Famicom in Japanese homes, pushing the machine to the home U.S. market seemed to be just a matter of time. It turned out to be rather a matter of effort and of micromanaging the marketing to a great degree of precision. Although Nintendo's sales are calculated as part of the toy market in Japan, Yamauchi unequivocally stated in 1986, "We do not create toys. We provide entertainment. And the world of entertainment does not care to distinguish between children and adult audiences. The only thing that matters is to entertain everyone" (Gorges 2011, 42; freely translated). That approach is easily verified for the Famicom in Japan, where one can find strip Mah-Jong and other erotic or pornographic games (entertainment for everyone, indeed), but had to be tweaked for the U.S. market.

Thinking of the Children: A Generational Divide

For Nintendo to reach American families, retailers had to accept selling its system first, and retailers were clearly not putting any hope in "video games," which had become something of a taboo word associated with a cultural practice seen as *passé* and a market thought to be burnt out amid the video game crash of 1983–1984. Nintendo of America's first NES version, presented at the Consumer Electronics Shows of 1984, had a keyboard and tape data recorder, which made it look too much like these "serious" home computers, which video game hardware manufacturers were now trying to push (notably the one firm caught in the eye of the storm, Atari). One solution then was to target another type of consumer, one that would enjoy the colorful characters that were Nintendo's strong suit after *Donkey Kong* and *Mario Bros.*

This is when the decision to market the console specifically to children, the core being 8- to 14-year-old boys, was made in a slightly different fashion than the marketing of the Famicom in Japan. On American shores, the family would quietly slip behind the children, and the Family Computer became a boys' toy (especially thanks to the publicized Zapper light gun and ROB the robot, tech toys *par excellence*). American parents could, like the Japanese, buy the home console for their children to play at home instead of going to these disreputable arcades. Second, the console could be pushed as an "entertainment system" that did more than play video games: It could be presented as an entertainment machine, like a VHS player or turntable.[2] Quite paradoxically, the NES had to *look* less like a toy and more like a machine on the surface, whereas in truth, at its core, it had to *function* more like a toy and less like a machine. This makes the NES something of an avatar of Nintendo's own identity, a material signifier of the firm's surface-and-core duality.

To spin the target demographics' enthusiasm in the right direction would require some delicate positioning on Nintendo's part: It had to impress the children while appearing as a reasonable and safe investment to their parents, who had experienced firsthand the video game crash. To paraphrase the authors of *Digital Play*, promoting the NES proved to be "an exquisite balancing act" based on children's "pester-power" ability to handle the "delicate negotiations" required for parents to accept buying the console for their children; "Parents had to be reassured about the nature of interactive games," all the while appealing to "children's rebellion and independence" (Kline, Dyer-Witheford and de Peuter 2003, 119). This independence came in by marketing games as enablers of power fantasies, with a campaign centered on a "paradigm-shifting" tagline by Nintendo of America's Gail Tilden (Harris 2014, 55): "Now you're playing with power!" This new direction went against the antagonistic taunting practices prevalent in video game marketing before (Therrien 2014, 560–561) and was better suited at reaching children. In true Nintendo duality, however, the surface discourse of "playing with power" hid the core reality that most Nintendo games were punishingly difficult.

Nowadays, claims that video games are "kids' stuff" or toys can occasionally appear in discourses but are usually met with eye rolls of annoyance or exasperation, like any cliché or retrograde view. Most people know that some video games are meant for kids but that video games as a whole cannot be reduced to that. But that awareness came progressively. In June 2002, for example, *The Economist* made a point of it: "Gaming is no longer the province of children and teenagers [...]. A generation that grew up with games has simply kept on playing" (The Economist 2002). This is a testament to the impact Nintendo has had on the industry and the cultural image of video games because in the 1980s, the idea of selling video games to kids was not self-evident. As Christopher Paul (2012) notes in a chapter titled "Video Games as 'Kid's' Toys," one origin point of video games is in research laboratories and their expensive, specialized computer equipment. The commercialization of this technology through leisure occurred with Atari's *Pong* and subsequent machines and led to the emergence of the second origin point to video games. As Dmitri Williams writes, "Game play in public spaces began as an adult activity, with games first appearing in bars and nightclubs before the eventual arcade boom. Then, when arcades first took root, they were populated with a wide mixing of ages, classes and ethnicities" (Williams 2006, 199).

This initial surge was quickly and increasingly confined to the young male audience as Carly Kocurek's historical account shows; from video game arcades hatched "an easily recognizable technomasculine archetype" of gaming, evidenced by the "video game world record culture" that "present a cohesive picture of gaming: young, male, technologically savvy, bright, and mischievous" (Kocurek 2015, xviii–xix). It must be noted, however, that "young" here does not mean "young children." Amusement arcades solely dedicated to video games were "a place that parents warned their kids to avoid because of perceptions about their clientele and sometimes seedy locations" (Paul 2012, 39). Video games may have been initially for men and women but they quickly shifted toward young men and women, then young men, and finally boys. Nevertheless, they were for big boys with basic economic sense, the capability to handle quarters, read and follow instructions, be tall enough to see the screen and manipulate the controls at an upright cabinet, and be left unsupervised in a public space for quite longer than what would be acceptable for young children. Video games were not for kids, and they were not toys, but rather an introduction to the computing processes of future technology, which the next generation of American workers would need (Kocurek 2015, chapter 1).

Arcades remained the prime revenue driver for the video game industry well after home video games emerged and remained especially so through the crash of 1983 and beyond. Kubey writes in 1982, "In the United States alone, consumers spend more on video games—about $9 billion a year, including some $8 billion for coin-op and $1 billion for home games—than on any other form of entertainment, including movies and records" (Kubey 1982, xiv). Much of that money was spent by young adults with disposable income and a taste for social entertainment, in the tradition of pinball parlors and bowling alleys. As home video game systems were developed and sold, from the beginning they were marketed to capitalize on the idea of "entertainment for the whole family" (Williams 2006, 197–199). Although some Atari 2600 games were appealing to children, or even specifically developed for them (such as *Kool-Aid Man*), children were not the primary consumer being targeted by the firm.

This is evident when looking at the firm's advertisements. One of the earliest television commercials, dated December 17, 1977, by a YouTube uploader,[3] showcases the 2600 (or rather the VCS, as it was known at the time) and *Combat*. Everyone seen in the commercial appears to be in their mid-30s and up; white hair is seen in the background crowd, and everyone is wearing a suit and tie. A compilation of Atari commercials, compiled by YouTube user memphiselle1[4] and lasting more than 30 minutes, can be described in a series of brief flashes of the first few minutes to provide further illustration. A boy and his mother play *Asteroids* together. Three men and three children play a variety of games. A man does business on his Atari home computer. A boy types in musical notation as the voice-over claims it is "simple enough for your child to use." A family is gathered around their TV playing Atari, while the father explains how it provides good home entertainment. In one of the most widely circulated commercials, a crescendo of people gather around the console, watching excitedly as more and more games are shown, starting with two boys and progressively adding their father, sister and mother, aunt and uncle, grandparents, and eventually a policeman and a pizza delivery guy. Children clearly belong in this marketing campaign, but they usually do so as part of the family unit and in service of social entertainment.

Outside the traditional promotional channels of advertisement was the Atari Club, which sent to Club members the *Atari Age* magazine, a publication that notified and informed them about all things Atari. This magazine is clearly meant for adults. *Atari Age*, vol.1 no.1 (May/June 1982, 2), starts off with a "celebrity corner" mock interview with Pac-Man, who reveals he had a "well-rounded education" and "graduated sphera cum laude," before doing stunt work in an enzyme detergent commercial. Baseball jokes ensue. On page 5, an article is titled "From Abu Dhabi to Venezuela, the World Plays Atari Games!" and discusses the recent South African Atari Tournament, an Atari Robot's demonstration success in Puerto Rico, and the world Asteroids championships recently held in Washington, DC. The Atari News, starting on page 6, are formatted after traditional newspapers and explain "what's an EPROM"—a nice case of technoliteracy, as seen in chapter 3—as well as presenting the Atari Computer Camps for "campers 10 to 18 years old"; "your child could be one of them!", the subtext seems to be whispering as we read. There's even a reprint of an Atari press release, starting thus: "Reinforcing its leadership position in offering cartridge versions of hit coin video games, Atari has signed an exclusive agreement with Centuri, Inc., for the rights to adapt current and future games created by Centuri, a leading American manufacturer of arcade games." This is dry enough to fit in *The Economist* rather than in any magazine aimed at children. Comparing this magazine's writing to that of *Nintendo Power* (from chapter 3) brings ample evidence that children fit in a peripheral manner to Atari's market positioning.

Nintendo's decision to market the NES to children in America is an important event in video game history, as it created a major generational divide. Kids born from the mid-1970s to the mid-1980s overwhelmingly took to Nintendo's console to the extent that Provenzo named them "Nintendo Kids" (and Kline, Dyer-Witheford, and de Peuter, "Nintendo generation"). As we will see, console video games in North America more or less followed that generation with increasingly mature games. A little more polemical, Sheff affirmed in his 1993 book's title that Nintendo "enslaved your children." Although not all games published on Nintendo's NES were made by the same teams or firms, they all had a certain feel of unity between them because of Nintendo's heavy regulations on content, so that a certain cultural "flair" could be taken out (a "Nintendo ethos" I will describe a little later). People born earlier and who played video games during the 1970s and early 1980s either had to play Nintendo and become big kids again (often experiencing social stigma) or seek refuge in the pastures of PC gaming, which could appear as spike-filled technical pits to the uninitiated. Many of them simply stopped playing video games, and a quiet rift started separating the digital play of the Nintendo generation from that of their parents, guardians, or elder siblings:

> One cohort effect is relatively easy to isolate: the generations that ignored video games in the late 1970s and early 1980s have continued to stay away. Those who played and stopped rarely returned; by 1984, baby boomers had dramatically decreased their play, probably because of the powerful social messages they were suddenly getting about the shame and deviancy of adult gaming. (Williams 2006, 205)

This generational divide is, in my opinion, obfuscated by the expression classically found in video game histories that "Nintendo resurrected the North American market" (Kline, Dyer-Witheford, and de Peuter 2003, 110; Williams 2006, 199; Harris 2014, 59; etc.). This may be true in the sense that Nintendo brought a financially sustainable market and model for the industry, like there was before the crash and its arrival. But "resurrection" has too many implications of continuity. The differences in economic and marketing models (see chapters 1 and 2), to say nothing of the cultural definition, role and impact of video games due to Nintendo's approach, are too profound to speak of a "resurrection" or "rebirth." Rather, we should think of Nintendo's North American arrival as the starting point of something new, a Second Coming after the Video Game Apocalypse of 1983–1984 (or so would the biblically themed periodization have it). This is the start of a distinct period in a cultural history of video games, a period that's larger than the NES, although it was born from it: the American Video Game ReNESsance.

The American Video Game ReNESsance

The ReNESsance is a regionally specific cultural period that designates the North American home video game market's redefinition following

Nintendo's success with the NES after the Crash of 1983. Although "American" in its name and origin, its influence rippled across the larger world. I define it as a period where the dominant social image of video games was equated with children's entertainment. Figure 6.1 charts the presence and strength of the period and identifies the four phases that shape it according to certain key events.

As a historical period, the European Renaissance is typically characterized positively as a return to the culture of antiquity, philosophy, and a thriving of the fine arts. Moreover, it is often envisioned as a transition toward the Age of Enlightenment with the likes of Spinoza, Voltaire, Hume, Newton, and the Scientific Revolution. The ReNESsance I am describing here has none of these implications. On the contrary, it is built on conservative commercial policies, restrictive licensing and partnership deals, and a top-down, highly hierarchical and authoritarian structuring of the video game industry (as we have seen in chapters 1 and 2). Although the term appears to be positive on the surface, in actuality we are as far away as possible from the strongly positive connotations of the Renaissance and its ideals. This contradiction is conscious wordplay meant to replicate Nintendo's own two-faced stance across the business-to-consumer and business-to-business spheres. For Nintendo to pull out the velvet glove and seduce consumers required that third-party developers be dealt with an iron hand.

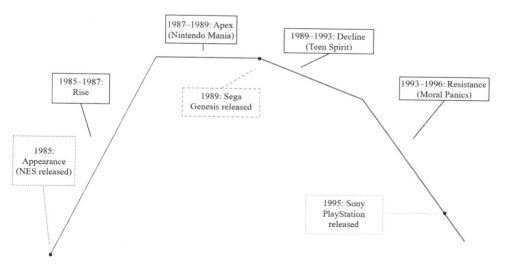

Figure 6.1 The American Video Game ReNESsance and its four phases: Appearance (1985), Rise and Apex (1985–1989), Decline (1989–1993), and Resistance (1993–1996).

Phases 1 and 2—Appearance, Rise, and Apex

The ReNESsance was foreshadowed by toy manufacturer Mattel's 1980 entry in the video game market, which put the Intellivision in its catalog of toys. Nintendo cemented the idea of the ReNESsance with the release and marketing of the NES in 1985 and 1986. The cultural movement progressively rises with the popularity of the console until it reaches its apex in 1987 and 1988, when the NES becomes the most popular toy and the United States is hit by "Nintendo mania": "In the U.S., 'playing Nintendo' replaced 'playing Atari' as the linguistic metonym for playing any videogame, not just software exclusive to Nintendo's console" (Altice 2015, 160).

Although Nintendo reached its apex in no small part thanks to the marketing and technological lock-in mechanisms that coerced developers and publishers, its stringent "content guidelines" played a role in cementing the unknown firm's brand reputation and forced all third-party games to conform to a shared "Nintendo ethos." In addition to Nintendo testing and approving every game developed by licensees for bugs or operational flaws, all games were prohibited from the following: sexually suggestive or explicit content; sexist language or depictions; random, gratuitous, and/or excessive violence; graphic illustration of death; domestic violence and/or abuse; excessive force in a sports game; ethnic, religious, nationalistic, or sexual stereotypes and symbols; profanity, obscenity, offensive language, and gestures; use or depiction of alcohol, smoking, and illegal drugs; and subliminal political messages or overt political statements (McCullough n.d., compiled from Schwartz and Schwartz 1991).

Much has been written about the effects of these content policies on third-party games and developers (Altice 2015, Arsenault 2012, Crockford 1993) and the absurd cases of censorship it led to—nude art sculptures covered up or entirely removed from games, crosses removed from gravestones, and so on (McCullough n.d.). I won't go over them here yet again, except to note that these policies proved necessary in accomplishing the NES's mission of seducing children while reassuring parents. The Nintendo ethos, broadly, revolved around an "epish" treatment of narrative (equal parts epic and childish), which has traditionally been described as indulging in power fantasies (Therrien 2014), and was visually encoded in vibrant, colorful graphics that favored a cartoonish visual style informed by Japanese *anime* and *manga* aesthetics (Picard 2008) partly because of the Famicom and NES's technical affordances.

Translation and localization issues and hiccups made it customary for players to decrypt important game clues encoded in messages almost impossible to decode. Through Nintendo games, children were also exposed to some elements of Japanese philosophy (honor, tradition, etc.), as well as some unique new discourses. Sheff opposed Disney's Mickey Mouse message ("We play fair and we work hard and we're in harmony...") with Mario's new values: "Kill or be killed. Time is running out. You are on your own" (Sheff 1993, 10). Messages aside, more children recognized Super Mario than Mickey Mouse (Sheff 1993, 9).

Phase 3—Decline: Genesis Does What Nintendon't

The problem with targeting a "Nintendo Generation" of 6- to 14-year-olds, Nintendo soon found out, is that kids grow up pretty fast, and their idols of worship are bound to change just as quickly. The Nintendo ethos was contested and ridiculed by Sega when it targeted teenagers with its Genesis promotions in 1989, precipitating the ReNESsance into a phase of decline. Sega's "edgy" promotional campaigns garnered attention and defined its personality through at least two tactics: aggressive comparative publicity campaigns, such as the now-iconic "Genesis Does What Nintendon't" advertisements, and the "Sega shout" signature, consisting of a half-shouted, half-shrieked "Sega!" rather than calmly but firmly pronouncing it. It screamed rebellion with an edgy and cool style.

Edgy, cool, fast, wacky, bizarre, rebel, trippy; these could all describe Sega's promotional signature. As the firm gained market share with games such as *Altered Beast*, insiders of video game culture knew, or would soon come to know, that games could deal with mature subject matters (and had sometimes done so for years, especially on the PC). I call this shift the "Teen Spirit" to reference the grunge movement that heavily defined the early 1990s in U.S. popular music and culture, and more specifically its origin point, Nirvana's 1991 hit song "Smells Like Teen Spirit." That was Sega's take on the spoony bards of Nintendo culture.[5]

Sega did not invent the edgy push for game marketing, of course. In the early 1980s, Atari had produced four television commercials exclusively for showing on MTV, the same cultural demographic that would be targeted by Sony and Nintendo some 15 years later. A commercial for *Pole Position* showed a buttoned-up, bowtie-wearing father driving his quiet and clean family around for a "Sunday drive" while an off-screen voice derided his social position as a "corporate executive." The plans were derailed by shaking the family from their car and dropping them into race cars so they could "play *Pole Position*." The rocking soundtrack, dizzying visuals, fast and disorienting action montage, and aftermath of the race showing the traumatized family members slowly walking while clutching car parts in shock and awe are all early embodiments of the rebellious rallying cry for a new kind of video game culture.

Sony's PlayStation marketing in 1995 would inscribe itself in the wake of Atari and Sega's 1980 and 1990 trail and succeed in repositioning games for a wider range of audiences. In this respect, on the level of global video game culture, Sony merely gave the final push to a historical marketing arc that Atari had flashed and Sega had developed with the marketing of its Sega Genesis to the "Teen Spirit." Just as the Seattle alternative rock bands' success had been co-opted by mainstream media and fashion industries that commercialized grunge culture, so would video games enter the spotlight with the "MTV Generation" and the PlayStation. In this light, the American Video Game ReNESsance temporarily put this movement on hold because of Nintendo's regressive marketing to children.[6]

The ReNESsance's influence declined due to Sega's efficient marketing campaign, especially given Nintendo's unconvincing attempts at responding to Sega's attacks: Against the witty "Sega Does What Nintendon't," all Nintendo could muster was "Nintendo Is What Genesisn't." Aside from Sega's influence, a second factor contributed to the decline of the ReNESsance: the release of *Tetris* as the bundled title for Nintendo's 1989 Game Boy. Sheff describes the surprising success the Game Boy has had with adults:

> Grown-ups flocked to *Tetris* too. Arakawa had predicted correctly; feedback from its customers told NOA that a third to a half of the *Tetris* players were adults, and Nintendo's presence in the adult market increased to such a degree that almost half (46 percent) of the Game Boy players in the West were adults. (Sheff 1993, 217)

Although both of these factors undermined the association of video games with children and chipped away at the ReNESsance as a cultural period, it still remained the dominant social image of video games in the 1990s due, in part, to Nintendo of America's content guidelines. They had been established for the Famicom and were still in full force, but as games substantially grew in graphical fidelity and plot complexity, more and more knotty issues showed up. The censorship of religious themes and symbols affected *Super Ghouls 'n Ghosts* by replacing crosses on gravestones with ankhs and the demon Samael's name with Sardius.

Capcom got off easy compared with Quintet for *ActRaiser*, a game whose plot revolves around the player being God and reclaiming the Earth from Satan. Apparently Nintendo of America was fine with the player controlling a delegate "angel" during the city-building phases, but God and Satan had to be renamed "The Master" and "Tanzra" (Tanzra also had his horns edited out). Another thing apparently fine with NoA was the possibility for the player in *Blackthorne* to fire his shotgun and kill slaves standing innocently (or, worse, chained to the wall) without consequence—but, crucially, without blood. The hemophobic Nintendo wasn't controlling games for ethical or moral ideas but simply for on-screen blood, gore, sex, and religious symbols, which is probably why it had Square alter *Final Fantasy II* so that Rosa, when captive, is threatened by a suspended wrecking ball rather than a scythe like in the Japanese original. When Cecil manages to rescue her, they hug rather than kiss (presumably to reduce "sexuality," which I personally find hilarious). Sprites for partially uncovered female enemies and characters in *Final Fantasy III*, like bare-breasted statues in the halls of *Super Castlevania IV*, got wardrobe upgrades.

As dialogue got increasingly verbose with the rise of story-driven games, direct references to death and other sensitive issues were carefully avoided, with varying degrees of success. In *Final Fantasy II*, all dialogue bits that hinted at Cecil and Rosa sleeping together were edited out, just like the "Porno mag" item that could be found in the secret programmers' room—proof, if any was needed, that Japanese games had not been defined as "kids' games" as much as in America. In *Final Fantasy III*, the spell "Death" and the enemy "Death Gaze" were renamed "Doom" and "Doom Gaze"; the spell "holy" was renamed "pearl," which didn't help players understand the logic of opposite elements (as in *Chrono Trigger*, where Crono was keyed to the element "Lightning" in the North American version, instead of "Heaven" in the Japanese version, which included both lightning and holy magic). Bars became cafés to avoid depicting alcohol. The inventory process could be endless—lists of alterations and pages dedicated to the topic can be found all over the Internet.[7] However, more than specific cases, what I wanted to illustrate was just how much Nintendo's overbearing attitude hung heavily over third-party licensees and stifled their creative aspirations. One game in particular, however, was about to cause changes so deep that it would create a chasm—or rather a "khasm." Before we get to that, we need context.

Interlude: CD-ROMs and FMV Games

Ever the technological stalwart of game culture, by the mid-1990s, the PC had seen a great adoption rate of CD-ROM players thanks to "killer apps" such as *The 7th Guest*, *Myst*, *Star Wars: Rebel Assault*, *Wing Commander III: Heart of the Tiger*, and *Phantasmagoria*. Interactive movies (also known as "Full-Motion Video" [FMV] games) were one of the newer up-and-coming genres that stood at the edge of current video games and provided a glimpse into what the "Future of Games" might look like. Magazines enthusiastically covered CD-ROM technology and the blending of games and cinema as the way forward to the future, in part, because such a framing provided a road to the cultural legitimization of video games.[8] *Nintendo Power* printed an article in April 1992 titled "Super NES Technology Update—CD-ROM" (*Nintendo Power* #35, April 1992, 70–71), in which it covered the 1992 Winter CES presentation of Nintendo and Philips's SNES-CD add-on. Screenshots from *The 7th Guest*, the hit FMV PC game for which Nintendo reportedly spent $500,000 to obtain the rights, appeared in the magazine, as the game and system were demonstrated in a private showing. The FMV train was moving fast, and it looked like games might integrate into mainstream culture soon.

Star Wars: Rebel Assault featured original footage digitized from the *Star Wars* films, and its 1995 sequel, *Star Wars: Rebel Assault 2: The Hidden Empire*, was the first time the *Star Wars* universe had seen live-action footage since *Return of the Jedi* in 1983. FMV games would try to deploy the film industry's "star power" as much as possible. *Wing Commander III* starred Mark Hamill as a starfighter pilot (this time *sans* lightsaber), with Malcolm McDowell and John Rhys-Davies as supporting cast. Tia Carrere could be seen in *The Daedalus Encounter*, and the David Duchovny/Gillian Anderson duo appeared in *The X-Files Game*. Games were on their way to something like "respectability" (i.e., cultural legitimization) thanks to these crossovers. Games were going mainstream (at least in this specific sector; in the larger home consoles market, the effect of the ReNESsance was still strong, and video games were seen as just that, games—and games for children, specifically).

Hollywood and Silicon Valley, it seemed, were destined to merge—a movement whose detractors were all too happy to prematurely christen as "Silliwood." One thing many gamers, reviewers, and magazine editors noticed is that going mainstream meant going simpler and blander. Their objections concerned the nature of the gameplay experience that CD-ROM technology afforded. The only thing you could do with film clips was start or stop them; once started, they would simply go on, and you would sit there without interacting. It had started in the arcades, where early LaserDisc games such as *Dragon's Lair* in 1983 or *Mad Dog McCree* in 1990 impressed audiences but ultimately fell short on exciting gameplay. Watch film clip and wait for the right moment, aim quickly and shoot, watch film clip that acts as reward or punishment, and wash, rinse, and repeat.

This basic template is ironically a system that Nintendo had used in a pioneering form of "interactive cinema" way back in 1974 with the electromechanical arcade machine *Wild Gunman*. A 16-mm projection apparatus would play a film scene on the screen, and when the gunman's eyes flashed brightly, players had to draw the light gun from the holster and quickly shoot the target. Depending on their speed, one of two film clips would be switched on by the machine, with the gunman either triumphing or dying. On a purely mechanical level, this simple branching system functioned exactly as a reflex testing machine that lights up a button and asks the player to tap it down as soon as possible, with a certain timed threshold resulting in failure. Of course, playing the game amounted to a much richer experience than simply tapping a button. Here we see a particular graphical regime, one that has since been deployed into quick time event scenes in modern games: the "timed trigger and reward." The main reason that people played these games was to enjoy the images being shown as the conflict or task to be accomplished was set up and the corresponding reward after successfully accomplishing the task. While the images are noninteractive (the player simply has to do something by some timed point or fail), their presence is key to the game experience and, indeed, is the game's *raison d'être*. The CD-ROM's storage capacity and random access to data provided the technical key for these games to be made in the domestic space.

Answering the Call of Cinema and TV

Nintendo passed on the opportunities of FMV games, leaving the Philips CD-i *Hotel Mario* and *Zelda* trilogy to die by the wayside, ideally with as little promotion as possible (see chapter 7). Nintendo did, however, partake in the Silliwood program through an ambitious experiment: making a film adaptation of *Super Mario Bros.* (1993). At first glance, that idea wasn't so bad. Nintendo characters had graced the small screen through multiple animated series, including *Captain N: The Game Master* (1989), *Super Mario World* (1991), and *The Adventures of Super Mario Bros. 3* (1990). These were all preceded by the *Super Mario Bros. Super Show!* (1989), which ran for three seasons and distinguished itself by alternating animation and live-action segments within each episode.

Naturally, the idea of having a live-action Mario jumping around was pretty quirky. Could Mario become live-action material? On the one hand, he was a human; on the other hand, he was the only human thing in the Mushroom Kingdom, a fantasy land rendered in cartoon form anyway. What would goombas, koopas, and Bowser even look like if Mario were an actor in a cap and overalls? The *Super Mario Bros. Super Show!* supplied as good an answer as any: Mario was Lou Albano, former wrestler and ring manager of Italian-American descent and fitting stature. The live-action segments would show Mario, Luigi, and various visiting celebrities in their Brooklyn plumbing business and depict their past life in the real world before they took a warp pipe to the Mushroom Kingdom and lived their grand adventures (the latter being animated segments). This solution had the advantage of taking the filming completely out of the fairy-tale setting, thereby suspending any questions of accuracy between the live-action show and the games.

The live-action solution would not fly, however, in making the transition from the small to the silver screen and from 10-minute comedic skits to a full-blown narrative. The fan site smbmovie.com chronicles the film's extensive solution-seeking work, which went through seven early script drafts by eight different writers in nine months. Production hit numerous roadblocks typical of the film industry: egos, filming schedules, misadjusted sets and props, and competing visions among creatives and financiers (Reeves 2013; Harris 2014, 317–323). Because producing a movie was squarely outside Nintendo's creative capability range, the firm had been completely hands off in the process. The disastrous result of the movie, a critical and box-office failure, no doubt reinforced the central Nintendo tenet of "never relinquish control." Either Nintendo would jump into film production and produce its own movies or it wouldn't have anything to do with them at all. Following its principles of staying lean in its software orientation, and facing the impossibility of laying a vertical hand over the filmmaking process like it had done with video game production, it quit.

In the end, Nintendo wouldn't go to the movies, and movies wouldn't come to Nintendo. However, some form of cinema found its way to a few third-party developers who pushed "cinematic" content on the SNES. If Nintendo couldn't integrate cinema in its core, then it would paste it over the surface.

The Seeds of Moral Panics

Digitized graphics started appearing in home video games around 1990, following the early push of rotoscopy made famous by Jordan Mechner's *Karateka* and *Prince of Persia*. Animation filmmakers had been using the rotoscope since the 1920s. The device was used to trace over previously filmed actors' movements, frame by frame; the technique allowed artists to replicate the lines of the silhouette and body exactly as they moved, on a frame-by-frame basis. Mechner had filmed his younger brother performing the basic motions needed for the game and had traced his silhouette for each frame in computer graphics. As a result, movement in *Prince of Persia* reached considerable fluidity and realism. The game's success spawned a number of variations, including *Another World*, *Flashback: The*

Quest for Identity, *Blackthorne*, *Nosferatu*, and *Lester the Unlikely*. These games would eventually be retroactively grouped into a subgenre: the "cinematic platformer" (note the name).

Digitization was about to push that logic further. The process was simple: Rather than having computer artists create graphics by filling in grids of pixels with colors, with one slightly different image for each frame of animation for each character, the developers would shoot actors against bluescreen backgrounds, filming them or taking photographs, and digitizing the picture frames one by one to make up a game's sprites and animations. Once the digitized pictures were in, it made no difference for programming: Sprites were sprites, assemblages of colored pixels organized in a grid, no matter what their ultimate origin had been. Individual frames could be touched up and special effects integrated into the animation. This technique avoided the issues with interactivity that FMV games had bumped into. The dissolving of motion into individual frames brought the source material into the realm of animation, which made the pictures as malleable as standard computer graphics.

One of the earliest games to have used the technique was Atari's *Pit-Fighter*, released for the arcades in 1990. Martial artists (and cheering spectators) had been filmed, the pictures digitized in computers, and animated in the game. Atari's poster (intended for arcade operators) claimed the game had been "Made entirely of DIGITALLY PROCESSED GRAPHICS for the ultimate in realism!" More interesting, it claimed a relation of kinship with the seventh art: "Camera 'zoom' and side-to-side 'pan' for a more cinematic look!" The idea was simple but the execution tricky because the core competencies of video game artists and programmers typically did not cover the various areas of filmmaking expertise required: the obvious issues of camera framing and operation, but also costumes, sets, make-up, lighting, digital photography editing, and so on. Moreover, convincingly integrating the shot characters into varied digital environments soon appeared all but impossible, especially because of lighting. Characters shot in bright light would appear to be in bright light anywhere in the game, even in game environments that were pictured as darker.

However imperfect they were, digitized graphics unquestioningly brought video games a step closer to the age-old quest for realism and achieved the literal technical benchmark of photorealism. That proved to be a step too close for some, who started paying closer attention to video games that showed "real people" bleeding and getting dismembered, their digital portraits accompanied by their digitized screams. "Welcome to the Next Level," as Sega would say.

From ReNESsance to Resistance: The *Mortal Kombat* Tipping Point

Nintendo's cultural fight with Sega—and with its own heritage to a degree—is best encapsulated in the *Mortal Kombat* fiasco. *Mortal Kombat* took the fighting game genre to new extremes—cranked it to 11, in colloquial speech. It combined the photorealistic digitized graphics of *Pit-Fighter* with the supernatural, physics-defying special moves of *Street Fighter II* and smeared buckets of blood and gore over it all, in the tradition of some particularly violent arcade games such as *Smash T.V.*[9]

Porting the game to home consoles was financially inevitable but culturally problematic given the role game consoles played in many American homes as a supervised alternative to the disreputable arcades. Sega's publishing philosophy was based on consumers' freedom of choice, and so appeared more amenable to this kind of game. As the company faced games with increasingly realistic violence, it created the Videogame Rating Council in 1993, a panel of psychology and media experts that would rate Sega games in one of three categories: GA for general audience, MA-13 for "mature" gamers 13 years or older, and MA-17 for adults. Where would *Mortal Kombat* land? Well, if a game where digitized actors can rip out the heart or spinal cord of their opponents amid pools of blood doesn't get the MA-17 rating, what could possibly justify it? However, the game had to get the MA-13 rating to sell to teenagers, Sega's main target. A wily stratagem let Sega have its cake and eat it too: The Genesis version conserved all the blood and gore of the highly violent arcade version but only if the player entered a "blood code" in the menu. Nintendo's SNES version was, for its part, irrevocably toned down, with characters losing gray "sweat" when hit instead of blood and similarly limited and less gory "fatality moves."[10]

The SNES version of *Mortal Kombat* was largely derided and tarnished Nintendo's image as a "kids' games" company, which played right into Sega's marketing strategy. Nintendo wasn't happy about this because even now it was trying to get rid of its heritage from the American Video Game ReNESsance. Gamers sure weren't happy about this either, as a reader letter from Mike Haney in the *Super NES Buyer's Guide* from March 1993 (months before the game was even released) illustrates:

> I have read that the mega-hot coin-op Mortal Kombat is going to be done by Acclaim for the Super NES. At first I thought that was great, but since the Big "N" has been known to insist that "excessive" blood and violence be removed from games for their systems, I don't know if the game is really going to be that great. We have something in this

country called "Freedom of choice." It is our right to choose what we watch on TV, or what games we play. I for one won't buy the game if it isn't the best translation possible. And, since it is supposed to be 16 megabit, I would believe that there should be enough memory to include all the characters, moves and even the fatalities. Also, since it is to be a high memory game, I refuse to pay $90 for a game that won't have the fatalities just because of Nintendo's archaic "no violence" policy. (*EGM* #44, March 1993, 6)

These realities took on a wholly new dimension during the 1993–1994 U.S. congressional hearings on the video game industry and offensive contents. At the initiative of Senators Herbert Kohl and Joseph Lieberman, the hearings examined games with disturbing contents—chiefly, *Mortal Kombat* and *Night Trap*, with their digitized graphics and live-action filmed actors—to decide whether they should be banned or regulated. If the video game industry wasn't willing to self-regulate its contents, then Congress would pass bills or form a regulatory agency to do so.

The hearings and the creation of the ESRB are often discussed as part of the general history of video games, but they have had a major impact on Nintendo, and on the cultural legacy of the NES and the ReNESsance more specifically. Nintendo claimed the moral high ground because it had always shut out all possibly controversial contents from its platforms; its version of *Mortal Kombat* had been sanitized, after all. Nintendo's approach was in truth already a mixed blessing: Although it preserved its image as a provider of "family-friendly" entertainment to the general public, it also alienated a large portion of its already maturing user base, as well as limiting the creative freedom of its third-party developers. Ultimately, Sega and Nintendo joined forces to pass a plan, which led to the creation of the Entertainment Software Rating Board (ESRB).

This news was bad for Nintendo because it dismantled the beneficial effects of its strategy in the public sphere. Nintendo had always been identified (and identified itself) as the console of choice for families and young children; Nintendo was a trusted brand, with exhaustive content guidelines that purportedly protected the children. Creating the ESRB leveled the playing field because Nintendo could no longer claim the moral high ground; any game for kids could appear on any platform, and with proper age classification, any game with mature contents could appear on any platform without harming the platform owner's reputation. The congressional hearings had crystallized in the public sphere what industry insiders had known for years: that video games were not kids' stuff. In the following months, Nintendo began shedding off its old skin. Seasons had come and gone, and the Nintendo Kids of yesteryear had grown and matured. They had fallen in with the wrong crowd, fallen prey to the bad influence of Sega. It was time to reclaim them.

Phase 4—Resistance: Rebellion in Dream Land

All the transitions between the phases of the American Video Game ReNESsance are fluid and imprecise to a degree, but the one between decline and resistance is particularly so. I would argue that the moment when Nintendo begins to fight against its own ethos marks the beginning of the resistance phase. It must be understood as two simultaneous processes: Nintendo resisting its own heritage, and the ReNESsance resisting and persisting in the public realm despite all attempts to move on because public perceptions do not change overnight with new marketing campaigns and slogans. Nintendo's first step was launching its "The Best Play Here" campaign (Elliott 1994), moving the target of marketing from children between 6 and 14 years of age to an "MTV generation" of 9- to 24-year-olds (Wesley and Barczak 2010, 20). In the process, Nintendo took a page or two from Sega's TV advertisement book. Taking a cue from the "Nintendo Is What Genesisn't" failure, I'd be tempted to describe the attempt as "Nintentries What Genedid."

A *Super Metroid* commercial shows this new direction. A scientist-looking young "geek chic" man explains that Nintendo wanted to make sure its latest *Metroid* game was the best ever before releasing it. He explains this while reining in a menacing Doberman ("Killer"), with subdued barks and growls, who attempts to chew the camera—us, in first-person, extreme, Sega Shout-style. Locked into a playtest room, the dog barks as light comes out of the door's window slit; an impressive rapid-sequence montage of gameplay against enormous bosses, explosions, and speed running illustrate the young man's commentary, who accentuates the "24 megs" of content that make up "Nintendo's biggest game ever." He then opens the door to reveal that the menacing Doberman has become a frightened Chihuahua before yelling, "Ship it!" The ad concludes with the tagline, "The best play here. Super Nintendo Entertainment System."

Fighting fire with fire, Nintendo stepped it up in July 1994 by launching an important promotional campaign around its new-found slogan: "Play It Loud." Teenagers could conceivably "rebel out" by playing Nintendo games at a high volume, hence disturbing their parents' tranquility. Conceivably, but embarrassingly, this is what good-boy bourgeoisie rebellion looked like. It was all the more hilariously inefficient if gamers were engaging in this rebellious attitude while playing their Game Boy with headphones. In 1995, Nintendo remarketed its popular handheld console in a variety of colored cases, christened the Play It Loud! series. Although the innards were the same (and should not be confused with the 1998 Game Boy Color hardware), the marketing embraced attitude—or rather wanted to. *Nintendo Power* put an ad with cool dudes (mysterious shades, black hair, yellow sunglasses, green punk hair) and gals (bold and flashy redhead, young woman with shaved head) (*Nintendo Power* #72, May 1995, 86–87). Surprisingly (and tellingly), the ad was advertising a contest to design an ad for the Game Boy Play It Loud! series. This strategy is as good as any when you have no idea how to market a product to a certain demographic: ask them for ideas. By this point, it seems obvious that Nintendo had no idea what its demographics were, let alone how to speak to them.

Still, the tone and target audience shifted. Many advertisements went into gross-out marketing—a full two-page spread opened many issues of *Nintendo Power* by showing a huge jar full of toenail clippings. Sometimes it was the iron stare of a grandmother handing out a huge platter of meat-loaf, with plenty of texture details thrown to the reader's face. Nintendo, through its advertisements and games such as *Killer Instinct*, was combating and resisting the ReNESsance's legacy, which persisted and resisted among entire groups of the general public for whom video games still were kids' toys.

One of the best illustrations of Nintendo's newfound coolness can be seen in *Donkey Kong Country*, a rhetorical incarnation of Nintendo's will in renewing its corporate identity by playing on "edgier" ground while enforcing conservative gameplay modes that capitalized on its own design expertise and history, in line with gamers' expectations. It all started before the game was even released. When *Nintendo Power* subscribers received their February 1994 issue of the magazine, they also got treated to a VHS tape titled "Donkey Kong Country Exposed." It started with a serious-looking "WARNING: The video you are about to see contains scenes of a graphic and animal nature. Anyone who may be offended by such material should leave the room now." The video then opened with a flash-cut montage of teenagers discussing, wearing backward baseball caps, athletic jerseys, or earrings. They went live-reporting behind the scenes for a look at the game, meeting developers who explained the technology. Their discussions ended on them agreeing that "it's a game that's ahead of its time," before a montage of in-game footage and playing teenagers was shown, with the "Play It Loud!" slogan presented to a suitably rocking rhythm of distorted guitars.

It's all in there: teenagers instead of kids, edgy look and promotion technique, and attitude through the slogan and music; all is set to break away from the "old" image of Nintendo. The game *Donkey Kong Country* did exactly the same in its introduction screen. An old bearded monkey played a gramophone record—that's Donkey Kong, the star of the old, quasi-mythical game—before getting promptly ejected by the new, hip, and cool Donkey Kong, who barged in with his stereo player and danced to a new, rocking soundtrack. We could almost hear him say to us, "Play It Loud!" Two of the most cutesy game heroes or franchises are emblematic of this shift to the "Teen Spirit" makeover. Kirby, the quintessential representative of Japan's *kawaii* aesthetics,[11] went from his traditional smiley, pinky, cloudy marshmallow self to a mean-looking thug aesthetic (well, as thuggish as a pink puff can possibly be), taking a mug shot at the Metro Police Department with stubble, bandage, angry eyes, and frown. "He used to be such a good boy," the title reads, before the text goes on:

> Sad. One day you're cute 'n cuddly. The next, you're burying your opponents and spitting on your enemies. Who's to blame? Bad parenting? One too many sitcoms? Either way, the mutant marshmallow is now on 16-bit in two games. [...] Yes, His Flabbiness is back in two new games for SNES. And this time he's here to separate the men from the cream puffs. (Nintendo of America 1995a)

Baby Mario, co-starring in *Super Mario World 2: Yoshi's Island*, also got the Play It Loud! treatment. A two-page ad paints the baby as "outta control," advising players to "put on a fresh diaper." Pictured, we find baby Mario's nursery room, wallpaper torn out, eggs smashed all over, window broken, and underwear drawer half-ripped open. A nice touch of Sega-esque competitor-denigrating marketing accompanies a screenshot: "Kicking, shrieking, crying, tantrums...and that's just the guys who bought new systems" (Nintendo of America 1995b).

After years of overbearing control and "content guidelines," mature games finally got their place at the Nintendo table in 1995. The extreme violence of *Mortal Kombat II* came to the Super NES wholly unaltered, and id Software could finally bring *Doom* over for dinner, with blood and gore intact—and even a blood-red cartridge. Nintendo did more than simply open the gates, however: It took a game that was under development at Rare (Nintendo's trusted second-party developer) and made it into its next poster franchise: *Killer Instinct*. No more confusion; Nintendo had found something to prove its "street cred" that it really wasn't a kids' games company anymore. Even the black cartridge said so—now *this* was different.

The new games fed into a renewed marketing circuit in obvious and somewhat entertaining ways. Examining the cover of Nintendo's Spring 1996 catalog for "Super Power Supplies" reveals some of the different products (clothes, magazines, keychains, watches, etc.) floating around a brain that has been partitioned between hit Nintendo games, all in psychedelic colors and style. Uncharacteristically from Nintendo, Mario is nowhere to be seen, at first. It turns out that he is there after all, only he's tucked away in the corner of the faceplate of a *Yoshi's Island* watch, itself appearing in a small bubble floating around. That's quite the demotion for a character that, just a few years ago, was touted as being more famous than Mickey Mouse among children. ("How art thou fallen from heaven, o Mario!", the Biblical analogy would now go) Flipping the catalog open does not reveal the traditional assortment of Mario pajamas, bedsheets, or lunchboxes either but rather the *Killer Instinct* products page. The first item listed is a "KI Motorcycle Jacket." "From Nintendo Kids to Nintendo Bikers" would have made a compelling headline.

After the Fall: The Nintendo Dark Age

Nintendo would rely on Rare to continue its soul-searching over the next years with the Nintendo 64. *GoldenEye 007* and *Perfect Dark*, a pair of celebrated shooters, were soon one-upped by *Conker's Bad Fur Day*, a twisted, irreverent take on cutesy cartoon characters gone haywire with guns, gore, profanity, alcohol, and scatological scenes, along with numerous popular culture and movie references to *The Matrix* and *Saving Private Ryan*, among others. It wasn't enough for Rare to put the ESRB Mature rating on the game box; an additional label at the bottom read: "ADVISORY: THIS GAME IS NOT FOR ANYONE UNDER AGE 17." If Nintendo had ever allowed a licensee to publish a game meant for a mature audience for the NES in 1989 or the Super NES in 1994, it would have insisted on having this label to clearly dissuade parents from buying the game for their children. But this is not the case in 2001 with *Conker*. Here, the logo is meant to intrigue the mature consumer—the 8–14 Nintendo Kid, now turned a twenty-something—into checking out what's such a big deal about this edgy game, not unlike the advisory for explicit lyrics found on music albums in the hip-hop, punk, hard rock, and heavy metal genres.

In hindsight, there's a clear way to frame these discursive me-too's: "Ninten's Stuck Where Genewas." It waded alone in the murky waters of its Dark Age, as we'll see in the next chapter, with the GameCube years exacerbating the firm's will to break away from its image of a "kiddie" games provider. The most telling sign of this can be found in the platform's game library, with violent and horror games appearing in much larger numbers: a 2002 remake of *Resident Evil*, *Resident Evil 0*, *Resident Evil 4*, *Hunter: The Reckoning*, and *Killer7* were all good indicators but not as much as Nintendo's publishing of its first-ever M-rated title, the horror game *Eternal Darkness: Sanity's Requiem* (Silicon Knights 2002). Eventually, Nintendo managed to "wake up" and returned to its roots with the Wii. "Entertainment for the whole family, together around the Wii," the ghosts of Famicom marketing whispered. The ReNESsance had been progressively phased out with the Dark Age, and finally a new day lay ahead, Nintendo's Wiivival.

> The difference in speed between the Space Shuttle and a snail is the
> same as the difference between ROM silicon chips and a CD-ROM, a
> difference of about 2 million times. [...] The next time someone tells
> you the CD-ROM is the wave of the future, tell them that the future
> doesn't belong to snails. (*Nintendo Power* #59, April 1994, 108)

On July 3, 2015, the Internet awoke to a weird story. Someone had recovered a long-lost prototype of the "Super NES CD-ROM." Pictures were posted, news sites reported all kinds of things, and authenticity was discussed, questioned, proved, and disproved, all at the same time. The Internet was ablaze with a fire so strong it could have roasted the top half of the exhibited machine—only because the bottom half of the machine was yellowed out, a normal consequence of the flame-retardant additive incorporated in its plastic shell, just as with the SNES. But the top half was pristine gray presumably because the flame-retardant chemical had not been incorporated in it. The Internet being what it is, message boards and comment spaces disregarded the facts and soon filled with "Obvious Photoshop is obvious," "Disgusting smokers, why didn't they put that Holy Grail in a safe," and so on.

Given that I was finishing the first draft of this book, and specifically this chapter, which focuses on the SNES-CD, I was surprised, puzzled, and worried that some heretofore unknown fact would turn up and completely invalidate everything I had written (these are the risks of working on the history of secretive corporations, I suppose). But what soon struck me the most was how the dead peripheral—a stillborn, no less—elicited a capital of sympathy among gamers. Soon, alternate histories turned up, various writers speculated on what would, might, or could have happened, how the (nonexistent) games would have stood out from their peers, and so on. The spoony bards hath awakened, and verily, their lyres pluckethed! The amount of interest the prototype generated is commensurate with the impact of its failure on Nintendo and on video game history in general. In a sense, this story shows that the SNES CD-ROM debacle encapsulates everything about the transformations of video game technology, culture, and marketing that would put an end to Nintendo's Silver Age.

The Future Was Multimedia

In the late 1980s, when NEC announced a CD-ROM player for its upcoming PC-Engine system, Nintendo got scared into developing a follow-up to the Famicom. This attests to the perceived importance of CD-ROM technology at the time. In the early 1990s, CDs were seen as a vital component of the "Future of Computers," a technological trajectory at the end of which lay vast fields ripe with possibilities.

Giovanni Dosi (1982) defined technological trajectories as trails of solutions that try to answer some engineering problem. That problem, in turn, is framed as part of a certain technical paradigm. In this framework, the home video game industry was operating at the time according to the technical paradigm of storage space maximization: Games were produced to fit on cartridges and thus had to maximize their usage of the limited storage space afforded by the cartridges' ROM. Game developers worked in that technical paradigm and sought solutions. One such solution was found, for example, in the technique of bank switching for Atari 2600 game development (Bogost and Montfort 2009b). Altice (2015) explains in great technical depth how Nintendo managed to cram so much data in its game cartridges to have its seminal *Super Mario Bros.* fit in only 40 kilobytes.

"Thinking outside the box," as the saying goes, eventually changed the terms of the problem by changing storage media altogether in favor of the CD-ROM. This completely reversed the technical paradigm. Game developers were not operating from the paradigm of storage space maximization but rather from the paradigm of storage space exploitation; developers moved from being constrained by cartridges that packed up to a whopping 32 megabits of space (4 megabytes), a technologically impressive feat for 16-bit standards, to CD-ROMs that offered at least 650 megabytes of memory. The new problem was that all this additional space had to be used somehow to demonstrate a game (or a platform)'s superior technology in the face of competitors. If *Super Mario World* could have 72 levels in 4 megabytes of storage, then having a *Super Mario World CD* with 11,638 levels just wouldn't cut it. This set in motion (quite literally with Full-Motion Video games) a trajectory of innovation that had been lying around dormant for years but could be made flesh thanks to the CD-ROM, a path that Nintendo had treaded in the past: the game console as multimedia entertainment device.

The idea that game technology would do something else, something *more* than only playing games, was not a new one when it started gaining traction in the early to mid-1990s. In fact, Nintendo had been actively pursuing it throughout the Famicom's life in Japan and attempted to do so as well for the NES in the United States. The Famicom's designed expandability could accommodate auxiliary services and complementary goods and functions. Japan was already seeing accessories meant to expand the system beyond playing games. The Family BASIC package comprised a cartridge that would allow users to program in a BASIC environment using the supplied Family Basic Keyboard and to store these user programs on the Famicom Data Recorder (a standard cassette tape recorder drive). Another high-profile peripheral was the 1988 Famicom Modem, which adults could use to trade stocks, bet on horse races, and access weather forecasts. Although these systems were not a huge success, they attest to the pursuit of such audience expansion goals by Nintendo, which attempted to reach out to family members other than the children and for activities other than playing games.

The World of Nintendo, as Provenzo noted in 1991, was bound to reach out into all kinds of other activities, which in hindsight works as a ghostly comeback of Nintendo's forays into other sectors in the 1963–1968 period, when the firm tried branching out into instant rice, taxis, a chain of love hotels, and so on. The idea of game consoles becoming multipurpose machines was seductive in the late 1980s, in part, because the market for home computers was still bustling—in Europe, personal computers such as the Commodore 64 and Sinclair ZX Spectrum were all the rage, just as the MSX computers in Japan had been a few years earlier. A trajectory of game consoles expanding to become home computers was in place, as *Newsweek* reported: "The biggest philosophical question among manufacturers at this year's CES: is the video game a mere toy, or a new communications medium? Nintendo clearly plots a course beyond entertainment for its machines" (*Newsweek*, June 17, 1990). *The Economist* reported on Nintendo's grand plans for the Brave New World of Nintendo on August 18, 1990, with an article titled "Wham! Zap! You just made a million":

This autumn Nintendo—the world's largest supplier of video games, with around 80% of the market—is set to launch a professional version of its best-selling "Famicon" (Japlish for "family computer"). Its Super-Famicon will be nothing less than a powerful business computer masquerading as a game-player.

The first of the Kyoto-based company's applications for adults will be a database package for its own distributors, who will be able to use their game-machines to dial in and find out what software products are available for Nintendo machines. This is only the beginning. Nintendo has teamed up with Fidelity Investment, an American fund manager, to develop software that will allow users to play the stock-market or to manage property. The Japanese company has also joined forces with AT&T to provide a communications network so that American households with a Nintendo in the living room can send video messages to one another. (*The Economist*, August 18, 1990, 60)

This trajectory, however, soon came under criticism. Couldn't the "Future of Games" just be full of games? *The Economist*'s report from January 19, 1991, tellingly titled "Back to Earth," nicely illustrates this quick turn-around. After pointing out that Nintendo's share price has dropped by half in 6 months and that the Super Famicom is a risky gamble for Nintendo, it weighs in against the multimedia strategy:

Perhaps the company's best hope is that Europe, where it only recently began selling its older model, will prove to be its next big market. This seems more promising than its other strategy of adapting machines for home banking or education. Video games are about addiction and fun, not learning.

Home computers constitute the first technical paradigm in the techno-logical trajectory of video game hardware serving for multiple different purposes[1], and the modern networked video game consoles with social media integration, video playback, and media server capacity are the latest (Sony's PlayStation line benefited greatly from this trajectory, with its consoles doubling as music CD, DVD, and Blu-Ray players). In between the early home computers and the later integrated games-and-media-and-network machines, however, was a substantial technical paradigm: the CD-ROM-based gaming console.

From 1991 to 1993, we find many game machines that were designed and sold as general multimedia devices: the Philips CD-i (1991), Commodore CDTV (1991), Tandy Visual Information System (1992), 3DO

Interactive Multiplayer (1993), and Pioneer LaserActive (1993). They were all able to play games but also to host edutainment software for the children, museum tours, encyclopedia, art galleries, and so on—incidentally, all kinds of things that would soon be available to everyone for free thanks to the Internet. There are probably many reasons that those platforms did not meet with success, but the rising availability of the Internet in the mid- to late 1990s (especially in the kind of techno-philic market these machines were aiming at) is surely one of them. Incidentally, I contend that these machines, taken together, should constitute the "generation 4.5" of video game historiography that I alluded to in the book's introduction. Their technological make-up, marketing initiatives, and cultural positioning exhibit distinct and common features that make them almost irrelevant as part of the "fourth generation of video game consoles."

Nintendo would be given the chance to partake in the multimedia future but would ultimately reject the SNES CD-ROM. The Super NES would concentrate on its status as a game-playing machine, in the classic sense of what video games had been up until now, upholding tried-and-true lessons. Still, the firm tip-toed in diversification efforts for the console through a range of accessories. The vast majority of them were intended for traditional gameplay purposes: specialized gamepads with auto-fire, wireless communications, slow-motion mode, programmable buttons, flight stick shape, and so on. A single-handed controller was released in Japan, specifically for playing RPGs or strategy games. Multitap adapters allowed up to five players to play together. Light guns included Nintendo's own Super Scope bazooka or Konami's Justifier. However, one of them pushed in the direction of multimedia: the Super NES Mouse, included with the important *Mario Paint*. The mouse was the quintessen-tial controller device for PCs that allowed one to browse documents, navi-gate complex graphical user interfaces, and have fine-tuned manual control over whatever it was they were doing. *Mario Paint* was a playful art studio where users could color, draw, make icons and sprites, animate pictures, and compose music. It was a suite of basic software like those found on a personal computer. It stands out from the SNES library and continues to enjoy success, two decades into the 21st century, thanks to musicians creating and uploading music made with the *Mario Paint* com-poser module.

Unique as it may stand, however, *Mario Paint* couldn't substitute for the wide range of software that CD-ROMs brought to the computers and multimedia devices of the 1990s. Unfortunately for Nintendo, rejecting the CD-ROM would not only close off the trajectory of multimedia computing but would also bring dire consequences to the traditional form of video games.

From Smokescreen to Vaporware: The SNES CD-ROM

When Nintendo formally announced its plans for a follow-up console to the Famicom in 1988, it was mainly a smokescreen in an attempt to combat the hype around NEC's PC-Engine. Ken Kutaragi, an engineer at Sony, initiated contact with Nintendo to share a sound chip he had been working on, which would be a dramatic improvement on the Famicom's. Asakura shows, through Kutaragi's notes from 1989 (Asakura 2012, 46–48), that he was pushing for a partnership with Nintendo as part of a long-term plan to get Sony in the games industry to concretize his vision of a "playstation," a mirror to the computer "workstations." Because NEC had announced (and eventually released in December 1988) a CD-ROM player add-on, the PC-Engine CD, Nintendo was afraid to lose its edge. Discussions with Sony turned to the development of a CD-ROM player for their next-in-kin Super Famicom, a logical solution given that the CD-ROM standard had been codeveloped by Sony and Philips.

Nintendo would get from Sony a Super Disc add-on for its Super Famicom, a heir to the Famicom's Disk System. The possibilities of CD-ROM storage would both expand the interactive possibilities of games and increase the technological appeal and life cycle of the console to the public. In return, Sony would get the possibility to develop and market its own Play Station machine (mind the space), a multimedia device that could read music, entertainment, educative, and multimedia CD-ROMs, as well as featuring a cartridge and controller port for playing Super Famicom games from Nintendo.

True to its business model of controlling the production chain, Nintendo asked Sony to develop a proprietary format for their software instead of using generic CD-ROMs. Sony complied, putting together the Super Disc format, a hybrid CD-ROM-in-a-plastic-disk-casing format, on the condition that it would control manufacturing and licensing for it. Surprisingly, Nintendo agreed, relinquishing an uncharacteristically high amount of control for its habits. At Sony, the terms of the agreement with Nintendo were largely seen as advantageous, leading to widespread disbelief (Akagawa 2013, 35–37). Why had Nintendo agreed to such conditions?

Most video game histories chronicle the events as follows: Late into development, when the CD-ROM add-on was ready to be revealed to the press, Hiroshi Yamauchi, for some reason, suddenly realized that the terms of the contract were too advantageous to Sony and declared this deal to have gone sour. Nintendo then secretly maneuvers to develop a partnership with Philips instead. Sony presents the SNES-CD and Play Station in a press announcement at the summer Consumer Electronics Show of 1991 on June 1. On June 2, Nintendo announces that it is rather pursuing a CD-ROM project with Philips. Scandal! Treason! Sony is humiliated. Later, at Sony in Japan, everyone has suffered from the "Philips Shock"; Ken Kutaragi pleads for Sony to pursue the game console project, meeting dissent from the conservative Sony board. Then he says, "Surely you won't let Nintendo get away with what they did to us?", and president Ohga slams his fist on the table, full of sound and fury, exclaiming "DO IT!"—that is, go on and do the PlayStation (minus the space, hence a wholly different product), and make Nintendo pay.

A number of crucial pieces are missing from this puzzle, however.[2]

Between a Rock and a Hard Place: The Sony-Philips Deals

The reason that Nintendo had agreed to the Sony deal was that it wanted to integrate a lockout chip in the Super Discs to continue with the noble tradition of its CIC and 10NES. Because Nintendo would own the chip and code that would serve as key for the software to run, it would effectively control licensing and production. Sony may have controlled the disks' hardware, but Nintendo would control the hardware-and-software lock needed to run the software on the disks. Sony, however, wanted such a lockout chip to be placed in the game console hardware rather than in the software disks and planned to protect the games and other software with data encryption instead (Dikmen, Rhizlane, and Le Roy 2011, 17). This solution was sound, and it was letting Sony control the flow of software—a big no-no in the Nintendo Economic System.

Sony may have had trouble understanding Nintendo's worries. At the time, Sony was not interested in producing video games (after all, Kutaragi had to work against the majority of the Sony board to develop the audio chip technology for Nintendo) but rather was pushing its multimedia and entertainment technologies and assets from its Sony Music and Sony Pictures subsidiaries. As Akagawa (2013, 34–35) relates, Sony's Play Station was envisioned as a way to get into the highly lucrative domestic karaoke machine market, a goal that makes perfect sense for the CD, music, and film powerhouse that the firm has always been. Moreover, as a manufacturer of televisions and VHS players (and co-developer of the CD-ROM format), Sony could stake an increased claim over the domestic, general entertainment electronics market and push videos on disc (especially music videos) to consumers. In this sense, the Super

Famicom compatibility might have been little more than a Trojan Horse for Sony, a way to seduce consumers that their children's video game machine might be replaced with a general device that would still allow them to play their games, as well as allowing adults to play or otherwise enjoy some entertainment.

If the future was to be all multimedia players, then Sony could reasonably end up being the best positioned firm in the world to profit from it. Since starting the collaboration with Nintendo in 1988, it had started moving from a technology company to being a technology and content company, acquiring CBS Records in 1987 and Columbia Pictures in 1989. Harris (2014, 136) gives this as the reason Nintendo backpedaled from the deal with Sony: It was afraid Sony would start developing content for the system, encroaching on its software-sided business model. It didn't help that Sony opened a software publishing branch in 1989, Sony Imagesoft, which would market games for Nintendo's platforms. That can't have been good news for Nintendo, which, as a self-party firm, treats third-party publishers as competitors more than allies, as we've seen in chapter 2.

These combined factors led Nintendo to seek additional leverage against Sony. Well, that and the legal bills that awaited Nintendo from Philips. One of the most interesting analyses of Nintendo's CD-ROM antics can be found in the book *La Bible Super Nintendo* (Audureau et al. 2013, 38–43), which is worth summarizing. Why would Nintendo reject the Sony project so late in the process and so unceremoniously? Incurring Sony's wrath could have led them to stop supplying the sound chip for the SNES, a key component to Nintendo's system. "In announcing its turnaround in June 1991, Nintendo not only publicly shames Sony, but also gambles on a considerable industrial risk" (Audureau et al. 2013, 40). It turns out that there's a longer history linking Nintendo with Philips, one that begins with an important event: Philips acquiring Magnavox in 1974, gaining them the all-important founding patent for video games that Ralph Baer had filed (U.S. Patent No. 3,659,284, known as "Television Gaming Apparatus"). Philips asserted the patent's reach by suing every major video game developer to obtain royalties on every video game system that was connected to a television.

When Nintendo of America entered the home video game market, Philips' lawyers proceeded to move against them for patent infringement. Nintendo of America, however, had just won their major case against the movie giant Universal Studios, which had unsuccessfully attempted to sue Nintendo for plagiarizing King Kong with its *Donkey Kong* game. Nintendo chose to fight Philips and the unbreakable Magnavox founding patent that had won against Atari, Sega, Bally, and others before. Nintendo strategized and attempted to sue Philips for inequitable conduct, demonstrating that cases of prior art existed for computer games before the filing of Baer's patent, and that they should have been disclosed when filing for the patent.[3] It didn't fly because Baer's patent was granted on the basis of making interactive applications on raster scan displays; TV display was the central point, and there was no prior art of games using TV displays. Checkmate.

After Nintendo's claim was rejected, Philips proceeded to sue them. The case was set to court in 1990 against impossible odds; it was just a matter of time before Nintendo lost, like every other console and arcade manufacturer before them. Nintendo wanted to settle and so had to offer something. It had just signed, on January 1, 1990, the contract for the Super Famicom CD add-on with Sony (Asakura 2012, 48) and was negotiating with the co-inventor of the CD-ROM. What had looked like a checkmate might turn around and offer a way out. Ralph Baer reveals that Nintendo paid $10 million to North American Philips in 1991 to cover all past patent infringements, a sum that he qualifies as "cheap" to resolve the issue. In all likelihood, that symbolic amount was part of a bigger deal between the Japanese and European firms which called for Nintendo to abandon its partnership with Sony and let Philips develop the Super NES CD-ROM add-on instead, as well as granting Philips the rights to publish video games starring two of Nintendo's most valuable intellectual properties, *Mario* and *Zelda* (which resulted in the infamous CD-i games *Hotel Mario*, *Link: The Faces of Evil*, *Zelda: The Wand of Gamelon*, and *Zelda's Adventure*). This episode led Audureau et al. to conclude: "More than a temporary nuisance, Philips is in truth a powerhouse in the industry, from a technological and legal standpoint" (Audureau et al. 2013, 41). The SNES-CD story certainly seems to support it.

After Nintendo's backstabbing episode, Sony nevertheless continued working with them. Dikmen, Rhizlane, and Le Roy claim these second-round negotiations happened because Sony threatened to sue Nintendo for breach of contract (2011, 18), whereas other accounts speak of Nintendo suing Sony instead. According to Akagawa, it would later be proved that the whole Philips deal was only intended by Nintendo to stall development on Sony's PlayStation (Akagawa 2013, 39). In any case, development work on the SNES-CD advanced substantially. *Electronic Gaming Monthly* mentioned definite plans in June 1992:

> One of the biggest surprises at the Winter Consumer Electronics Show was Nintendo's announcement of some of the specifications for their

upcoming Super Nintendo CD-ROM drive. Their press release stated that their unit would be in the stores as early as January 1993, and that it would sell for only about $200! Add in the fact that almost all of the specifications they published equalled or exceeded the ones for Sega's Mega CD-ROM, while the price was only about half of what Sega's unit was selling for at that time in Japan ($370). (*EGM* #35, June 1992, 48)

What ultimately happened is that Nintendo dealt with both firms to honor its agreements simultaneously. In October 1992, Sony and Nintendo announced the Play Station, set to "combine Nintendo's Super NES home video game system with a CD-ROM drive" (*The New York Times* 1992), for which Nintendo would control licensing over all game software, while Sony would deal with non-game software (multimedia encyclopedias, music, educational titles, etc.). In parallel, Philips would be manufacturing a CD-ROM add-on to the Super Famicom and Super NES—the SNES Nintendo Disk Drive—whose software would be compatible with Philips' CD-i player.

These plans were all set to go. *Electronic Gaming Monthly* had a feature on the Super NES CD in their March 1993 issue, discussing technical specs and claiming that development had been recently finalized at Nintendo of Japan. The general "gaming gossip" section even stated: "As you'll read in this ish, the Super NES CD-ROM is far from vaporware!" (*EGM* #44, March 1993, 46) Nothing materialized, however, and the project of a CD-ROM add-on just went up in smoke. The whole project had started as a strategic necessity to stay relevant in an era dominated by CD-positive games futurology, which Nintendo's competitors NEC and Sega fully embraced. But as months passed, Nintendo observed the occasional misfortunes and general low performance of the Sega CD add-on, which was adopted by fewer than 10% of Mega Drive owners (*Screen Digest*, March 1995, 60). Nintendo passed up on CD-ROM technology, pulling through the years with expansion chips in its SNES cartridges and pushing for its next console, a 64-bit system initially known as "Project Reality" that would become the Ultra 64 and finally the Nintendo 64. It would use cartridges, good old proprietary cartridges, with their high barriers to entry, guaranteed profit margin, and manufacturing locks, on which the Nintendo Economic System hinged.

The CD-ROM debacle led to a new discourse surfacing; because Nintendo wasn't going to have CD-ROM technology, it could reject it wholesale. Articles appeared where Nintendo decried CDs' loading times and argued for a "purity" and "back to basics" approach—a natural ambition for a firm whose business revolves around reiteration rather than innovation. *Nintendo Power* famously compared the difference in speed between cartridges and CD-ROMs to the difference between the travel speed of a space shuttle and a snail (as seen in the chapter's epigraph). Even better, the appeal to speed was also a recuperation of Sega's main war horse in marketing the Genesis as a system that was all about speed (see chapter 3). Nintendo's newfound discourse was, in a sense, a jujutsu move on Sega's brand identity, using its own strength against itself.

Although Nintendo did have a point, it was given somewhat of an undue importance by the Japanese giant, especially when compared with the digital soundtracks, sprawling environments, lush prerendered 3-D cinematics, or Full-Motion Video clips that CD-ROM games allowed. Nintendo might not have been interested in making games based on these new, CD-dependent features, but many of its third-party licensees were. Additionally, cartridge production costs were much higher to begin with and inevitably translated to a higher price point for the consumer, which together with Nintendo's stringent quality assurance process stymied experimentation and the development of risky, innovative game concepts. Silverware and spoony bards were fine as a dining experience and brought in good money, but a variety of other offers would simply never exist in this context. Many third-party game developers were enthused by the possibilities of CD-ROM storage and ultimately left Nintendo and worked mainly or entirely on rival consoles—notably Capcom, Konami, and Squaresoft.

The Rise and Fall of the Licensees

Initially, Nintendo had set on the path of closed platforms with the Famicom. It had opened to others by necessity, not by choice (Gorges 2011, 49), and put up stringent control mechanisms to tolerate licensees. Now, after Sega had shown up, it had started working on its attitude with the Super NES, but it amounted to little more than accepting them in its garden. It sure didn't make a platform *for* them. One place where this was perfectly clear was in the documentation for developers, which Nintendo provided.

Nowadays, a slew of measures to help third-party developers support a platform are considered to be a baseline requirement. However, it was not the case for earlier platform owners. In an interview with Masami Ishikawa, who designed the Sega Mega Drive, two answers are given that illustrate the mindset of the time:

How did developers create games for the Mega Drive? Did Sega supply development kits or frameworks?

MI [Masami Ishikawa]: As far as I know, they were using ZAX Z80 emulators to develop game programs. It was nothing like modern-day software development environments, which are equipped with libraries and SDKs. I recall that programmers were studying the source codes of the test program I made for debugging in order to develop each function.

[...]

Did games developers and designers have any input into how the hardware was designed?

MI: The process was not like it is today—we did not ask software developers for opinions. We simply had a one-way meeting when we finished drafting the specs. (Stuart 2014)

Nintendo and Sega's documentation for their 8- and 16-bit consoles, for instance, consist of little more than lists of addresses and dry data, devoid of any explanations and contextual information. Moreover, the documents have been translated from Japanese into an overly cryptic and byzantine form of English that anyone who has played 8-bit video games will readily recognize.[4] As a matter of fact, Australian developer Beam Software got its authorization from Nintendo and became one of the first foreign developers for the Famicom by reverse-engineering the Famicom and producing quality documentation in better English, which Nintendo eventually started distributing to its third-party developers.[5] Parsing out Nintendo's Super NES documentation may have felt more like deciphering an inventor's private notes than reading an instruction manual explicitly written with an effort to be helpful, resulting in a difficulty of access that was further compounded by the "silverware" architecture of specialized components requiring specialized knowledge to handle correctly (to say nothing of the platform's legal and financial barriers to entry described in chapters 1 and 2). As a result, all it took was a developer-friendly platform and business model to steal Nintendo's thunder, leaving it alone to dine on its precious silverware. This is what happened between the mid-1980s and the mid-1990s.

The following figures compare data on the sales of games by publisher for different platforms. For each platform, I took the listed total worldwide, cumulative-to-date sales for software titles, as tallied on the VGchartz website. I then made a list of all million sellers (titles that have sold more than 1 million copies), a common benchmark for noteworthy and profitable games, the goal of any game publisher in the hit-driven video games market.[6] I then tallied up the total count of software sales for each publisher by adding up the sales from these million sellers. Figures 7.1–7.4 represent not how many games were made but how many "hit" game copies were sold by each publisher.

As the data show, the spread of sales is limited on Nintendo's consoles, particularly when compared with Sony's PlayStation. The Super Famicom is also the platform where third-party licensees sold the most copies of games compared with Nintendo—in other words, where they encroached on Nintendo's software-side garden the most. The Nintendo 64 numbers show the isolation in which Nintendo found itself. Why was there a lack of third-party game developers to support the Nintendo 64? Because by the mid-1990s, most of them had left the Nintendo playground for the greener

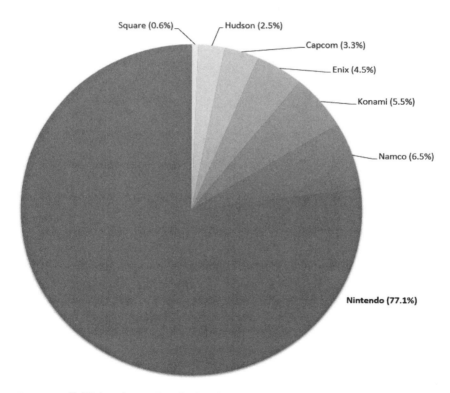

Figure 7.1 Publisher shares of total sales of million-sellers for the Famicom/NES. (Total: 233.68 million copies)

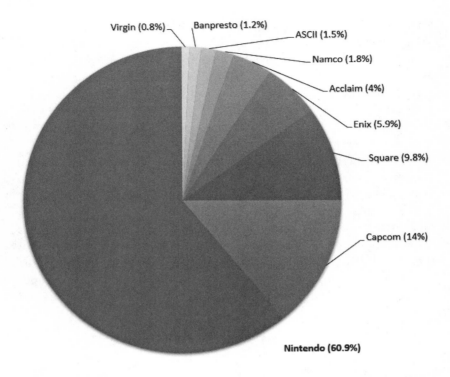

Virgin (0.8%)
Banpresto (1.2%)
ASCII (1.5%)
Namco (1.8%)
Acclaim (4%)
Enix (5.9%)
Square (9.8%)
Capcom (14%)
Nintendo (60.9%)

Figure 7.2 Publisher shares of total sales of million-sellers for the Super Famicom/Super NES. (Total: 143.6 million copies)

pastures of Sony, who wowed them with two key technologies that were all the rage in the 1990s: high-powered real-time polygonal 3-D processing and the CD-ROM as a high-capacity storage media. Beyond the "wow" factor, however, Sony seduced them because it actually courted them.

The Sony Creative Expansion (SCE) Model

When Sony entered the video game industry in 1994, its policies shifted the positioning of third-party developers and publishers from outside the platform ecosystem to inside its boundaries. In this respect, Sony leaned further away from vertical integration and more toward the horizontal form characteristic of the network organization. This was entirely different from Nintendo's system and pushed Sega's openness further. The PlayStation was not there primarily for Sony to publish its own games (symptomatically, its launch in the United States did not include a pack-in game, contrary to about every other major video game console so far) but was a game machine destined to play a wide host of different games, just

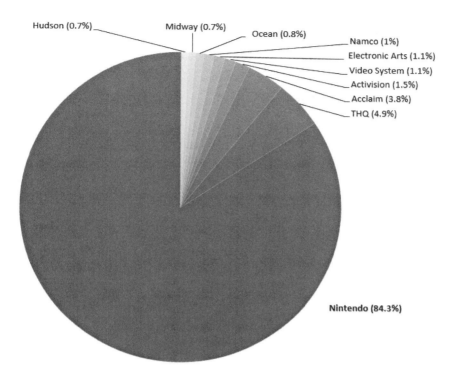

Hudson (0.7%)   Midway (0.7%)   Ocean (0.8%)

Namco (1%)
Electronic Arts (1.1%)
Video System (1.1%)
Activision (1.5%)
Acclaim (3.8%)
THQ (4.9%)

Nintendo (84.3%)

Figure 7.3 Publisher shares of total sales of million-sellers for the Nintendo 64. (Total: 142.75 million copies)

like the record, VHS, and CD players were not manufactured for a particular film studio or record label to push its entertainment products.

Like Nintendo, Sony would control the manufacturing and distribution of licensed games. Like Sega and unlike Nintendo, it would sell the system at a loss to build market share and make money on subsequent software titles. Unlike both Sega and Nintendo, it would not make its own games the core of the PlayStation's business proposition but rather put extensive effort into making things easy for third-party developers and publishers. Where Nintendo was a reluctant gatekeeper that carefully screened anyone who showed up to enter its walled garden, Sony not only opened wide the licensing gates (like Sega) for any game to be made as long as the developer paid the fee, but went an extra mile by offering rides and guided tours to make sure everyone would be comfortable.

From Platform Owner to Platform Provider
Although this shift in emphasis may seem subtle, it leads to a major difference in the role of the platform owner. Whereas Atari, Nintendo, and

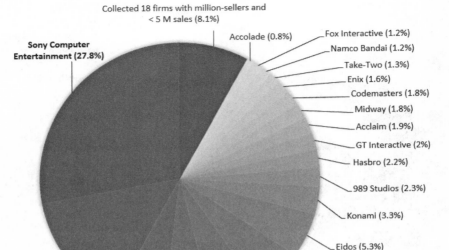

Collected 18 firms with million-sellers and < 5 M sales (8.1%)

Accolade (0.8%)

Sony Computer Entertainment (27.8%)

Fox Interactive (1.2%)

Namco Bandai (1.2%)

Take-Two (1.3%)

Enix (1.6%)

Codemasters (1.8%)

Midway (1.8%)

Acclaim (1.9%)

GT Interactive (2%)

Hasbro (2.2%)

989 Studios (2.3%)

Konami (3.3%)

Eidos (5.3%)

THQ (5.7%)

Electronic Arts (14.2%)

Activision (5.8%)

Square (5.9%) Capcom (5.8%)

Figure 7.4 Publisher shares of total sales of million-sellers for the PlayStation. (Threshold: 5 million copies; total: 426.65 million copies)

Sega were platform owners—game developers and publishers that also developed and sold game machines and accepted some licensed third parties for complementary goods—Sony stepped in as a platform provider. Instead of being a game developer, the platform provider is a technological supplier and production facilitator for game developers and publishers, playing the role of the middle man between consumers buying games and the parties that make them. It had to develop its own games, of course, to kick-start the adoption of its platform, but internal game production was a means toward an end rather than the other way around.[7] Whereas Nintendo distinguishes itself from other platform owners through its software orientation, Sony can be said to have adopted a service orientation. As a technology company with no expertise in game development, it approached the video game industry from the perspective of a hardware manufacturer and standard bearer, providing services to other firms that would produce the content. Sony's template became the new blueprint for subsequent entrant Microsoft, which adopted the model with its Xbox console.

Sony's plan had all the right tools to accomplish this revolution. On the development side, they assembled an internal team solely dedicated to helping out third-party developers and listening to their feedback. Moreover, they supplied a software development kit to game developers, with proper documentation, sample code, and detailed instructions to help them work with the intricacies of the hardware. More important, they also innovated by providing software libraries to developers, modular parts of code supplied to deal with common features that developers often needed to implement—a kind of basic building block. This new proposition in the world of home consoles initially required adaptation from developers, who had to trust the platform provider and work from the tools it provided them instead of writing every single part of their code from scratch. Developers quickly got over their sentiment of losing control however when they realized how streamlined it made development: They could now stage a structure with Lego bricks instead of spending their time melding their own plastic pieces.

This was a different kind of brick-handling than what licensees had been subjected to in the Kyoto firm's imperial garden.

Bricks in the Network Wall: The Nintendo Economic System

The Nintendo Economic System, with its various criss-crossing policies, constructed a hybrid organizational structure that straddled the categories of hierarchical and network structures in a demonstration of what Melissa Schilling qualified as modular organizational forms relying on contract manufacturing to engage in "loose couplings" (Schilling 2003b). Jennifer Johns (2005) has similarly detailed the global and international production networks of video games for both the hardware and software sides of the market.

Hierarchical and bureaucratic structures allow a firm to be more focused and efficient in attaining its goals. A common form of business-to-business relationship in this context is for a firm to attempt vertical integration, which consists of buying or taking control over most or all stages of a given product's life, from production to consumption—for instance, a console manufacturer deciding to acquire a semiconductor manufacturer rather than purchasing its semiconductors. The downsides of vertical integration are that it decreases a firm's flexibility and concentrates risk because the corporation owns every segment of the product chain. For example, if a new technology suddenly renders semiconductors obsolete, then the vertically integrated firm is stuck with useless semiconductor factories and needs to spend resources dealing with this. On the upside, vertical integration increases coordination and control over the market, supply, and profit margins; a vertically integrated firm depends on fewer intermediaries, which is a rare and valuable freedom in business.

Among the many other types of organizational structures, the network is the most pertinent to understand Nintendo. The network structure increases cost-efficiency by having component suppliers, distributors, and all other actors involved along the product delivery chain undercut each other through competition; it also distributes risk among all participating firms. In the tech industry, this advantage is particularly important because technology firms need to venture into research and development (R&D) and new technological developments all the time, always risking that its manufacturing facilities get stuck on a bad technology gamble. This is why the tech industry is particularly volatile for investors. It's also worth noting, following Casey O'Donnell, that although network structures are typically regarded as being less hierarchical, it is not an automatic principle:

> Too often networks are talked about as inherently open, better, or different than hierarchical systems, yet networks can be just as hierarchical. There is nothing fundamental about networks that make them naturally flat or more open. They must be constructed in ways that enable flatness or openness. (O'Donnell 2011, 95)

Nintendo has made extensive use of the network structure in developing a "fabless" ("fabrication-less") production model: "At Nintendo, we do not own the production factories that manufacture our products. All production processes are outsourced to external suppliers and production factories (production partners)" (Nintendo Co. 2016b). Normally, the trade-off is that the network structure limits the firm's control over its partners' processes, thus preventing tight integration and resultant economies and introducing delays in manufacturing as the different partner organizations each negotiate their own schedules. A semiconductor manufacturer may reduce the production volume of a chip Nintendo needs to start producing a new standard, leaving Nintendo empty-handed or facing chip shortages—which is exactly what happened in 1988 (Lazzareschi 1988).

But Nintendo's business architecture has managed to minimize almost every disadvantage and achieve a best-of-both-worlds situation, a vertically integrated network—a wall. The first, counterintuitive element we need to acknowledge to truly understand Nintendo's positioning is that Nintendo is not a technology company. It lets technological firms such as Cisco, Intel, Silicon Graphics, IBM, and so on innovate and take the risks, along with the commensurate rewards, to develop the right technologies. Then, as these firms sell their new technologies at premium prices to recoup their R&D expenses, it looks at the "last-gen tech," those seasoned or withered technologies in an industry where everyone else is using the top-of-the-line novelties. In this, Nintendo occupies a unique place as an entertainment company with a "software orientation," contrary to its modern competitors Sony and Microsoft, which are technology companies that leave most of the software to third-party licensees.

Nintendo's reliance on hardware suppliers organized as a network would normally rob them of the advantages of vertical integration—controlling costs and supply. But in fact, Nintendo still manages to control costs and supply by resorting to "old" tech because the rate at which new technology costs go down is appreciable. The other way of bringing down costs is to place large orders, which allows streamlining of the process, stability, and predictability—all desirable features for a production firm. The resulting economies of scale can confer enormous advantages that make ownership of the production process through vertical integration almost irrelevant. As an indication of the scale we are talking about, Steve Jobs explained that the same 68000 processor used in the Apple Lisa had its price shaved off by 80% for the large quantities ordered for the Apple Macintosh (Sen 2012, 32:00). These are not questions of details. Nintendo's phenomenally large initial order for the Famicom from semiconductor supplier Ricoh resulted in such rock-bottom costs that the firm managed to market the Famicom at a price point no competitor could match.

Now, if Nintendo's strategy is so good, then why don't other firms opt for it too? Part of the answer is that Sony and Microsoft are large tech companies, with games being only part of their activities; developing, manufacturing, and selling technology products is their main business. The other part of the answer lies with Nintendo's unique fiscal policy of accumulating savings and holding onto them. Whereas corporations typically take on strategic debt and invest capital in the hope of creating growth and generating ever-increasing returns on investment, Nintendo stockpiles cash and assets. Inoue wrote in 2010: "In December 2008, its cash and cash-equivalent assets totaled more than one trillion yen" (Inoue 2010, 100)—the equivalent of $11 billion. That's with absolutely no debt to repay, an anomaly in the modern corporate world. These cash reserves are essential for Nintendo to place large orders from committed manufacturing partners: "For a fabless company that doesn't own manufacturing facilities, the cash is important as a guarantee of credit" (Inoue 2010, 101).

The combined effects of these elements help us appreciate how Nintendo built its Super Power. Through its immense cash assets, it secured very advantageous prices on older and cheap components, alleviating the downsides of not practicing vertical integration and freeing it from long-term commitment to any technology. It also allowed Nintendo to market consoles without subsidizing and needing to recoup their hardware losses, and the nonstandard architectures gave Nintendo a lead time on third-party developers to sell its own games. This more than enviable position was the result of former president Hiroshi Yamauchi betting the bank (literally) on the Famicom/NES, investing all profits from the hugely lucrative Game and Watch portable systems to develop the Famicom (Gorges 2011). As the gamble paid off with immense profits, Yamauchi resisted the temptation of diversifying the company's activities, creating more products, borrowing money, and making acquisitions (a decision probably informed by its failed diversification attempts in the 1960s and 1970s). Instead, he put all Nintendo's money in a war chest to weather the inevitable storms to come in the video game industry's notorious boom-or-bust business. He was going to need it, time and again, but especially so against the biggest shock Nintendo would face: Sony's PlayStation.

Behind the "Sony Shock": Technological and Commercial Innovation

What happened in the closing years of the Super NES's life was a marketing and distribution revolution to which Nintendo failed to respond. This marked the second time Nintendo failed to react appropriately as the incumbent market leader (Subramanian, Chai, and Mu 2011, 230), following Sega's successful Genesis push in North America. Both of these situations confirm the important impact of two factors studied by Melissa Schilling (2002): a learning orientation, which Nintendo lacked because of the glittering NES gold and shiny SNES silverware, and an appropriate timing of entry, which the big N was too slow in seizing. Innovation from competitors sent them reeling.

Veryzer's model of technological innovation (1998) considers a firm's technological capability as separate from its commercial capability; innovations may likewise inscribe themselves in technological continuity/discontinuity and commercial continuity/discontinuity. Subramanian, Chai, and Mu (2011) summarize technological discontinuity as taking place "when a new functionality is introduced in an innovation that is beyond the scope of the industry's existing technological knowledge base" and commercial discontinuity "when existing customers change the way they perceive and use the innovation" or "if the innovation is capable of attracting a new set of customers as its potential users." The Super NES, as should be clear by now, is continuous on both counts. Moreover, as I've demonstrated, Nintendo remained on course and resisted every new technologically discontinuous innovation that appeared during the SNES years, while also enforcing commercial continuity through its Nintendo Economic System as much as it could get away with. This may explain just how badly Nintendo was struck by Sony's entry in the video games market, an entry that was founded on a double discontinuous innovation with the PlayStation, both technological and commercial.

Sony contributed to the structure of the home video game market by giving more creative support to game developers but also because its CD-ROM technology and distribution infrastructures changed the fundamental dynamics of the market's supply and demand by dramatically lowering the manufacturing cost of game software and considerably augmenting the flexibility of its distribution. In this sense, Sony resolved some of the most important tensions inherent in marketing disruptive technologies: establishing customer-oriented distribution and distribution-oriented pricing (Moore 2014, 197–212). The production of cartridges involved long delays, high initial production volumes, and fixed shipment sizes, resulting in a general lack of agility in responding to the demands of the market and a need for nothing less than clairvoyance in predicting the market's demand, as Malik (1997) details:

> While the Sony PlayStation uses CD-ROMs, Nintendo 64 uses cartridge-based games. CDs are preferred by developers for a variety of reasons. For starters, a CD can hold up to 650 megabytes of data, while a cartridge's storage capacity is only 16 megabytes.
>
> In addition, Nintendo makes these cartridges in Japan and it takes about three months for developers to lay their hands on the blanks, which means the game developers have to second-guess the demand and run the risk of making a costly mistake. Blank cartridges sell for around $35, while blank CDs sell for about $6.
>
> Wrong forecasts may leave developers with either huge excess inventories or not enough copies of a hot title. In comparison, CDs have a turnaround time of less than two weeks. "CDs give higher margins to third-party developers, one of the main reasons they are attracted to the Sony PlayStation platform," adds IDC's Zinsmeister.
>
> A higher installed base, which means higher volumes, a bigger library of titles and a cheaper medium, gives Sony a price advantage. The company can sell PlayStation games for about $35 in retail outlets,

while Nintendo games are in the $75 price range thus limiting sales. The problem is exacerbated by Nintendo's demographics—most N64 players are in the 8-to-14-year-old age group. Kids generally don't have $75 burning a hole in their pockets. (Malik 1997)

In contrast, "PlayStation CD-ROMs could be produced in required quantities in as little as one week, and shipped in less than 24 hours thanks to Sony Music's efficient distribution service. And we could even produce very small orders of tens of copies" (Akagawa 2013, 106). CD-ROMs allowed a model of "repeat business," where game quantities could be ordered repeatedly as they were sold instead of huge (and risky) quantities determined from trying to guess demand months ahead of time. This occasioned a paradigm shift from production- to customer-oriented distribution: Consumer demand would pull in additional production as needed instead of top-heavy production trying to push its products down on consumers.

Beyond Distribution and into Genre Innovation
This also translated into a platform more conducive to innovative games. Cartridges were produced using mask ROM, a type of memory that required the programming code to be locked down and converted into a mask, which would imprint the instructions into the chips themselves at the time of manufacturing. Producing the mask was time-consuming and costly. Combined with Nintendo's restrictive supply planning, the Nintendo Economic System was elitist and exacting, built to support high quantities of relatively few titles by developers with enough financial means to support the upfront costs to meet minimum order quantities. Sony gave more creative freedom to developers by lowering the entry barriers to the market, and its model was based on providing access to a large quantity of games. It achieved this goal by maintaining the game developers' profit margins and cutting its own, all the while cutting the game's retail price to consumers by almost half. These terms and pragmatic conditions stood in stark contrast to Nintendo's, as table 7.1 shows.

The model would work if consumers kept on spending as much money on games as before. The same amount would get them almost twice as many games, which would amount to total royalties to Sony about the same as Nintendo could get but would double game developers' profit margins (and possibly distribute them across twice as many game developers). Hence, Sony's strategy also worked as a mitigating factor to the video game industry's hit-driven market, where it is typically assumed that 20% of the games make 80% of the profits (Kline, Dyer-Witheford, and de Peuter

Table 7.1 Cost and price breakdown for producing a game on Super Famicom and Sony PlayStation, derived from Asakura 2012, chapter 4.

	Super Famicom	PlayStation
Retail price (for consumers)	$98	$58
Manufacturing cost	$15	$1.50
Royalty (to platform owner)	$15	$7.50
Equipment amortization cost	$10	$10
Advertising	$6	$6
Risk insurance on stocks	$5	None
Developer profit margin	$10	$10
Wholesaler profit margin	$12	$6
Retailer profit margin	$25	$17

2003, 113). The commercial affordances of Sony's PlayStation promoted innovation and risk-taking, as much as its technological affordances of increased storage space in CD-ROMs and real-time polygonal 3-D graphics.

When looking at table 7.1, it would seem that wholesalers and retailers would be refractory to Sony's pricing strategy, given the important reductions in their profit margins. Despite the raw numbers, however, the logistics of production and distribution proved highly desirable for them. Unlike product development and production, the sales and retail world revolves around product circulation and transition; inventory has to be managed, storage space is wasted space, and the ideal good is one that arrives in timely fashion, in the quantities ordered, and that flies off the shelf quickly to get more goods in and out. Nintendo cartridges were always selling but notoriously difficult to plan for, with turnaround calculated in months and quantities in fractions of registered orders. PlayStation games would net them less margin per unit, but they were priced at a sweeter spot for the customer, meaning more units would sell. They took less physical space, thus lessening the impact of unit margins in terms of volume. These combined factors led to Sony's platform being more attuned to distributors' pricing needs than previously with cartridges (especially proprietary cartridges exclusively manufactured by a platform owner who could blacklist them for going six cents below the suggested retail price, as seen in chapter 1).

This was, as Asakura (2012, 110–115) detailed, Sony's PlayStation Revolution: a technological revolution that appealed to game developers and a commercial revolution that appealed to them as well as retailers and distributors. Gamers, as the end users, were all happy to join the movement when they saw the quality and quantity of games on offer. The bricks

had been taken out of the Nintendo Economic System walls and reconfig-
ured as a paved road on the ground. The sun shone through, its rays
dancing through the vivacious gardens of Sony, basking in the glow of a
new Golden Age.

Into Twilight

One by one, Nintendo's former subjects, useful in bringing secondary
revenue and expanding their installed base, became Sony contributors.
All the weight they had gained by publishing on Nintendo's platforms suddenly shifted around, magnifying Sony's presence. Konami graced the
PlayStation with emblematic releases such as *Suikoden*, *Castlevania: Symphony of the Night*, *Metal Gear Solid*, *Dance Dance Revolution*, and *Silent Hill*,
while the N64 received the "alright" *Castlevania 64*, *Quest 64*, and *Hybrid
Heaven*. Capcom developed its *Resident Evil* and *Breath of Fire* series, as well
as its Mega Man and Street Fighter characters on Sony's platform, whereas
Nintendo had to wait more than a year for ports of *Mega Man Legends* and
Resident Evil 2. However, nothing hurt as bad as Square, with whom Nintendo had collaborated for *Super Mario RPG* and had done tests for Nintendo 64 hardware. Square brought its *Final Fantasy*, *Mana*, and *Chrono*
series to the PlayStation. In the end, these developers wanted CD-ROM
storage and creative freedom, and Nintendo wouldn't give it to them.
Licensee support plummeted as everyone left the Nintendo garden and
its obscuring walls for the evergreens of the Sony kingdom. There had
been the Resurrection with the NES first, then the Second Coming with
the SNES, and the Crusades against Sega; now, finally, the Exodus was
playing out.

Nintendo had committed to its self-party strategy. It wasn't interested
in adopting technical standards such as data storage media from other
corporations, preferring to retain absolute control over manufacturing
instead. It opted for a strategy of technological leapfrogging (Schilling
2003a) with a 64-bit processor, looking to embed technological superiority into the name of the console. In retrospect that was quite a leap to
attempt, given that 64-bit cores would reach widespread adoption in PCs
only a full decade later in 2006, when Intel released the Core 2 Duo processor for mainstream computers. Here, Nintendo may have been swept
in by the marketing "bit wars" (Therrien and Picard 2015), which focused
on consoles' bit power (as seen in chapter 3), or it may have stumbled into
Wesley and Barczak's "performance trap" (Wesley and Barczak 2010). Did
customers need 64 bits of power? No, they needed great games. Nintendo
was all about making great games, so it did not need a large supply of

third-party games. It may well be that Nintendo underestimated the draft of partners it would have to face. After all, developers and publishers had always put up with Nintendo's ways, eventually. But pride comes before a fall and arrogance was never too far off, as Jeff Ryan perhaps best captured when describing the transition from the Super NES to the Nintendo 64:

> With enough great games, Nintendo would be able to ride out the lack of third-party developers. Who cared if the shelf was mostly Nintendo for the first few years? Most of the other games merely gave the illusion of choice. ... N64 gamers, like SNES and NES gamers before them, wanted Nintendo games. They wanted Mario, and Link, and little else. (Ryan 2012, 188)

Conclusion: Silver Linings and Golden Dawns

> The game the console manufacturers are fighting is the same old battle that other companies fought at the start of the Internet, of a walled garden over open access. In the end, in my opinion, it is inevitable that the open world will kill the closed one. (Nicholas Lovell, cited in Chatfield 2011)

The Super NES's life may seem to have ended shortly after the release of the Nintendo 64, at least in the marketing practices and North American video game industry. Nintendo of America stopped shipping SNES cartridges in 1997 after a last batch of 14 games. 1998 saw the return of *Frogger*, with few changes from the 1981 original—a fitting conclusion to a console all about reiteration, and that was it. Nintendo tried to prolong its newly minted 16-bit victor in 1997 with a new, smaller, and cheaper SNES, the SNES 2 (or technically known as the SNS-101 model). The system was meant for the laggards (Moore 2014), people who for various reasons would not make the move to the 32- or 64-bit generation or who had missed out on the SNES. Japan would also see the revised system in 1998, this time called the Super Famicom Jr.

In Japan, Nintendo repeated the Famicom Disk Writer experience with a 16-bit "Nintendo Power" cartridge, a rewritable Super Famicom flash cart that could host any game that did not require an expansion chip (admittedly, quite a restriction). The service launched in 1997 and might have been Nintendo's attempt at stirring its own revolution in distribution to match Sony's CD-ROM upheaval; a rewritable cartridge eliminated stocks, distributors, wholesalers, and everything. The Nintendo Power system helped the Super Famicom remain remarkably active in its late life, with 28 games produced for the Japanese market in 1997 (compared with America's 14), 18 in 1998, 19 in 1999 (to be fair, 8 of them being in the *Picross* series), and a final release in 2000 with *Metal Slader Glory: Director's Cut*—the same year Sony released the PlayStation 2, to put things in perspective.

The other key Japanese peripheral was the Satellaview, launched in 1995 and discontinued in 2000. It fit underneath the SFC thanks to the expansion port and integrated satellite communications and download into a daily schedule of gaming. Digital magazines could be read, games could be downloaded, and, perhaps curiously by modern standards, games could be played through broadcast during certain time periods that became special events or a regular "gaming programming" schedule. The Satellaview was Nintendo's integrated proposition to answer the multimedia and networking paradigms that were taking the computing and video gaming world, all the while retaining its absolute control.

Next Generations

The youth of today and tomorrow may not get to experience the Super NES as people did in the 1990s. Even if some of them might get their hands on a functional SNES and cartridges, they will be playing the games with at least 25 more years' worth of games in their thumbs and behind their eyes. Most of them will play SNES games in emulators such as SNES9X or ZSNES, content with the various *ad hoc* modifications that these emulators use to support certain games that use nonstandard programming routines and tricks of the original hardware—notably, the work that was done in expansion chips. (byuu 2011, 1) Few of them will probably see the point in choosing *higan*, an emulator by byuu first known as *bsnes* that strives for cycle-accurate emulation at the cost of considerably higher computing requirements. Nevertheless, byuu's dedication to the integral, hardware-specific ideal is commendable, and his research into reverse-engineering low-level quirks in the SNES's functioning is helping the technically oriented get a firmer grasp on the system's unique affordances.

Still, more young gamers will probably be playing enhanced remakes of "old" SNES games or perhaps their spiritual successors, homages to the Queen of 16 bits by talented game developers who were influenced by the console. The rise of independent or "indie" games in the mid 2000s, thanks to digital distribution and the democratization of game development tools, resulted in a number of titles that fall into this category. *Axiom*

Verge and *Cave Story* pushed the 2-D platformer action-adventures of the *Metroid* and *Castlevania* series, whereas *Scott Pilgrim vs. the World: The Game* evoked the beat-them-alls of the 1990s (starting with *River City Ransom* on the NES). All of these games offer a curious assemblage of retro aesthetics: The music and sound uses chip sounds and techniques from the 1980s, but the graphics are done in 16-bit SNES style and color palettes. Other games such as *Terraria* and *Stardew Valley* have picked up the visual style of the SNES without the 8-bit sounds.

Beyond specific indie games, the SNES's graphics left behind a stylistic legacy that has reached widespread representation and acceptance. In 2011–2012, the Grand Palais museum of Paris hosted an exhibition on the history of video games, whose visual identity revolved around a picture of the Grand Palais's surroundings populated by game characters from various eras. They were all rendered as sprites on an isometric background, with a color palette that evoked the SNES. The exhibition's curators proposed a periodization of video game history in the accompanying book and described the 1983–1990 period with the keyword "pixel," whereas the 1990–1995 period is designated as "pixel art" (Clais, Alves, and Dubois 2011). This periodization is congruent with the main thesis we explored in the book: that the Super NES was a refinement, an iterative enhancement of what the NES offered. It brought pixels to the status of art form.

Parallel Lives

Beyond the legacy it left, the Super NES persists and lives on. In 2016, Square-Enix published a remastered version of its Super Famicom game *Romancing SaGa 2* for mobile platforms, making it available in English for the first time, 23 years after its original Japanese release. In 2013, a game was published for the long-thought-dead console: *Nightmare Busters* (Arcade Zone 2013), a game that had been developed in 1994 and got shelved when publishing was canceled. It finally found its way, and design-wise it plays like a time capsule from 1994. (Kohler 2014) Super Fighter Team, the publisher, was also joined by Piko Interactive, a developer and publisher of games for older systems that has published or acquired multiple games since its founding in 2013.

The homebrew scene has a role to play in this as well. The practice of ROM hacking is one way by which gamers extend the life of classic Super NES games by developing fan translations for Japanese games and alternate versions of games with different levels, gameplay possibilities, graphics overhauls, or even full-blown new adventures. The portal romhacking.net currently lists 22 hacks for *The Legend of Zelda: A Link to the Past*, 96 for *Super Metroid*, and 150 for *Super Mario World*. *Zelda3: Parallel Worlds* provides a complete new adventure, one that proved too challenging to many gamers. This spurred PuzzleDude to develop a hack of the hack, *Zelda 3: Parallel Remodel*, which preserves the essence of the hacked *Zelda* but lowers the difficulty.

Even more interesting cases of hybrid, ghostly extensions keep popping up. byuu's *higan* emulator features support for an expansion chip, the Media Streaming Unit (MSU1), which allows the Super NES to access data of up to 4 GB in size. Essentially, it functions as a bridge to receive the data that would normally, according to plan, be sent to the SNES through Sony's SNES-CD. Matthias Dagler (d4s) has created a *Super Road Blaster* ROM, a port of *Road Blaster* (*Road Avenger* on the Sega CD) for byuu's MSU-1-equipped virtual SNES. In July 2016, possible worlds, parallel worlds, and alternate realities converged into *Super Boss Gaiden*, a homebrew game that was released for the SNES and the SNES-CD. Although currently only one person in the world owns an SNES-CD, a game exists that is compatible and operational on the prototype for a platform that never existed. Or has it not existed, in the eyes of spoony bards and thanks to Nintendo's super power, even if the silverware was nowhere to be seen?

From Darkness to Light

This book may have been about the "dark side" of the Super NES and Nintendo, but as I wrote at the beginning, there's no arguing with the SNES's lasting appeal and ongoing esteem. Nothing in this book will change that, and I plan to continue enjoying the SNES games that I have known for 20-some years now. If anything, the Super NES shows us that, although we may always look forward to new, original ideas, we may overvalue innovation as a criterion of historical relevance. Certainly academics and typical video game historians are prone to value "firstness" above all else, whereas gamers and sometimes game reviewers may appreciate the umpteenth iteration in a series or genre.[1] This discrepancy might form a rift between the ongoing historical accounts and research and the past practices and current appreciation of the gaming heritage across a wide spectrum of gamers. In time, this rift might feed back into a misinformation echo chamber of its own (Therrien and Picard 2014), as academics and historians bring the "firsts" into the spotlight and devalue reiterations, although they may be more representative of the gaming practices of the period. Although I have consistently minimized the innovative aspects of the SNES and its games library in this book and showed how in almost every case its innovations came from some other prior art, this should be no reason to ignore the impact these various reiterations have had.

The SNES also alludes to ethical questions of obsolescence and supersession, in line with the work of James Newman (2012). In answering the ever-forward push toward more, new, never-before-seen experiences, we might overlook and indeed stifle the possibilities to reach deeper into already treaded waters. In a paradoxical reversal of Nintendo's surface-and-core duality at the end of this book, a platform owner bent on reiteration and a platform made of conservative technology, exclusionary marketing policies, and enforcing a homogenizing culture may end up favoring the in-depth exploration of certain design ideas and experiences.

Call it a triumph of human creativity over corporate business if you will. Through the various forms of its afterlife, gamers, homebrewers, hackers, and next-generation game developers are collectively exploring the creative affordances that had been left latent in the SNES, finally free from the chains of marketing constraints—free from Nintendo's Super Power. It is as if the SNES encouraged us to dwell in 2-D, challenging (but not impossibly so), relatively short or bite-size game experiences. For a while longer, perhaps, to reach further along the ideas and aesthetics of the late 1980s and early 1990s, and to bring them to perfection, instead of skipping ahead and surfing along the surface of constantly shifting ludic proposals in a search for golden ages that glitter and fade as new dawns break.

In the end, silver is stronger, and it's up to all of us spoony bards to keep its shine. That may be our own Super Power.

Notes

Introduction

1. I am being hyperbolic here to drive the point home. In fact, Nintendo can do (and has done) well even with plummeting home console market share, given the formidable gold mine the Game Boy became and the incredible accumulated treasury the firm has banked on (see chapter 7).
2. These numbers are disputed by Sega fans, who claim the total was higher if counting alternative hardware releases and combining sales of add-ons and other related hardware, for extended time periods, and other caveats. Some even claim that, in truth, Sega won the war. This goes to show how deeply zealous the devotees were (and still are) to their platform and corporation, as I explore later in chapters 3 and 6. The key issue is that Sega's Genesis sales are woefully undocumented.
3. I thank Nick Montfort for the idea of framing the Super NES era as a "silver age"; the analogy became the basis of this book's argument following his insightful suggestion.
4. Harris' "History of NOA" (Nintendo of America) chapter, subtitled "a story told in 8 bits," has its 8 bits named after "great men": Arakawa, Lincoln, and so on, all the way down to no. 8, "Nintendo Power." This bit is the only one that is not a person and, disturbingly, the only one that should have been named for a woman, as the main person behind *Nintendo Power* was Gail Tilden.

Chapter 1: Establishing the Nintendo Economic System (NES)

1. Things are changing as modern consoles increasingly feature networked applications and communications. Owning a WiiU or a PS4, for instance, gives access to lists of friends and news from them, video or voice chat, gameplay watching and streaming services, and so on.

2. For a more thorough account of the Famicom's birth, see Altice (2015, 11–17).

3. For detailed hard numbers on the NES (and, more largely, the home video game U.S. market), see Hill and Jones (2012); for the Nintendo of America insider point of view, see Sheff (1993); for an account bridging the NES in America and Famicom in Japan, see Gorges (2011) or Altice (2015) for a Platform Studies approach.

4. The *Shoshinkai* was "Japan's main association of toy industry retailers [...], a multitiered distribution network" (Harris 2014, 326) that Nintendo had progressively come to control because its products were such a large part of the toy industry. See Gorges (2011, 49) or Harris (2014, 326–327) for more.

Chapter 2: Minutes to Midnight

1. This trickling has occurred most imperfectly, as when *EGM* showed a picture of the Super Famicom and "Famicom adaptor" prototypes from the November 21, 1988, press conference but labeled them as the "Super Famicom and the original Famicom" instead (*EGM* #2, July/August 1989, 39).

2. The text is available on the MobyGames database (http://www.mobygames.com/game/super-mario-world/cover-art/gameCoverId,79893/). Some highlights will illustrate the tone: "Mario's off on his biggest adventure ever. [...] Guide Mario and Yoshi through nine peril-filled worlds [...]. Use Mario's new powers and Yoshi's voracious monster-gobbling appetite as you explore 96 levels [*sic*] filled with dangerous new monsters and traps. [...] Mario's back, and this time he's better than ever!"

3. Incidentally, this factor is tied to the games as well, as it allows more games to be stored on the console or more complex games that will utilize the added storage to create new experiences. That said, modern game consoles are increasingly pushing a number of auxiliary features that may result in intrinsic valuation. See the discussion on "multimedia" in chapter 6.

Chapter 3: "Now You're Playing with Power ... Super Power!"

1. *Lewis Galoob Toys, Inc. v. Nintendo of America, Inc.*, U.S. District Court for the Northern District of California—780 F. Supp. 1283 (N.D. Cal. 1991). http://law.justia.com/cases/federal/district-courts/FSupp/780/1283/1445354/.

2. Translated as *Paratexts. Thresholds of interpretation* (Genette 1997). The actual first appearance of the word is in *Introduction à l'architexte* (1979).

3. Dunne 2016 substantially develops this point and devotes the paper to this topic.

4. For a more in-depth discussion, see: http://www.gamepilgrimage.com/content/smashing-myth-about-speed-and-power.

5. https://trademarks.justia.com/745/34/melt-o-vision-74534584.html.

Chapter 4: Beyond Bits and Pixels

1. Because this chapter focuses on the technical material hardware, I have tried to use "SFC" and "Super Famicom" to describe what is inside both the Japanese and North American/European systems. When I use "SNES" or "Super NES," I

refer specifically to the North American console, which usually distinguishes itself from the Japanese system by its exterior casing design, controller, logo and color scheme, promotional materials and 1991 launch, and linguistic or cultural alterations in its game library.

2. See, for instance, the thread "Advantages of SNES hardware vs. Genesis hardware," started by "Jeckidy" on the *Sega-16 Forums*, with 2166 messages from 2012 to 2015. In-depth topics also abound on the NesDev forums (http://forums.nesdev.com), and particularly the SNESdev subforum.

3. The article with the interview is widely cited across the Internet, but at the time of writing, the Nintendojo site returns a 404 error. I'm citing a March 24, 2016, archival copy from the Internet Wayback Machine (https://web.archive.org/web/20160324155943/http://www.nintendojo.com/archives/interviews/view_plain_item.php?1130801472).

4. I have used words that I esteem to be common and more likely to get the point across, such as "first-person" or "isometric," but I want to note that the Game FAVR paper that Côté, Larochelle, and I wrote is mainly a terminological contribution to a standardized vocabulary that rejects many of these terms. See Arsenault, Côté, and Larochelle (2015) for more.

5. Readers interested in the detailed workings of sprites, tiles, memory management, and other programming techniques should search online for the SNES game development documentation, the Super Nintendo Development Wiki, and the NESDEV forums or turn to Nathan Altice's *I AM ERROR* for a legible and extensive description of Famicom programming, which the Super Famicom largely reprises (namely, the PPU's raw 8:7 aspect ratio, scrolling mechanisms, vertical blank [VBLANK], and object attribute memory [OAM] cycling considerations).

6. See *EGM* #28 (November 1991, 160): "From the initial games that we've previewed, a combination of flicker and game slow down has occurred that severely detracted from our overall enjoyment of the games. This is especially true when the game throws more objects on the screen to make contest [sic] even more challenging. Game players don't want to finish their new games overnight and when some of the titles actually get easier, because of unexpected slow-down, it defeats the purpose."

7. Note that three-color sprites do not translate into three-color characters because characters could be assembled from multiple sprites; a metasprite could thus feature more than three colors.

8. It is obviously difficult to provide general estimates for the wide library and relative diversity of games that appeared on the console (see http://www.gamepilgrimage.com/content/sega-genesis-vs-super-nintendo and some of the sources behind).

9. See Furniss (1998, 18–19) or Cavalier (2011) for more details.

10. Atmospheric perspective consists of applying colors that are increasingly close to a unified blue/green tint as represented objects are farther away to imitate the effect of the atmosphere on color. *Dragon View* makes exemplar use of the technique by shading the 3-D environment in appropriate hues, contributing to establish an impression of depth and distance to the spaces.

11. See a paper I previously published with Audrey Larochelle (Arsenault and Larochelle 2014) for examples and an expanded discussion on what we called "layered Z-space."

12. YouTube user NicksplosionFX has compiled every Super Famicom/SNES title screen playing out in a single 9-hour video titled "Super Press Start."

13. Exact citation from my notes taken during Skot Deeming's presentation at the Université de Montréal, "Skot Deeming présente: Microfabricants. Les débuts du développement 'fait maison' sur le ZX Spectrum," March 23, 2016, on the exhibit held at the *Carrefour des arts et des sciences*, titled "Micromakers: The Beginnings of Homebrew Development on the ZX Spectrum."

Chapter 5: The Race to 3-D

1. This section proceeds from and summarizes some earlier work (see Arsenault and Larochelle 2014 for more details).

2. Isometric projection is a specific type of axonometric projection, founded on equal angles for all three axes of the representation. Most video games do not use 60-degree angles because this causes imperfect ratios for vertical and horizontal pixels, which results in jagged lines. Accommodating monitor resolutions often makes game developers turn toward dimetric projection (one angle for two axes, a different one for the third axis) or, more rarely, trimetric projection (all three axes use a different angle). This means most axonometric games emphasize two or one dimension(s) over the other(s), as reduced angles imply an axis with reduced range (see Arsenault and Larochelle 2014 for an expanded discussion).

Chapter 6: The American Video Game ReNESsance

1. Japanese criminal groups that can be imperfectly but succinctly described as the "Japanese mafia."

2. This logic also extended to "game paks" and their packaging (Altice 2015, 108–109).

3. Zantor135, "Atari 2600 commercial December 17 1977." https://www.youtube .com/watch?v=YJNbhekKShI. Published December 28, 2011.

4. memphiselle1, "Atari 2600 Commercials (Ultimate Collection)." https://www .youtube.com/watch?v=2jQ01NSC6Gs. Published September 14, 2014.

5. Incidentally, Nirvana's song can be heard at the end of a "trainumentary" short film created for the Sega test department, "This Is SEGA TEST," at the 24:00 mark.

6. DigThatBoxRETRO, "Pole Position—Atari Video Game Commercial— Atari 5200—1983 MTV Commercial." https://www.youtube.com/watch?v =kiEj4RNpYME. Published August 15, 2010.

7. A special mention goes out to *Illusion of Gaia* for tackling some quite disturbing themes. In the city of Freejia, the player can report a hiding slave laborer to a slaver in exchange for a precious Red Jewel. Visiting the labor market, with kids chained behind bars, nets this reply from a slaver: "These laborers are the same age as you. Remember. There are people everywhere who live this way." One

laborer talks with Will: "I've tried not to think. The more I think, the more empty I become … ." Chilling.

8. The Ludiciné research group at Université de Montréal, led by Bernard Perron and of which I was a part, had a three-year research project studying the genres of interactive films and full-motion video games (Perron 2012, Perron et al. 2008).

9. Interestingly, the SNES port of the arcade game, *Super Smash T.V.*, retained most of the original's violence, even if some "blood fountain" effects were removed from bosses. This is rather uncharacteristic from Nintendo in 1991. Hypothetically, the top-down view might have minimized the perception of violence. In any case, it reinforces the argument for considering the implications of digitized graphics.

10. *Super Street Fighter II* would, in 1994, also recolor the portraits of beaten characters to display gray or white "sweat" instead of red blood.

11. *Kawaii* is the "cute" style found in fashion, cosmetics, *anime*, manga (and anything, really), as exemplified by Pikachu or Hello Kitty.

Chapter 7: The CD-ROM That Would Not Be

1. See Jimmy Maher's Platform Studies book on the Commodore Amiga, *The Future Was Here*, for an expanded discussion of these issues.

2. The story is complicated, usually partially described, and the overlapping scenes and episodes make it difficult to describe with certainty in extensive detail. My account is based on Akagawa (2013), Asakura (2000), Dikmen, Rhizlane, and Le Roy (2011), Harris (2014), Audureau et al. (2013), and the consoledatabase.com entry for "SNES CD-ROM." It should be regarded as the best possible offer I can come up with at the time of writing and one that integrates most of the facts, anecdotes, suppositions, and hearsay that was available to me in writing rather than a complete and definitive sequence of events to be accepted as "the truth".

3. *Nintendo of America Inc. v. Magnavox Co.*, U.S. District Court for the Southern District of New York - 707 F. Supp. 717 (S.D.N.Y. 1989). http://law.justia.com/cases/federal/district-courts/FSupp/707/717/1574608/

4. Altice goes in depth into the localization and translation practices of the NES in the aptly-titled *I AM ERROR* (2015).

5. Thanks to Melanie Swalwell for this illustrative piece of information.

6. The threshold of 1 million copies is, like all thresholds, arbitrary to a degree. However, it does account for the hit-driven nature of the games market and represents a comfortable profit margin that allows amortization of development costs, a minimum of return on investment for the publisher, the means to pursue other projects or grow for the developer, as well as attracting a following among gamers and gaining notoriety and positive exposure. The indie game *Game Dev Tycoon* provides a nice simulation of these dynamics and shows how a game developer may be kept in a continual struggle for survival and stagnation with sales that are "just good."

7. See Akagawa (2013, 99–124) for more on this from Sony personnel.

Conclusion: Silver Linings and Golden Dawns

1. This insight stems from collective research conducted by Bernard Perron, Carl Therrien, Guillaume Roux-Girard, Simon Dor, Andréane Morin-Simard, Hugo Montembeault, Pascale Thériault, Pierre-Marc Côté, Mikaël Julien, and Francis Lavigne as part of a research project on the history and theory of video game genres, funded by the Social Sciences and Humanities Research Council of Canada. Findings, including the games being cited and remembered for different genres by various discursive communities, are bound to appear on the LUDOV website (http://ludov.ca/), the video games observation and documentation university lab.

References

Adams, Ernest. 2009. The Designer's Notebook: Sorting Out the Genre Muddle. *Gamasutra*. July 9. http://www.gamasutra.com/view/feature/132463/the_designers_notebook_sorting_.php.

Akagawa, Ryôji. 2013. *La révolution PlayStation : Les hommes de l'ombre*. Translated by Florent Gorges and Fabien Nabhan. Toulouse: Pix'n love Editions.

Altice, Nathan. 2015. *I Am Error: The Nintendo Family Computer/Entertainment System Platform*. Cambridge, MA: MIT Press.

Apperley, Thomas, and Darshana Jayemane. 2012. Game Studies' Material Turn. *Westminster Papers in Communication and Culture* 9 (1): 5–25.

Arsenault, Dominic. 2009. Video Game Genre, Evolution and Innovation. *Eludamos (Göttingen)* 3 (2): 149–176.

Arsenault, Dominic. 2012. Nintendo Entertainment System. In *The Encyclopedia of Video Games: The Culture, Technology, and Art of Gaming*, edited by Mark J. P. Wolf. Santa Barbara, CA: ABC-Clio.

Arsenault, Dominic, Pierre-Marc Côté, and Audrey Larochelle. 2015. The Game FAVR: A Framework for the Analysis of Visual Representation in Video Games. *Loading ...* 9 (14). http://journals.sfu.ca/loading/index.php/loading/article/view/155.

Arsenault, Dominic, and Audrey Larochelle. 2014. "From Euclidean Space to Albertian Gaze: Traditions of Visual Representation in Games Beyond the Surface." *DiGRA '13—Proceedings of the 2013 DiGRA International Conference: DeFragging Game Studies* 7 (August). http://www.digra.org/wp-content/uploads/digital-library/paper_242.pdf.

Asakura, Reiji. 2013. *La révolution PlayStation—Ken Kutaragi*. Trans. O. Braillon. Toulouse: Pix'n Love.

Audureau, William, Greeg Da Silva, Rodolphe Gicquel, Michaël Guarné, Stéphane Hersin, Jean-Baptiste Jarraud, Régis Monterrin, et al. 2013. *La Bible Super Nintendo*. Toulouse: Pix'n Love.

Bangeman, Eric. 2006. Sony Taking Big Hit on Each PS3 Sold; Xbox 360 in the Black. *Ars Technica*. November 16. http://arstechnica.com/gaming/2006/11/8239/.

Barton, Matt, and Bill Loguidice. 2008. A History of Gaming Platforms: Atari 2600 Video Computer System/VCS. *Gamasutra*. February 28. http://www.gamasutra.com/view/feature/131956/a_history_of_gaming_platforms_.php.

Benchoff, Brian. 2015. Winning the Console Wars – An In-Depth Architectural Study. *Hackaday*. November 6. http://hackaday.com/2015/11/06/winning-the-console-wars-an-in-depth-architectural-study/.

Bogost, Ian. 2008. Persuasive Games: Windows and Mirror's Edge. *Gamasutra*. December 23. http://www.gamasutra.com/view/feature/132283/persuasive_games_windows_and_.php.

Bogost, Ian, and Nick Montfort. 2009. Platform Studies: Frequently Questioned Answers. In *Proceedings of the Digital Arts and Culture Conference*. http://escholarship.org/uc/item/01rok9br.

Brandenburger, Adam M, and Barry J. Nalebuff. 1997. *Co-Opetition*. New York: Currency-Doubleday.

Buchanan, Levi. 2009. Genesis vs. SNES: By the Numbers. *IGN*. March 20. http://www.ign.com/articles/2009/03/20/genesis-vs-snes-by-the-numbers.

byuu. 2011. Accuracy Takes Power: One Man's 3GHz Quest to Build a Perfect SNES Emulator. *Ars Technica*. August 9. http://arstechnica.com/gaming/2011/08/accuracy-takes-power-one-mans-3ghz-quest-to-build-a-perfect-snes-emulator/.

Cario, Erwan. 2013. *Start!: La grande histoire des jeux vidéo*. Paris: La Martinière.

Carlyle, Thomas. 1993. *On Heroes, Hero-Worship, and the Heroic in History*. Berkeley, CA: University of California Press. (1841).

Cavalier, Stephen. 2011. *The World History of Animation*. Berkeley, CA: University of California Press.

Chatfield, Tom. 2010. *Fun Inc.: Why Games Are the 21st Century's Most Serious Business*. London: Virgin.

Cifaldi, Frank. 2010. This Day in History: Nintendo Settles with the FTC. *1Up.com*. April 10. http://www.1up.com/news/day-history-nintendo-settles-ftc.

Cifaldi, Frank. 2012. Nintendo Power: Remembering America's Longest-Lasting Game Magazine. *Gamasutra*. December 11. http://www.gamasutra.com/view/feature/183233/nintendo_power_remembering_.php.

Clais, Jean-Baptiste, Douglas Alves, and Philippe Dubois. 2011. *Game Story: Une histoire du jeu vidéo*. Paris: RMN-Grand Palais.

Clements, Matthew T, and Hiroshi Ohashi. 2005. Indirect Network Effects and the Product Cycle: Video Games in the U.S., 1994-2002. *Journal of Industrial Economics* 53 (4): 515–542.

Collins, Karen. 2008. *Game Sound: An Introduction to the History, Theory, and Practice of Video Game Music and Sound Design*. Cambridge, MA: MIT Press.

Consalvo, Mia. 2006. Console Video Games and Global Corporations: Creating a Hybrid Culture. *New Media & Society* 8 (1): 117–137. doi:10.1177/1461444806059921.

Consalvo, Mia. 2007. *Cheating: Gaining Advantage in Videogames*. Cambridge, MA: MIT Press.

Covell, Chris. n.d. Super Famicom: December 1988. The First Super Famicom Demonstration. *Japanese Secrets!* http://www.chrismcovell.com/secret/SFC_1988Q4.html.

Covell, Chris. n.d. Super Famicom: July 1989. The Second SFC Demonstration. *Japanese Secrets!* http://www.chrismcovell.com/secret/SFC_1989Q3.html.

Covert, Colin. 1983. Atari, Inc. The Early Years (An Unauthorized History). *TWA Ambassador Magazine.* November.

Crockford, Douglas. 1993. The Untold Story of Maniac Mansion. *Wired.* April 1. https://www.wired.com/1993/04/nintendo-2/.

Damisch, Hubert. 1987. *L'origine de la perspective.* Paris: Flammarion.

Decuir, Joe. 1999. 3 Generations of Game Machine Architecture. Slides presented at the Classic Gaming Expo. http://www.atariarchives.org/dev/CGEXPO99.html.

DeMaria, Rusel, and Johnny L. Wilson. 2002. *High Score!: The Illustrated History of Electronic Games.* Berkeley, CA: McGraw-Hill/Osborne.

DeWinter, Jennifer. 2015. Japan. In *Video Games around the World*, edited by Mark J. P. Wolf, 319–344. Cambridge, MA: MIT Press.

Dikmen, Laure, Hamouti Rhizlane, and Frédéric Le Roy. 2011. L'instabilité des relations coopératives dans un environnement hypercompétitif : Le Cas Sony—Nintendo. In *Vingtième Conférence de l'Association Internationale de Management Stratégique (AIMS)*. Nantes (France). http://www.strategie-aims.com/events/conferences/4-xxeme-conference-de-l-aims/communications/1251-quand-la-cooperation-est-creatrice-de-la-rivalite-le-cas-sony-nintendo/download.

Donovan, Tristan. 2010. *Replay: The History of Video Games.* East Sussex, UK: Yellow Ant.

Dosi, Giovanni. 1982. Technological Paradigms and Technological Trajectories: A Suggested Interpretation of the Determinants and Directions of Technical Change. SSRN Scholarly Paper. Rochester, NY: Social Science Research Network. https://papers.ssrn.com/abstract=1505191.

Dosi, Giovanni, and Richard R. Nelson. 1994. An Introduction to Evolutionary Theories in Economics. *Journal of Evolutionary Economics* 4 (3): 153–172.

Dunne, Daniel J. 2016. Paratext: The In-Between of Structure and Play. In *Contemporary Research on Intertextuality in Video Games*, edited by Christophe Duret and Christian-Marie Pons, 274–295. Hershey, PA: Information Science Reference.

Elliott, Stuart. 1994. Nintendo Turns Up the Volume in a Provocative Appeal to Its Core Market: Teen-Age Males. *The New York Times.* July 1. http://www.nytimes.com/1994/07/01/business/media-business-advertising-nintendo-turns-up-volume-provocative-appeal-its-core.html.

Elmer-Dewitt, Philip. 1991. Hold On to Your Joysticks. *Time.* June 10. http://content.time.com/time/magazine/article/0,9171,973136,00.html.

Eyes, David, and Ron Lichty. n.d. Programming the 65816. Including the 6502, 65C02 and 65802. Western Design Center, Inc. https://wiki.nesdev.com/w/images/7/76/Programmanual.pdf.

Finn, Mark. 2002. Console Games in the Age of Convergence. In *Computer Games and Digital Cultures Conference Proceedings*, edited by Frans Mäyrä, 45–58. Tampere (Finland).

Forman, Ellen. 1989. Nintendo Zaps Blockbuster: Reproduction of Game Instructions Spurs Copyright Lawsuit. *The Sun-Sentinel.* August 13. http://articles

.sun-sentinel.com/1989-08-13/business/8902250572_1_nintendo-blockbuster
-video-games.

Fowler, Alastair. 1982. *Kinds of Literature: An Introduction to the Theory of Genres and Modes*. Oxford: Clarendon.

Fulton, Steve. 2009. Electronic Games: The Arnie Katz Interview. *Gamasutra*. December 28. http://www.gamasutra.com/view/feature/132614/electronic _games_the_arnie_katz_.php.

Furniss, Maureen. 1998. *Art in Motion: Animation Aesthetics*. Bloomington, IN: Indiana University Press.

Gallagher, Scott, and Seung Ho Park. 2002. Innovation and Competition in Standard-Based Industries: A Historical Analysis of the U.S. Home Video Game Market. *IEEE Transactions on Engineering Management* 49 (1): 67–81.

Genette, Gérard. 1982. *Palimpsestes: La littérature au second degré*. Paris: Éditions du Seuil.

Genette, Gérard. 1987. *Seuils*. Paris: Éditions du Seuil.

Genette, Gérard. 1997. *Paratexts: Thresholds of Interpretation*. Translated by Richard Macksey and Jane E. Lewin. Cambridge: Cambridge University Press.

Gorges, Florent. 2008. *L'histoire de Nintendo (Volume 1, 1889–1980): Des cartes à jouer aux Game & Watch* . Châtillon : Pix'n Love.

Gorges, Florent. 2009. *L'histoire de Nintendo (Volume 2, 1980–1991): L'étonnante invention: les Game & Watch* . Châtillon : Pix'n Love.

Gorges, Florent. 2011. *L'histoire de Nintendo (Volume 3, 1983–2003): Famicom/Nintendo Entertainment System* . Châtillon : Omaké Books.

Gorges, Florent, Julien_C, Caféine, Angel, Julo, and RaHan. 2009. La Saga de la Super Nintendo. Retour sur le parcours d'une console culte. Vol. 84. *Gameblog* podcast. http://www.gameblog.fr/podcast_87_podcast-n-84-la-saga-de-la-super -nintendo.

Gowan, Evan. 2010. Star Fox 2. *SNES Central*. March 24. http://snescentral.com/ article.php?id=0077.

Gowan, Evan. 2012. Super Mario FX. *SNES Central*. February 4. http://snescentral .com/article.php?id=1032.

Gowan, Evan. 2016. Release of the Super NES. *SNES Central*. August 21. http:// snescentral.com/article.php?id=0945.

Grant, Robert M. 2005. Rivalry in Video Games. In *Cases to Accompany Contemporary Strategy Analysis*, 5th ed., edited by Robert M. Grant and Kent E. Neupert, 211–232. Malden, MA: Blackwell.

Gray, Jonathan. 2010. *Show Sold Separately: Promos, Spoilers, and Other Media Paratexts*. New York, NY: New York University Press.

Gretz, Richard T., and Suman Basuroy. 2013. Why Quality May Not Always Win: The Impact of Product Generation Life Cycles on Quality and Network Effects in High-Tech Markets. *RETAIL Journal of Retailing* 89 (3): 281–300.

Guinn, Jeff. 1991. Son of Nintendo "Super Nintendo" Promises to Make America's Favorite Video Game Even Better—But at a Cost. *Fort Worth Star-Telegram*. June 1. http://articles.sun-sentinel.com/1991-06-01/features/9103010474_1_game -deck-super-nintendo-kathy-blackmon.

Harris, Blake J. 2014. *Console Wars: Sega, Nintendo, and the Battle That Defined a Generation*. New York, NY: It Books.

Harris, John. 2007. Game Design Essentials: 20 Difficult Games. *Gamasutra*. August 23. http://www.gamasutra.com/view/feature/130063/game_design_essentials _20_.php.

Herman, Leonard. 1994. *Phoenix: The Fall & Rise of Home Videogames*. Springfield Township, NJ: Rolenta Press.

Hill, Charles W. L., and Gareth R. Jones. 2012. *Strategic Management: An Integrated Approach*. 10th ed. Mason, OH: South-Western College Pub.

Hubner, John, and William Kistner. 1983. What Went Wrong at Atari? *InfoWorld*. November 28.

Ichbiah, Daniel. 2004. *La Saga des Jeux Vidéo: De Pong à Lara Croft*. Paris: Vuibert. (1997).

Inoue, Osamu. 2010. *Nintendo Magic: Winning the Videogame Wars*. New York, NY: Vertical.

Jeckidy. 2012. Advantages of SNES Hardware vs. Genesis Hardware. *Sega-16 Forums*. http://www.sega-16.com/forum/showthread.php?22265-Advantages-of -SNES-hardware-vs-Genesis-hardware.

Johns, Jennifer. 2006. Video Games Production Networks: Value Capture, Power Relations and Embeddedness. *Journal of Economic Geography* 6 (2): 151–180.

Juul, Jesper. 2002. The Open and the Closed: Games of Emergence and Games of Progression. In *Computer Games and Digital Cultures Conference Proceedings*, edited by Frans Mäyrä. Tampere (Finland). http://www.digra.org/digital -library/publications/the-open-and-the-closed-games-of-emergence-and -games-of-progression/.

Kalata, Kurt. 2009. Konami Shoot-Em-Ups. *Hardcore Gaming 101*. July 10. http:// www.hardcoregaming101.net/konamishooters/konamishooters.htm.

Katz, Michael L, and Carl Shapiro. 1986. Technology Adoption in the Presence of Network Externalities. *Journal of Political Economy* 94 (4): 822–841.

Kent, Steven L. 2001. *The Ultimate History of Video Games: From Pong to Pokémon and Beyond—The Story Behind the Craze That Touched Our Lives and Changed the World*. New York, NY: Three Rivers Press.

Kline, Stephen, Nick Dyer-Witheford, and Greig De Peuter. 2003. *Digital Play: The Interaction of Technology, Culture, and Marketing*. Montréal: McGill Queens University Press.

Kocurek, Carly A. 2015. *Coin-Operated Americans: Rebooting Boyhood at the Video Game Arcade*. Minneapolis, MN: University of Minnesota Press.

Kohler, Chris. 2004. *Power-up: How Japanese Video Games Gave the World an Extra Life*. Indianapolis, IN: BradyGames.

Kohler, Chris. 2014. Nightmare Busters Is an Awesome New Game for … Super Nintendo? *Wired*. January 16. https://www.wired.com/2014/01/nightmare -busters/.

Kubey, Craig. 1982. *The Winners' Book of Video Games*. New York, NY: Warner Books.

Lamarre, Thomas. 2009. *The Anime Machine: A Media Theory of Animation*. Minneapolis, MN: University of Minnesota Press.

Lane, Philippe. 1991. Seuils éditoriaux. *EspacesTemps* 47–48: 91–108.

Lazzareschi, Carla. 1988. High-Tech Crisis Forces Publishers to Make Tough Choices: Shortage of Memory Chips Hurting Video Game Makers. *Los Angeles Times*. May 26. http://articles.latimes.com/1988-05-26/business/fi-5306_1 _chip-shortage.

Lunenfeld, Peter. 1998. *The Digital Dialectic: New Essays on New Media*. Cambridge, MA: MIT Press.

MacDonald, Charles. 2000. Sega Genesis VDP Documentation. https://emu-docs .org/Genesis/Graphics/genvdp.txt.

Maher, Jimmy. 2012. *The Future Was Here: The Commodore Amiga*. Cambridge, MA: MIT Press.

Malik, Om. 1997. The Game: Sony PlayStation versus Nintendo64. *Forbes*. September 19. http://www.forbes.com/1997/09/19/feat.html.

Marchand, André, and Thorsten Hennig-Thurau. 2013. Value Creation in the Video Game Industry: Industry Economics, Consumer Benefits, and Research Opportunities. *J. Interact. Mark. Journal of Interactive Marketing* 27 (3): 141–157.

Margetts, Chad, and M. Noah Ward. 2010. Nintendojo Interview with NES Case Designer Lance Barr. *Nintendojo.com*. http://www.nintendojo.com/archives/ archives/interviews/view_item.php?1130801472=.

Maslow, Abraham H. 1966. *The Psychology of Science: A Reconnaisance*. New York, NY: Harper and Row.

McCullough, John James. 2016. Nintendo's Era of Censorship. http://jjmccullough .com/Nintendo.php.

Mecheri, Damien. 2014. *Video Game Music—Histoire de la musique de jeu vidéo*. Toulouse: Pix'n Love.

Mielke, James. 2016. The Disappearance of Yu Suzuki. *1Up.com*. http://www.1up.com/ features/disappearance-suzuki-part-1.

Montfort, Nick, and Mia Consalvo. 2012. The Dreamcast, Console of the Avant-Garde. *Loading...* 6 (9). http://journals.sfu.ca/loading/index.php/loading/article/view/ 104.

Moore, Geoffrey A. 2014. *Crossing the Chasm: Marketing and Selling Disruptive Products to Mainstream Customers*. New York, NY: HarperCollins.

Nelson, Richard R., and Sidney G. Winter. 1982. *An Evolutionary Theory of Economic Change*. Cambridge, MA: Belknap Press of Harvard University.

Newman, James. 2012. *Best Before: Videogames, Supersession and Obsolescence*. Milton Park, Abingdon, Oxon, New York: Routledge.

Newsweek. 1990. Nintendo and Beyond. *Newsweek*. June 17. http://www.newsweek .com/nintendo-and-beyond-206470.

Nintendo Co. 2016a. Hardware and Software Sales Units (as of June 30, 2016). *Investor Relations Information, Nintendo Co. Website*. https://www.nintendo.co.jp/csr/ en/q_and_a/qa3.html.

Nintendo Co. 2016b. Q&A: Business Partner Relations. *Investor Relations Information, Nintendo Co. Website*. https://www.nintendo.co.jp/csr/en/q_and_a/qa3.html.

Norman, Donald A., and Roberto Verganti. 2013. Incremental and Radical Innovation: Design Research vs. Technology and Meaning Change. *Design Issues* 30 (1): 78–96.

O'Donnell, Casey. 2011. The Nintendo Entertainment System and the 10NES Chip: Carving the Video Game Industry in Silicon. *Games and Culture* 6 (1): 83–100.

Palmer, J. 1989. Joy Toy Nintendo's Future Not All Fun and Games. *Barron's National Business and Financial Weekly*. June 26.

Parish, Jeremy. 2015. *Good Nintentions: 30 Years of the Nintendo Entertainment System*. Middletown, DE: GameSpite Publishing, LLC.

Paul, Christopher A. 2012. *Wordplay and the Discourse of Video Games: Analyzing Words, Design, and Play*. New York, NY: Routledge.

Perron, Bernard. 2012. Interactive Movies. In *The Encyclopedia of Video Games: The Culture, Technology, and Art of Gaming*, Volume 1, edited by Mark J. P. Wolf, 322–324. Westport, CT: Greenwood Press.

Perron, Bernard, Dominic Arsenault, Martin Picard, and Carl Therrien. 2008. Methodological Questions in "Interactive Film Studies." *New Review of Film and Television Studies* 6 (3): 233–252.

Picard, Martin. 2008. Videogames and Their Relationship with Other Media. In *The Video Game Explosion: A History from PONG to PlayStation and Beyond*, edited by Mark J. P. Wolf, 293–300. Westport, CT: Greenwood Press.

Picard, Martin. 2010. Pour une esthétique du cinéma transludique: figures du jeu vidéo et de l'animation dans le cinéma d'effets visuels du tournant du XXIe siècle. PhD. thesis, Université de Montréal. https://papyrus.bib.umontreal.ca/xmlui/handle/1866/3735.

Picard, Martin. 2013. The Foundation of Geemu: A Brief History of Early Japanese Video Games. *Game Studies* 13 (2). http://gamestudies.org/1302/articles/picard.

Picker, Randal. 2010. The Razors-and-Blades Myth(s). *Law & Economics Working Papers*. September. http://chicagounbound.uchicago.edu/law_and_economics/562.

Pollack, Andrew. 1993. Market Place; Nintendo's Dominance in Games May Be Waning. *The New York Times*. April 23, Business. http://www.nytimes.com/1993/04/23/business/market-place-nintendo-s-dominance-in-games-may-be-waning.html.

Provenzo, Eugene F. 1991. *Video Kids: Making Sense of Nintendo*. Cambridge, MA: Harvard University Press.

Reeves, Ben. 2013. Mario's Film Folly: The True Story Behind Hollywood's Biggest Gaming Blunder. *Game Informer*. May 28. http://www.gameinformer.com/b/features/archive/2013/05/28/mario-s-film-folly-the-true-story-behind-hollywood-s-biggest-gaming-blunder.aspx.

Reisinger, Don. 2008. The SNES Is the Greatest Console of All Time. *CNET*. January 25. https://www.cnet.com/news/the-snes-is-the-greatest-console-of-all-time/.

Retro Gamer. 2013. Super Nintendo. *Retro Gamer*. December 28. http://www.retrogamer.net/profiles/hardware/super-nintendo/.

Retro Gamer. 2015. Your Greatest Game of All Time. *Retro Gamer* 150: 62. December.

Roberts, Sam. 2009. The Rumored SuperGrafx Conversion. *Light Sword Cyber Mainframe*. http://lscmainframe.kontek.net/features/supergrafx/index.html.

Rockenberger, Annika. 2014. Video Game Framings. In *Examining Paratextual Theory and Its Applications in Digital Culture*, edited by Nadine Desrochers and Daniel Apollon, 252–285. Hershey, PA: Information Science Reference.

Ryan, Jeff. 2012. *Super Mario: How Nintendo Conquered America*. New York, NY: Portfolio/Penguin.

Schatz, Thomas. 1981. *Hollywood Genres: Formulas, Filmmaking, and the Studio System*. Philadelphia: Temple University Press.

Schilling, Melissa. 1999. Winning the Standards Race: Building Installed Base and the Availability of Complementary Goods. *European Management Journal* 17 (3): 265–274.

Schilling, Melissa. 2002. Technology Success and Failure in Winner-Take-All Markets: The Impact of Learning Orientation, Timing, and Network Externalities. *Academy of Management Journal* 45 (2): 397–398.

Schilling, Melissa. 2003a. *Technological Leapfrogging: Lessons from the U.S. Videogame Industry*. SSRN Scholarly Paper ID 2533203. Rochester, NY: Social Science Research Network. https://papers.ssrn.com/abstract=2533203.

Schilling, Melissa. 2003b. Factors Driving the Adoption of Increasingly Modular or Increasingly Integrated Forms. In *AAAI Technical Report SS-03–02*. https://www.aaai.org/Papers/Symposia/Spring/2003/SS-03-02/SS03-02-027.pdf.

Schilling, Melissa. 2006. Game Not Over: Competitive Dynamics in the Video Game Industry. In *The Business of Culture: Strategic Perspectives on Entertainment and Media*, edited by Joseph Lampel, Jamal Shamsie, and Theresa K. Lant, 75–103. Mahwah, NJ: Lawrence Erlbaum Associates. https://www.researchgate.net/publication/298787146_Game_not_over_Competitive_dynamics_in_the_video_game_industry.

Schwartz, Steven A., and Janet Schwartz. 1994. *Parent's Guide to Video Games*. Rocklin, CA: Prima Pub.

Szczepaniak, John. 2013. The Making of: *Super Castlevania IV*. *Retro Gamer* 119, 30–35.

Shankar, Venkatesh, and Barry L. Bayus. 2003. Network Effects and Competition: An Empirical Analysis of the Home Video Game Industry. *Strategic Management Journal* 24 (4): 375–384.

Sheath. 2010. 1989–1990: Competing with Speculation. *Game Pilgrimage*. April 26. http://www.gamepilgrimage.com/content/1989-1990-competing-speculation.

Sheff, David. 1999. *Game Over: Nintendo's Battle to Dominate Videogames*. London: Hodder & Stoughton. (1993).

Sloan, Daniel. 2011. *Playing to Wiin*. Chichester: John Wiley and Sons.

Smith, Tony. 2002. "Megahertz Myth." *The Guardian*. February 28. https://www.theguardian.com/technology/2002/feb/28/onlinesupplement3.

Stuart, Keith. 2014. *Sega Mega Drive/Genesis: Collected Works*. Edited by Darren Wall. London: Read-Only Memory. Reprinted excerpt available online. http://www.kotaku.co.uk/2014/10/30/sonic-helped-sega-win-early-90s-console-wars.

Stuart, Keith. 2015. Nintendo: NES to Smartphone, It's Been about One Thing—Control. *The Guardian*. March 17. https://www.theguardian.com/technology/2015/mar/17/nintendo-smartphone-iphone-nes-control-satoru-iwata-dena.

Subramanian, Annapoornima M., Kah-Hin Chai, and Shifeng Mu. 2011. Capability Reconfiguration of Incumbent Firms: Nintendo in the Video Game Industry. *Technovation* 31 (5–6): 228–239.

Takahashi, Dean. 2011. The Making of the Xbox: Microsoft's Journey to the Next Generation (part 2). *VentureBeat*. November 15. http://venturebeat.com/2011/11/15/the-making-of-the-xbox-part-2/.

Terdiman, Daniel. 2009. Is the Video Game Industry Recession-Proof? *CNET*. January 9. https://www.cnet.com/news/is-the-video-game-industry-recession-proof/.

The Economist. 1990. Wham! Zap! You Just Made a Million. *The Economist*. August 18.

The Economist. 1991. Back to Earth. *The Economist*. January 19.

The New York Times. 1992. Sony to Aid Nintendo. *The New York Times*. October 13, Business. http://www.nytimes.com/1992/10/14/business/sony-to-aid-nintendo.html.

Therrien, Carl. 2014. From the Deceptively Simple to the Pleasurably Complex: The Rise of Cooperative Address in the History of Video Games. In *The Handbook of Digital Games*, edited by Marios C. Angelides and Harry Agius, 548–572. Piscataway, NJ: IEEE Press.

Therrien, Carl. 2015. Inspecting Video Game Historiography Through Critical Lens: Etymology of the First-Person Shooter Genre. *Game Studies* 15 (2). http://gamestudies.org/1502/articles/therrien.

Therrien, Carl, and Martin Picard. 2014. Techno-Industrial Celebration, Misinformation Echo Chambers, and the Distortion Cycle. *Kinephanos, Journal of Media Studies and Popular Culture*. History of Games International Conference Proceedings. January. http://www.kinephanos.ca/2014/history-of-games/.

Therrien, Carl, and Martin Picard. 2015. Enter the Bit Wars: A Study of Video Game Marketing and Platform Crafting in the Wake of the TurboGrafx-16 Launch. *New Media & Society*. April.

The Seattle Times. 1991. Nintendo Price-Fixing Case Settled. *The Seattle Times*. April 11.

Tomasson, Robert E. 1991. Nintendo to Pay $25 Million in Rebates on Price Fixing. *The New York Times*. April 11, Business. http://www.nytimes.com/1991/04/11/business/nintendo-to-pay-25-million-in-rebates-on-price-fixing.html.

tsr. 1996. Ed Logg Interview: Tetris ... Forever. *Atari HQ*. 2000. http://www.atarihq.com/tsr/special/el/el.html.

Veryzer, Robert W. 1998. Discontinuous Innovation and the New Product Development Process. *Journal of Product Innovation Management* 15 (4): 304–321.

Weber, Jonathan. 1992. Jury Sides With Nintendo in Suit Brought by Atari. *The Los Angeles Times*. May 2. http://articles.latimes.com/1992-05-02/business/fi-1361_1_video-game-market.

Wesley, David T. A., and Gloria Barczak. 2010. *Innovation and Marketing in the Video Game Industry: Avoiding the Performance Trap*. Farnham, UK: Ashgate.

Willcox, Jaimes K. 1991. Video Games Power Up. New 16-Bit Game Systems Are Twice as Good. *Popular Mechanics*. December.

Williams, Dmitri. 2002. Structure and Competition in the U.S. Home Video Game Industry. *International Journal on Media Management* 4 (1): 41–54.

Williams, Dmitri. 2006. A Brief Social History of Game Play. In *Playing Video Games: Motives, Responses, and Consequences*, edited by Peter Vorderer and Jennings Bryant, 197–212. Mahwah, NJ: Lawrence Erlbaum Associates.

Winter, Sidney G. 1984. Schumpeterian Competition in Alternative Technological Regimes. *Journal of Economic Behavior & Organization* 5 (3–4): 287–320.

Wong, Kevin. 2013. How We Played With Power: The Secret History of "Nintendo Power." *Complex Mag*. http://ca.complex.com/pop-culture/2013/12/how-we-played-with-power-secret-history-of-nintendo-power.

Wyatt, Patrick. 2012. StarCraft: Orcs in Space Go Down in Flames. *Code of Honor*. September 27. http://www.codeofhonor.com/blog/starcraft-orcs-in-space-go-down-in-flames.

Young, Carolin C. 2014. Silverware. In *The Oxford Encyclopedia of Food and Drink in America*, edited by Andrew F. Smith, 256–263. New York: Oxford University Press.

Magazines

Billboard Magazine. November 12, 1994.

Computer and Video Games #123. February 1992. Future Publishing.

EGM² #1. July 1994. Sendai Publishing.

Electronic Gaming Monthly #1, May 1989. Sendai Publishing.

Electronic Gaming Monthly #2. July/August 1989. Sendai Publishing.

Electronic Gaming Monthly #15. October 1990. Sendai Publishing.

Electronic Gaming Monthly #28. November 1991. Sendai Publishing.

Electronic Gaming Monthly #35. June 1992. Sendai Publishing.

Electronic Gaming Monthly #40. November 1992. Sendai Publishing.

Electronic Gaming Monthly #44. March 1993. Sendai Publishing.

Electronic Gaming Monthly #57. April 1994. Sendai Publishing.

Electronic Gaming Monthly #59. June 1994. Sendai Publishing.

Electronic Gaming Monthly #63. October 1994. Sendai Publishing.

JV—Culture jeu vidéo. Printemps 2016. "Hors série—Génération Super Nintendo." Paris (France).

N-Force #10. April 1993. Europress Impact.

Nintendo Power #16. September/October 1990. Nintendo of America.

Nintendo Power #25. June 1991. Nintendo of America.

Nintendo Power #26. July 1991. Nintendo of America.

Nintendo Power #29. October 1991. Nintendo of America.

Nintendo Power #35. April 1992. Nintendo of America.

Nintendo Power #52. September 1993. Nintendo of America.

Nintendo Power #53. October 1993. Nintendo of America.

Nintendo Power #59. April 1994. Nintendo of America.

Nintendo Power #72. May 1995. Nintendo of America.

Screen Digest. March 1995. p.60.

Audiovisual Materials

The Adventures of Prince Achmed. Lotte Reiniger, 1926.

The Adventures of Super Mario Bros. 3. TV series directed by John Grusd, 1990 (1 season). United States: NBC.

Atari 2600 Commercials (Ultimate Collection). memphiselle1, 2014. *YouTube*. https://www.youtube.com/watch?v=2jQ01NSC6Gs.

Atari 2600 Commercial December 17 1977. Zantor135, 2011. *YouTube*. https://www.youtube.com/watch?v=YJNbhekKShI.

Captain N: The Game Master. TV series directed by Michael Maliani, John Grusd, Kit Hudson, and Chuck Patton (3 seasons). United States, Canada: NBC.

The Enchanted Drawing. James Stuart Blackton, 1900.

Fantasmagorie. Émile Cohl, 1908.

Gertie the Dinosaur. Winsor McCay, 1914.

Humorous Phases of Funny Faces. James Stuart Blackton, 1906.

Jurassic Park. Steven Spielberg, 1993.

The Matrix. The Wachowskis, 1999.

Pole Position—Atari Video Game Commercial—Atari 5200—1983 MTV Commercial. DigThat-BoxRETRO, 2010. *YouTube.* https://www.youtube.com/watch?v=kiEj4RNpYME.

Saving Private Ryan. Steven Spielberg, 1998.

Snow White and the Seven Dwarfs. Walt Disney, 1937.

Star Wars: Episode IV—A New Hope. George Lucas, 1977.

Star Wars: Episode V—The Empire Strikes Back. Irvin Kershner, 1980.

Star Wars: Episode VI—Return of the Jedi. Richard Marquand, 1983.

Steve Jobs: The Lost Interview. Paul Sen, 2012.

Super Mario Bros. Rocky Morton and Annabel Jankel, 1993.

The Super Mario Bros. Super Show! TV series directed by Dan Riba, 1989 (1 season). United States: First-Run Syndication.

Super Mario World. TV series directed by John Grusd, 1991 (1 season). United States: NBC.

Super Press Start. NicksplosionFX, 2014. *YouTube.* https://www.youtube.com/watch?v=w9V-A_26soM.

Terminator 2: Judgment Day. James Cameron, 1991.

This Is SEGA TEST. John Jansen, 1996.

Games Cited

This is not a critical and complete ludography of SNES/SFC games but rather a list of games cited within the book. As such, the information within is trimmed and edited to make it simple and accessible for the purpose of the book—to identify which games and which version(s) are being discussed. More information on individual games, game versions, and companies can be obtained through further research on reference websites such as *MobyGames* or *Wikipedia*, as needed.

The list is American-centric partly because the book is American-centric too. Games are listed in alphabetical order of North American titles (i.e., *Final Fantasy III* instead of *VI* and *Out of This World* instead of *Another World*). For each game, the version or port being listed depends on the book's arguments when discussing them. Disparities in title, release year, developer, or publisher are given when pertinent. Platforms have been streamlined. All computers, including the Amiga, Atari ST, ZX Spectrum, PC-88, PC-98, IBM-PC compatibles, Macintosh and Apple, DOS and Windows operating systems, and so on, have been concatenated into a global "PC" term. NES and SNES often include Famicom and Super Famicom but not the opposite.

Finally, the names of developers and publishers have been brought down to their basic, stable roots to standardize and keep the list simple and readable. For publishers, corporation, or society types, divisions, subsidiaries, and so on have been ignored (Nintendo LLC, Nintendo of America, and Nintendo Co, Ltd. are all "Nintendo"). For developers, internal team names, company suffixes, and individual celebrity persons have been ignored (Nintendo EAD, Nintendo R&D1, and Shigeru Miyamoto are all "Nintendo"). Last, supplementary particles such as "Games," "Software," "Entertainment," "Studios," and so on have often been eliminated. I have tried to ensure that the various names remain specific enough to be searchable in the future.

4-D Boxing. PC: 1991. Distinctive Software (dev), Mindscape (pub).

ActRaiser. Super NES: 1991. Quintet (dev), Enix (pub). Original release in Japan: 1990.

Adventure. Atari 2600: 1980. Atari (dev), Sears (pub).

Adventure Island. NES: 1988. Hudson Soft (dev), Hudson Soft (pub).

Age of Empires. PC: 1997. Ensemble Studios (dev), Microsoft (pub).

Akalabeth:World of Doom. PC: 1980. Richard Garriott (dev), California Pacific Computer (pub).

Alone in the Dark. PC: 1992. Infogrames (dev), I motion (pub).

Altered Beast. Arcade: 1988. Sega (dev), Sega (pub). Ported to the Sega Genesis in 1988.

Ant Attack. PC: 1983. Sandy White (dev), Quicksilva (pub).

Asteroids. Atari 2600: 1981. Atari (dev), Atari (pub). Original release on arcade: 1979

Axelay. Super NES: 1992. Konami (dev), Konami (pub).

Axiom Verge. PlayStation 4: 2015. Thomas Happ (dev), Thomas Happ (pub). Ported to PC and other consoles.

Battle Cars. Super NES: 1993. Malibu Interactive (dev), Namco (pub).

Battletoads in Battlemaniacs. Super NES: 1993. Rare (dev), Tradewest (pub).

Berzerk. Arcade: 1980. Stern Electronics (dev), Stern Electronics (pub).

Blackthorne. Super NES: 1994. Blizzard Entertainment (dev), Interplay (pub).

Bomberman. NES: 1987. Hudson Soft (dev), Hudson Soft (pub).

Breath of Fire. Super NES: 1994. Capcom (dev), Square (pub). Original release published by Capcom in Japan: 1993.

Brett Hull Hockey '95. Super NES: 1994. Radical Entertainment (dev), Accolade (pub).

Bucky O'Hare. NES: 1992. Konami (dev), Konami (pub).

Cannon Fodder. Super NES: 1994. Sensible Software (dev), Virgin Interactive (pub). Original release on PC in 1993.

Castlevania. NES: 1987. Konami (dev), Konami (pub).

Castlevania 64. Nintendo 64: 1999. Konami (dev), Konami (pub).

Castlevania II: Simon's Quest. NES: 1988. Konami (dev), Konami (pub).

Castlevania III: Dracula's Curse. NES: 1990. Konami (dev), Konami (pub).

Castlevania: Dracula X. Super NES: 1995. Konami (dev), Konami (pub).

Castlevania: Symphony of the Night. PlayStation: 1997. Konami (dev), Konami (pub).

Cave Story. PC: 2005. Studio Pixel (dev), Studio Pixel (pub).

Chrono Trigger. Super NES: 1995. Square Soft (dev), Square Soft (pub).

Clay Fighter. Super NES: 1993. Visual Concepts Entertainment (dev), Interplay (pub).

Conker's Bad Fur Day. Nintendo 64: 2001. Rare (dev), Nintendo (pub).

Contra III: The Alien Wars. Super NES: 1992. Konami (dev), Konami (pub).

Dance Dance Revolution. Arcade: 1998. Konami (dev), Konami (pub).

Defender. Arcade: 1981. Williams Electronics (dev), Williams Electronics (pub).

Donkey Kong. Arcade: 1981. Nintendo and Ikegami Tsushinki (dev), Nintendo (pub). Ported to the Famicom in 1983.

Donkey Kong Country. Super NES: 1994. Rare (dev), Nintendo (pub).

Doom. Super NES: 1996. id Software (dev), Williams Entertainment (pub). Original release published by id Software on PC in 1993.

Dragon Quest V. Super Famicom: 1992. Chunsoft (dev), Enix (pub).

Dragon View. Super NES: 1994. Kemco (dev), Kemco (pub).

Dragon's Lair. Arcade: 1983. Advanced Microcomputer Systems (dev), Cinematronics (pub).

Drakkhen. Super NES: 1991. Kemco-Seika (dev), Infogrames (pub). Original release developed and published by Infogrames on PC in 1989.

Dungeon Master. Super NES: 1993. FTL Games (dev), JVC (pub). Original release on Atari ST in 1987.

E.T. the Extra-Terrestrial. Atari 2600: 1982. Atari (dev), Atari (pub).

E.V.O.: Search for Eden. Super NES: 1993. Almanic (dev), Enix (pub). Original release in Japan: 1992.

Earth Defense Force. Super NES: 1992. Jaleco (dev), Jaleco (pub).

Eternal Darkness: Sanity's Requiem. GameCube: 2002. Silicon Knights (dev), Nintendo (pub).

Eye of the Beholder. PC: 1994. Westwood (dev), Capcom (pub). Original release published by SSI (Strategic Simulations Inc.) on PC in 1991.

FarmVille. Web: 2009. Zynga (dev), Zynga (pub).

Final Fantasy II. Super NES: 1991. Square (dev), Square (pub). Original release in Japan titled *Final Fantasy IV*.

Final Fantasy III. Super NES: 1994. Square (dev), Square (pub). Original release in Japan titled *Final Fantasy VI*.

Final Fantasy Mystic Quest. Super NES: 1992. Square (dev), Square (pub).

Final Fantasy Tactics. PlayStation: 1998. Square (dev), Sony Computer Entertainment (pub).

Final Fight. Super NES: 1991. Capcom (dev), Capcom (pub). Original release on arcade in 1989.

Flashback: The Quest for Identity. Super NES: 1993. Delphine Software (dev), U.S. Gold (pub). Original release on Amiga in 1992.

Frogger. Super NES: 1998. Konami (dev), Majesco (pub). Enhanced remake of the original release for the arcade published by Sega in Japan in 1981.

F-Zero. Super NES: 1991. Nintendo (dev), Nintendo (pub). Original release in Japan in 1990.

GoldenEye 007. Nintendo 64: 1997. Rare (dev), Nintendo (pub).

Gradius III. Super NES: 1991. Konami (dev), Konami (pub). Released in Japan in 1990. Original release on arcade in 1989.

Hang-On. Arcade: 1985. Sega (dev), Sega (pub).

Home Pong. Dedicated console: 1975. Atari (dev), Sears (pub).

Hotel Mario. CD-i: 1994. Philips (dev), Philips (pub).

Hunter: The Reckoning. GameCube: 2002. High Voltage Software (dev), Interplay (pub).

Hybrid Heaven. Nintendo 64: 1999. Konami (dev), Konami (pub).

Hyperzone. Super NES: 1992. HAL Laboratory (dev), HAL Laboratory (pub). Original release in Japan in 1991.

I, Robot. Arcade: 1984. Atari (dev), Atari (pub).

Illusion of Gaia. Super NES: 1994. Quintet (dev), Enix (pub). Original release in Japan in 1993.

Indiana Jones' Greatest Adventures. Super NES: 1994. Factor 5 (dev), JVC (pub).

Jim Power: The Lost Dimension in 3-D. Super NES: 1993. Loriciel (dev), Electro Brain (pub).

Joe & Mac. NES: 1992. Data East (dev), Data East (pub). Original release on arcade in 1991.

John Madden Football. Sega Genesis: 1990. Electronic Arts (dev), Electronic Arts (pub).

Jungle Hunt. Atari 2600: 1983. Atari (dev), Atari (pub). Original release on arcade by Taito in 1982.

Jurassic Park. Super NES: 1993. Ocean (dev), Ocean (pub).

Karateka. PC: 1984. Jordan Mechner (dev), Brøderbund (pub).

Kid Icarus. NES: 1986. Nintendo (dev), Nintendo (pub).

Killer Instinct. Super NES: 1995. Rare (dev), Nintendo (pub). Original release published by Midway on arcade in 1994.

Killer7. GameCube: 2005. Capcom (dev), Capcom (pub).

King Arthur's World. Super NES: 1993. Argonaut (dev), Jaleco (pub). Original release in Japan in 1992.

Kirby Super Star. Super NES: 1996. HAL Laboratory (dev), Nintendo (pub).

Kirby's Dream Land 3. Super NES: 1997. HAL Laboratory (dev), Nintendo (pub).

Knight Lore. PC: 1984. Ultimate Play the Game (dev), Ultimate Play the Game (pub).

Lemmings 2: The Tribes. Super NES: 1994. DMA Design (dev), Psygnosis (pub). Original release on PC in 1993.

Lester the Unlikely. Super NES: 1994. Visual Concepts Entertainment (dev), DTMC Inc. (pub).

Link: The Faces of Evil. CD-i: 1993. Animation Magic (dev), Philips (pub).

Lufia II: Rise of the Sinistrals. Super NES: 1996. Neverland (dev), Natsume (pub). Original release in Japan in 1995.

Mad Dog McCree. Arcade: 1990. American Laser Games (dev), American Laser Games (pub).

Mario Bros. Famicom: 1983. Nintendo (dev), Nintendo (pub). Original release on arcade.

Mario Paint. Super NES: 1992. Nintendo (dev), Nintendo (pub).

Maze War. PC: 1974. Steve Colley, Greg Thompson, Howard Palmer, Dave Lebling, Mark Horowitz, and George Woltman (dev).

Mega Man Legends. Nintendo 64: 2000. Capcom (dev), Capcom (pub). Original release on PlayStation in 1997.

Mega Man X. Super NES: 1993. Capcom (dev), Capcom (pub).

Mega Man X2. Super NES: 1995. Capcom (dev), Capcom (pub).

MegaRace. PC: 1993. Cryo Interactive (dev), Software Toolworks (pub).

Menzoberranzan. PC: 1994. DreamForge Intertainment (dev), Strategic Simulations Inc. (pub).

Metal Gear Solid. PlayStation: 1999. Konami (dev), Konami (pub).

Metal Slader Glory: Director's Cut. Super NES: 2000. HAL Laboratory (dev), Nintendo (pub). Released on Nintendo Power hardware system.

Metroid. NES: 1987. Nintendo (dev), Nintendo (pub). Original release on the Famicom Disk System in Japan in 1986.

Might & Magic III: Isles of Terra. Super NES: 1995. New World Computing (dev), FCI (pub). Original release published by New World Computing on PC in 1991.

Mortal Kombat. Super NES: 1993. Midway (dev), Acclaim (pub). Ported on the Sega Genesis. Original release published by Midway on arcade in 1992.

Mortal Kombat II. Super NES: 1994. Midway (dev), Acclaim (pub). Original release published by Midway on arcade in 1993.

Myst. PC: 1993. Cyan (dev), Brøderbund (pub).

NCAA Basketball. Super NES: 1992. Sculptured Software (dev), Nintendo (pub).

New Super Mario Bros. Nintendo DS: 2006. Nintendo (dev), Nintendo (pub).

NHL Stanley Cup. Super NES: 1993. Sculptured Software (dev), Nintendo (pub).

Night Driver. Arcade: 1974. Atari (dev), Atari (pub).

Night Trap. Sega CD: 1992. Digital Pictures (dev), Sega (pub).

Nightmare Busters. Super NES: 2013. Arcade Zone (dev), Super Fighter Team (pub).

Nobunaga's Ambition. Super NES: 1994. KOEI (dev), KOEI (pub). Released in Japan in 1993. Original release titled *Nobunaga no Yabō: Zenkokuban* on PC in Japan in 1986.

Nosferatu. Super NES: 1994. SETA (dev), SETA (pub).

Ogre Battle: The March of the Black Queen. Super NES: 1994. Quest (dev), Enix (pub). Original release in Japan in 1993.

Out of This World. Super NES: 1992. Delphine Software (dev), Interplay (pub). Original release on Amiga in 1991. European title: *Another World*.

OutRun. Arcade: 1986. Sega (dev), Sega (pub).

Pac-Man. Atari 2600: 1982. Atari (dev), Atari (pub). Original release on arcade developed and published by Namco in 1980.

Perfect Dark. Nintendo 64: 2000. Rare (dev), Rare (pub).

Phantasmagoria. PC: 1995. Sierra On-Line (dev), Sierra On-Line (pub).

Pilotwings. Super NES: 1991. Nintendo (dev), Nintendo (pub). Original release in Japan in 1990.

Pit-Fighter. Super NES: 1991. Atari (dev), THQ (pub). Original release published by Atari on arcade in 1990.

Pitfall!. Atari 2600: 1982. Activision (dev), Activision (pub).

Pole Position. Arcade: 1982. Namco (dev), Namco (pub).

Populous II: Trials of the Olympian Gods. Super NES: 1993. Bullfrog (dev), Imagineer (pub). Original release published by Electronic Arts on PC in 1991.

Prince of Persia. Super NES: 1992. Arsys (dev), Konami (pub). Original release on PC developed and published by Brøderbund in 1989.

Q*Bert. Arcade: 1982. Gottlieb (dev), Gottlieb (pub).

Quake. PC: 1996. id Software (dev), id Software (pub).

Quest 64. Nintendo 64: 1998. Imagineer (dev), THQ (pub).

R.C. Pro-Am. NES: 1988. Rare (dev), Nintendo (pub).

Rad Racer. NES: 1987. Square (dev), Nintendo (pub).

Rally-X. Arcade: 1981. Namco (dev), Midway (pub). Original release published by Namco in Japan in 1980.

Ravenloft: Stone Prophet. PC: 1995. DreamForge Intertainment (dev), Strategic Simulations Inc. (pub).

Ravenloft: Strahd's Possession. PC: 1994. DreamForge Intertainment (dev), Strategic Simulations Inc. (pub).

Resident Evil. GameCube: 2002. Capcom (dev), Capcom (pub).

Resident Evil 2. Nintendo 64: 1999. Capcom (dev), Capcom (pub). Original release on PlayStation in 1998.

Resident Evil 4. GameCube: 2005. Capcom (dev), Capcom (pub).

Resident Evil Zero. GameCube: 2002. Capcom (dev), Capcom (pub).

River City Ransom. NES: 1990. Technos (dev), Technos (pub). Original release in Japan in 1989.

Robotron: 2084. Arcade: 1982. Vid Kidz (dev), Williams Electronics (pub).

Rock n'Roll Racing. Super NES: 1993. Silicon & Synapse (dev), Interplay (pub).

Romancing SaGa 2. Super Famicom: 1993. Square (dev), Square (pub).

RPM Racing. Super NES: 1992. Silicon & Synapse (dev), Interplay (pub).

Scott Pilgrim vs. the World: The Game. PlayStation Network and Xbox Live Arcade: 2010. Ubisoft (dev), Ubisoft (pub).

Secret of Mana. Super NES: 1993. Square (dev), Square (pub).

Seiken Densetsu 3. Super Famicom: 1995. Square (dev), Square (pub).

Sewer Shark. Sega CD: 1992. Digital Pictures (dev), Sony Imagesoft (pub).

Sid Meier's Civilization. Super NES: 1994. MicroProse (dev), KOEI (pub). Original release published by MicroProse on PC in 1991.

Silent Hill. PlayStation: 1999. Konami (dev), Konami (pub).

SimAnt. Super NES: 1993. Imagineer (dev), Maxis Software (pub). Original release developed by Maxis Software and released on PC in 1991.

SimCity. Super NES: 1991. Nintendo (dev), Nintendo (pub). Original release developed and published by Maxis Software on PC in 1989.

SimCity 2000. PC: 1994. Maxis Software (dev), Maxis Software (pub).

Smash Tennis. Super NES: 1993. Namco (dev), Namco (pub).

Sonic the Hedgehog. Sega Genesis: 1991. Sega (dev), Sega (pub).

SOS. Super NES: 1994. Human Entertainment (dev), Vic Tokai (pub). Release titled *Septentrion* in Japan.

Soul Blazer. Super NES: 1992. Quintet (dev), Enix (pub).

Space Battle. Intellivision: 1979. APh Technological Consulting (dev), Mattel Electronics (pub).

Space Harrier. Arcade: 1985. Sega (dev), Sega (pub).

Space Harrier 3-D. Sega Master System: 1988. Sega (dev), Sega (pub).

Star Fox. Super NES: 1993. Argonaut and Nintendo (dev), Nintendo (pub).

Star Fox 64. Nintendo 64: 1997. Nintendo (dev), Nintendo (pub).

Star Wars: Rebel Assault. PC: 1993. LucasArts (dev), LucasArts (pub).

Star Wars: Rebel Assault 2: The Hidden Empire. PC: 1995. LucasArts (dev), LucasArts (pub).

Star Wars: The Empire Strikes Back. Atari 2600: 1982. Parker Brothers (dev), Parker Brothers (pub).

Stardew Valley. PC: 2016. ConcernedApe (dev), Chucklefish Games (pub).

Starglider. PC: 1986. Argonaut (dev), Rainbird Software (pub).

Street Fighter II Turbo. Super NES: 1993. Capcom (dev), Capcom (pub). Original release on arcade in 1992 titled *Street Fighter II Turbo: Hyper Fighting*.

Street Fighter II: The World Warrior. Super NES: 1992. Capcom (dev), Capcom (pub). Original release on arcade in 1991.

Street Fighter II': Special Champion Edition. Sega Genesis: 1993. Capcom (dev), Capcom (pub). Original release on arcade in 1992 titled *Street Fighter II': Champion Edition*.

Stunt Race FX. Super NES: 1994. Nintendo and Argonaut Software (dev), Nintendo (pub).

Stunts. PC: 1990. Distinctive Software (dev), Brøderbund and Mindscape (pub).

Suikoden. PlayStation: 1995. Konami (dev), Konami (pub).

Super Boss Gaiden. Super NES and Super NES-CD: 2016. Chrono Moogle and Dieter von Lazer (dev).

Super Castlevania IV. Super NES: 1991. Konami (dev), Konami (pub).

Super Ghouls 'n Ghosts. Super NES: 1991. Capcom (dev), Capcom (pub).

Super Mario All-Stars. Super NES: 1993. Nintendo (dev), Nintendo (pub).

Super Mario Bros. NES: 1985. Nintendo (dev), Nintendo (pub).

Super Mario Bros. 3. NES: 1990. Nintendo (dev), Nintendo (pub). Original release in Japan in 1988.

Super Mario Kart. Super NES: 1992. Nintendo (dev), Nintendo (pub).

Super Mario RPG: Legend of the Seven Stars. Super NES: 1996. Square (dev), Nintendo (pub).

Super Mario World. Super NES: 1991. Nintendo (dev), Nintendo (pub). Original release in Japan in 1990.

Super Mario World 2: Yoshi's Island. Super NES: 1995. Nintendo (dev), Nintendo (pub).

Super Metroid. Super NES: 1994. Nintendo and Intelligent Systems (dev), Nintendo (pub).

Super Road Blaster. Super NES + MSU1: 2012. Matthias "d4s" Nagler (dev). Original release titled Road Blaster, developed and published by Data East on arcade in 1985.

Super R-Type. Super NES: 1991. Irem (dev), Irem (pub).

Super Smash T.V. Super NES: 1991. Williams Entertainment (dev), Acclaim (pub). Originally titled *Smash T.V.*, developed and published by Williams Electronics on arcade in 1990.

Super Soccer. Super NES: 1992. Human Entertainment (dev), Nintendo (pub). Original release titled *Super Formation Soccer* and published by Human Entertainment in Japan in 1991.

Super Star Wars. Super NES: 1992. Sculptured Software and LucasArts (dev), JVC (pub).

Super Star Wars: The Empire Strikes Back. Super NES: 1993. Sculptured Software and LucasArts (dev), JVC (pub).

Super Street Fighter II. Super NES: 1994. Capcom (dev), Capcom (pub). Original release on arcade in 1993 titled *Super Street Fighter II: The New Challengers*.

Teenage Mutant Ninja Turtles IV: Turtles in Time. Super NES: 1992. Konami (dev), Konami (pub). Original release on arcade in 1991.

Tempest 2000. Atari Jaguar: 1994. Llamasoft (dev), Atari (pub).

Terraria. PC: 2011. Re-Logic (dev), Re-Logic (pub).

Tetris. Game Boy: 1989. Bullet-Proof Software (dev), Nintendo (pub).

The 7th Guest. PC: 1993. Trilobyte (dev), Virgin Interactive (pub).

The 7th Saga. Super NES: 1993. Produce (dev), Enix (pub).

The Daedalus Encounter. PC: 1995. Mechadeus (dev), Virgin Interactive (pub).

The Legend of Zelda. NES: 1987. Nintendo (dev), Nintendo (pub). Original release on the Famicom Disk System in Japan in 1986.

The Legend of Zelda: A Link to the Past. Super NES: 1992. Nintendo (dev), Nintendo (pub). Original release in Japan in 1991.

The X-Files Game. PC: 1998. HyperBole Studios (dev), Fox Interactive (pub).

Thunder Spirits. Super NES: 1991. Technosoft (dev), Seika (pub). Original release published by Sega on arcade in 1990.

Tokimeki Memorial. Super Famicom: 1996. Konami (dev), Konami (pub). Original release on PC-Engine in 1994.

Tomcat Alley. Sega CD: 1994. Code Monkeys (dev), Sega (pub).

Top Gear. Super NES: 1992. Gremlin Graphics (dev), Kemco (pub).

Top Landing. Arcade: 1988. Taito (dev), Taito (pub).

Tunnels of Doom. Texas Instruments TI-99/4A: 1982. Texas Instruments (dev), Texas Instruments (pub).

U.N. Squadron. Super NES: 1991. Capcom (dev), Capcom (pub). Original release on arcade in 1989.

Utopia: The Creation of a Nation. Super NES: 1993. Gremlin Graphics (dev), Jaleco (pub). Original release developed by Celestial Software and published by Gremlin Interactive on PC in 1991.

Virtua Fighter. Arcade: 1993. Sega (dev), Sega (pub).

Virtua Racing. Sega Genesis: 1994. Sega (dev), Sega (pub). Original release on arcade in 1993.

Vortex. Super NES: 1994. Argonaut Software (dev), Electro Brain (pub).

Wild Gunman. Arcade: 1974. Nintendo (dev), Nintendo (pub).

Wing Commander III: Heart of the Tiger. PC: 1994. Origin Systems (dev), Origin Systems (pub).

Winning Run. Arcade: 1988. Namco (dev), Namco (pub).

X. Game Boy: 1992. Nintendo and Argonaut Software (dev), Nintendo (pub).

Xevious. Arcade: 1983. Namco (dev), Atari (pub). Original release published by Namco in Japan in 1982.

Ys III: Wanderers from Ys. Super NES: 1992. Nihon Falcom (dev), American Sammy (pub). Original release published by Nihon Falcom on PC in Japan in 1989.

Zaxxon. Arcade: 1982. Sega (dev), Sega/Gremlin (pub).

Zelda II: The Adventure of Link. NES: 1988. Nintendo (dev), Nintendo (pub). Original release in Japan in 1987.

Zelda: The Wand of Gamelon. CD-i: 1993. Animation Magic (dev), Philips Interactive (pub).

Zelda's Adventure. CD-i: 1995. Viridis (dev), Philips Interactive (pub).

Zelda3: Parallel Remodel. Super NES emulators and homebrew channels: 2012. Euclid, SePH, and PuzzleDude (dev).

Zelda3: Parallel Worlds. Super NES emulators and homebrew channels: 2007. Euclid and SePH (dev).

Index